D0069543

"*Carrying her own psychic wounds with a feisty grace, Szarke's Callie Lindstrom expresses remarkable empathy and insight in telling the stories of troubled others in her life. This beautifully detailed, soulful work is a touch gritty and a touch angry over insensitivity and unfairness in the world it describes. And yet there is as well an underlying love for people and place in these stories, and a sort of joy emergent through the depth and honesty in Szarke's telling of them.*"
—Joe Paddock, *poet, oral historian, author of* Circle of Stones

"*Of all the writers I know, few possess more discipline and commitment to the craft than Connie Szarke. That dedication is apparent in all of her writing but especially so in her delicately drawn characters. She obviously loves her main character, Callie, now grown up since* Delicate Armor, *and you'll love her too.*"
—Stephen Wilbers, *author, columnist, and writing instructor*

Lady
in the Moon

"Keep on dancing dg

[signature]

Lady in the Moon

• A NOVEL IN STORIES •

Connie Claire Szarke

Heron Bay Publishing
Minneapolis

Copyright © 2016 Connie Claire Szarke. All rights reserved.

Published by Heron Bay Publishing, Minnesota
www.heronbaypublishing.com

PUBLISHER'S NOTE: This is a work of fiction. Names, characters, places, and incidents are the products of the author's imagination or are used fictitiously. Any resemblance to actual events or persons, living or dead, is entirely coincidental.

Without limiting the rights under copyright reserved above, no part of this publication may be reproduced, stored in or introduced into a retrieval system, or transmitted, in any form or by any means (electronic, mechanical, photo-copying, recording or otherwise), without the prior written permission of both the copyright owner and the above publisher of this book.

Designed by Dorie McClelland, springbookdesign.com
Book illustration designed by Freepik.com

ISBN: 978-0-9885363-4-0

Printed in the United States of America

To the memory of Penny, Sam, Teco, Kelsey Kady Shadywood Lady, Laddy Berger, Scout Salvatore, Topaz, Pola, & Amer.

And to Kipp the Piper Man & Lexi-Callie Rose.

Also by CONNIE CLAIRE SZARKE

Delicate Armor, second edition, novel #1 in the Callie Lindstrom series, Heron Bay Publishing, 2014, Midwest Book Award Finalist & Winner of the Jeanette Fair Memorial Award—Tau State, sponsored by Delta Kappa Gamma

A Stone for Amer, novel #2 in the Callie Lindstrom series, Heron Bay Publishing, 2013

Stone Wall, a stand-alone short story set in Ireland, Red Dragonfly Press, 2012

Omertà, a stand-alone short story set in Sicily, Heron Bay Publishing, 2015

Contents

*The apple cannot be stuck back on the Tree of Knowledge;
once we begin to see, we are doomed and challenged to seek
the strength to see more, not less.*
—*Arthur Miller*

1

On the Road to Knowing It All

Human beings . . . or cosmic dust—
we all dance to a mysterious tune, intoned
in the distance by an invisible piper.
—Albert Einstein

"WE'RE GOING TO TURN right around and go home," Will announced after dropping Hannah and Nellie off at the curb. For their part, the two elderly women didn't even wave goodbye as they toddled up to the house, much less extend an earlier invitation to stay overnight.

Will tightened his seatbelt. "Hit the road, Cal, we're heading for home."

"But Dad, it's three hundred and fifty miles back to Long Lake. Seven hundred miles in one day? I'm not sure I can do that." In the rear-view mirror, Callie noticed new stress lines and her pupils still dilated after the unsettling encounter with her dad's cousins, especially Nellie, whose judgmental remarks about Uncle Amer made Cal spout off in his defense right there in the middle of the cemetery, ending with "Amer was a somebody! He was *family*, for God's sake!"

"We'll stop in one of these small towns for the night if we have to," said Will. "I won't stay another minute with those old biddies."

"I don't think they're keen on it either, Dad. "

1

IT WAS DURING THE AUTUMN of 1986 when Callie and her father traveled to the Swedish Cemetery in Rockford, Illinois, intent on locating a tombstone for Uncle Amer, dead since 1919. Because of a falling-out with his cousins over what was found inside that cemetery—or rather *not* found—Will insisted on leaving.

Early that evening, he and Cal found rooms in Spring Green, Wisconsin, and over supper, discussed Hannah and Nellie's side of the family, their conservative upbringing, closed minds, negative attitudes toward whatever or whoever didn't fit into their views of life, resulting in those terrible comments about Uncle Amer.

As Will Lindstrom came to understand his uncle's lifestyle, he vacillated, albeit slightly, between acceptance and criticism. Above all, however, he was troubled by the fact that no tombstone had ever been set.

"I thought you'd come to terms with it, Dad, back there: We'd remember Amer in other ways."

"I thought so too. But damn it all, his brothers broke their promise." Will folded his napkin, laid it on the table, and passed a hand over the left side of his face. "To think they never followed through with their part of the agreement, made him go without a marker all these years—those tight-fisted swine. And my cousins? Dropped right out of the same friggin' mold."

"It's up to us then, Pops."

"Guess so. I don't know. We'll see. Have to think about it . . . what to do."

The next morning, after a breakfast of fried eggs and crispy bacon washed down with grapefruit juice and steaming hot coffee at the Spring Green Cafe, Callie drove past Frank Lloyd Wright's Taliesin, and the curious House on the Rock, before stopping for gas at the edge of town.

The fuel pumps bordered on a grassy stretch across from a Day's Inn, where a mangy old dog, unleashed, alone, and not far from the highway, was sniffing along the base of an elm tree, one of the few still standing after disease wiped out most of them. Scattered beneath the naked branches lay shriveled leaves and wilted grass. These, plus whatever else landed on the ground that morning, would eventually meld into the soil, along with the inevitable snows of winter.

"That dog over there, under the tree," said Callie, standing next to a gas pump, "I wonder where he belongs."

"Who knows?" said Will.

"Wonder where he came from, where he's heading."

"Maybe he just wandered off."

This dog reminded Callie of the old lab who plodded across the street each day, trying to speed up as a car approached, but barely able to make it to the other side. Cal always pulled up next to him, rolled her window down, and shouted "Hey, Blackie!" Cloudy eyes and the set of his mouth conveyed a sad look of disappointment in the betrayal by a trembling body on arthritic legs. Yet when Blackie glanced up at Cal, he offered a proud tilt of his head, calling to mind the great hunting dog he had once been.

"Let's hope this one hasn't been ditched," she said, reaching for the gas pump. "Turned out to fend for himself."

Will pointed toward the motel. "I'd say he spent the night in one of those rooms, came outside to freshen up a bit. He's definitely out here on business."

Observing the mongrel as he licked his paw and washed his muzzle, Callie chirped, "*Oui, Oui! Sa toilette!*" fancying up the conversation with a touch of the French she'd learned as a girl. Her teacher: the neighbor boy who lassoed *his* dog and got pulled all over Masterton on roller skates, hollering, "*Allez! Allez le chien!*"

Callie leaned against the car while gas drizzled into the tank from a clunking black pump. She recalled the happy face of that long-ago retriever and how he loved towing his boy Danny, making those metal strap-on wheels click faster and faster over cracks in the sidewalks.

"According to the morning paper, there'll be a Hunter's Moon tonight, Pops; with all that light we can take our time getting home."

The promise of a deep buttery moon would top off Callie's long day behind the wheel—provided the clouds didn't interfere. Her father called it the Hunter's Moon, because, as he said, "that's exactly what it does each October—provides light for a hunter and his dog."

"Or," she reminded him, recalling that field where a young girl galloped her pony with a sheepdog racing alongside, "a hunter and *her* dog!"

"Of course, Cal. That goes without saying."

"Or not."

In Callie's case, however, it was no time for taking aim with a shotgun, but for simply roaming a huge field with her own dog, Piper, as she did a year ago. And the year before that. It was a time to ponder whatever thoughts and memories surfaced in her mind: Sporadic enlightenment was what she called those rapid moments of reflection, like darting ripples glinting in the sunshine. Memories for Callie were movies of the mind—recall, edit, scene change, laugh, wipe away the tears.

She recalled those walks with a dancing Piper, amazed at the powerful hunter's moonbeam and how it cast itself over bent cornstalks, clumps of earth, crowns of oak groves next to fields, an abandoned bird's nest in the crook of a bare branch, a beetle bug crawling in the dirt.

While Piper raced ahead through harvested rows, occasionally looking back to make sure she was close behind, Cal let her thoughts run too, back to the lives of farmers and small town folks she knew as a child—their looks and voices, the stories they told, their upsets, how some of them argued and pounded on the counter in her dad's office, then left the stately Maywood County Courthouse to maneuver along Masterton's Main Street, back to their cars and trucks and tractors, their farmyards and fields—some men tired and bowlegged in their overalls, others sprightly and tall, dressed in suits and fedoras. A few of those lives had reached well beyond Callie's hometown, even as far away as another country.

Remembering all those many struggles and successes helped Callie to size up her own life now that she had made it through what seemed like an underwater tunnel plugged at both ends. Although she had gone from tiptoeing to skipping ahead and shouldering her way through, it had taken a long while to get to where she was now—slightly more at ease and confident after catching a glimpse of her new direction. To arrive there had been like scrambling out of that tunnel and swimming straight up from the oozy bottom of a deep pond through whirlpools and deadly entanglements of dense weeds. That's what she thought about while hiding in darkened rooms to escape Jim's verbal attacks, his kicking at doors, and the slamming of books and kitchenware. While crouched next to her piano or silent behind the shower curtain or wedged inside a closet, Callie imagined what it would be like to escape that tunnel and reach clear water. One day, she would burst through the surface, gasp for air, and be greeted by chortling geese riding the waves, and gulls swooping down from a limpid, blue sky, celebrating in a safe place after such a long time fending off threats and abuse. Before reaching clear water, Cal felt like a stagnant river that might never find its way to the sea.

Callie replaced the dripping nozzle, plucked her receipt from the slot, and watched the old dog rub his face with a paw. "*Le chien* doesn't have a collar. Maybe he wandered in off the highway from some farm place. I don't see anyone else around."

"Excepting that vehicle parked over there," said Will, "in front of the motel entrance. From the looks of it, she could use an oil change."

"And a new filter."

Dark exhaust spewed from the tail pipe of a deep blue van. Its sliding door stood open, revealing guitar cases and speakers.

The dog ambled over to the idling vehicle, hesitated for a moment, and then hauled himself up to the passenger seat. A young man exited the motel, carrying another guitar case. He skirted his car, slid the door closed, grooved back to some tune in his head, slipped in behind the wheel, and inched around the circle directly in front of Callie and Will.

With his forearm resting on the rolled-down window ledge, the gray-faced dog sat up tall, his rheumy eyes looking off into the distance, as he likely had done a hundred times before. The driver and his pal turned onto the highway and sped out of sight.

"Wonder how much longer that old pooch has got," said Will.

With a lively tune playing in her own head, Callie soft-shoed back to the driver's seat, feeling uplifted from what she'd just witnessed, relieved to see that, although long in the tooth and homely with age, the dog was not alone on the prairie.

"He has a pretty good job, so who knows? With all that music going on around him, he could last for quite a while."

"Yup. Obvious what's keeping him a-going. Gotta have a purpose in life." Will rubbed the side of his face where a surgery from several years earlier had left a mean scar and a deep indentation in his cheek, along with some paralysis. Strands of white hair brushed the collars of his dress shirt and rust-colored suit jacket. "You know, Cal, for some time now, although I hate to admit it, I've been feeling a bit like that old dog looks—pretty much along for the ride."

Callie tucked her credit card inside her purse, turned the key, stared straight ahead, planted her foot on the gas feed, plunged it to the floor, and intentionally revved the car engine several times over.

Will scowled at her. "What the . . . ?"

"He's not along for the ride, Pops," she said, shifting out of neutral and pulling forward. "He owns that passenger seat."

Leaving the gas station to turn north, in the direction of La Crosse, Callie accidently ran over a chunk of curb, eliciting the familiar "Ip-ip-ip" from her father: It made her feel like a kid again.

"Sorry!" she said with a short laugh. "Anyhow, he's the navigator too. Probably telling his driver to slack up and sing a song: 'Woof woof!' Watch where you're drii-ving, tra-la."

"How many times do I have to tell you to keep an eye out for curbs, Cal? Not to mention all those center islands you've backed over since forever; actually, since you started driver's training back in Masterton. I swear, one of these days, you're going to break an axel. Or at the very least, throw the tires out of alignment. Again!"

"Tra-la, tra-la," she sang, checking her seatbelt and patting the champagne-colored dashboard of her dad's Cadillac. "Two hundred and fifty miles to go for home."

"Let's hope we can make it intact," said Will.

Just as she reveled in rowing a small boat across a wide lake, Callie loved the compact security of an automobile, especially one that still smelled new. Once the doors were closed, it provided protection, offered a simple place that took her where she needed to go—where she wanted to go—agreeable, confined quarters with surrounding views and jazzy music on the radio. The few distractions and minimal housekeeping inside a car allowed memories and impressions to settle in, accompanied by the hum of a well-lubed engine and the ticking of tires on patched asphalt.

The first car she could recall was her parents' 1936 Nash. Although Cal was born eight years later, that black Nash remained in the family until 1950. To her, the steering wheel was like a miniature Ferris wheel and as slender as a hula-hoop. Positioned like the eyes on a praying mantis, the headlights sat high over the long front bumper. En route to Tepeeotah and her grandparents' lake cottage, young Callie sat in the passenger seat with the window rolled down, chin resting on folded arms, the summer air warm with the aroma of cottonwoods and sugar maples, cow pies, freshly turned field dirt, and grubbed tree stumps on Iver Knutson's farmland. In autumn, she caught the whiff of harvested oats, shelled corn, windrows of drying hay, and mounds of leaves swept together by the wind. When she could smell the mossy backwaters of Lake Shetek, she knew they had arrived and would soon be bobbing about in their fishing boat.

Through the open window of that Nash, Callie's eyes danced along with the dip and rise of highline wires. Her gaze rose to the sky where she imagined herself clinging to the back of a mallard or a goose, soaring to who–knows-where.

"Remember our old Nash, Dad?" she asked, lowering the volume on the radio. "I loved that running board."

"Ha! What a prize! My Nash 400. Paid six hundred and sixty-five dollars for her; a lot of money in those days."

"What did the 400 stand for?"

"How far she could go on a tank of gas."

"No kidding! Too bad we can't get that kind of mileage nowadays."

"Did I ever tell you about the time we were driving down to Sioux City, Iowa? To see my brother?"

"Tell me again."

"It happened a little more than a year after you were born. Emily was holding you in the front seat, and Liz, about eight, was stretched out in the back. Which, by the way, could be converted into a bed for camping. Oh, that was some vehicle, that sedan. Even though it was considered middle-line, to me it spelled 'luxury.'"

"You used to be a car salesman. Right, Dad?"

"Well, yes." Will paused for a second. "Does it still show?"

"Yup, it does."

"Anyhow, there we were, driving along a gravel road when all of a sudden the rear end jumped, flew up, and jolted back down again. I thought we'd hit something big or plunged into a deep rut. But I couldn't spot anything in the rear view mirror and so we just kept a-going until she slowed down after a bit and plumb stopped—as if we'd run out of gas."

Ready for the punch line, Callie relaxed, her right hand resting easy atop the steering wheel.

"A semi-truck driver, who'd been following us for quite some distance, stopped behind our stalled Nash and hopped out, laughing his head off. 'I wanted to see how far you'd get,' he shouted, 'without a gas tank!'

"You see, the straps had rusted through and down it went; found the thing a ways back, in tall grass alongside the road."

"How far did we get without it?"

"About a mile or so, as I recall. We loaded the tank into our trunk and got towed to the nearest town. Only needed a couple of hours to get it strapped back on and hooked up, before making it to Sioux City."

"And that's the one time when Uncle Ray and Aunt Eloise actually invited us into their house?"

"Yup. But she was a corker even then. Snarly woman."

Callie remembered her parents' more recent trips, between 1981 and '83, when Will and Emily, on their way to California, had pulled up in front of 2214 Oak Street, Sioux City, Iowa. Each time, they could see Ray and Eloise peaking through the curtains downstairs or cracking the blinds upstairs, refusing to come to the door. On the last try, in 1985, Will's brother, bent and slow as a garden snail, finally came out of his house. Although he had no wallet on him, Ray invited Will and Emily out for lunch, while Eloise, rankled and aflame, stood before her picture window, casting a malevolent glare that might have shattered glass and set the lawn on fire.

"It's been nearly twelve months to this very day since I've seen or heard from my brother," said Will. "I tried calling a few times, to no avail. Hard to imagine him being in an old folk's home, but that's likely where he's living now—unless Eloise did him in."

"You'll have to try contacting him again, Dad."

"Probably. Even though there's no marker, I sure wish Ray could have seen where Uncle Amer lies, especially since he never made it to the funeral all those years ago. Never had the chance to say goodbye. Amer was like another dad to us boys, you know."

"Us boys," Cal repeated with a smirk, remembering the boxing match between her dad and uncle so very long ago. Not even a punch to the stomach or jaw, or a pair of broken glasses lying twisted among the acorns. Just Uncle Ray rolling down the hill and into the lake.

When Callie, as a young girl, had put on a boxing glove and pranced around the yard with a next-door neighbor boy in Masterton, she ended up with a bloody nose and ran home crying. Somehow, though, she'd felt proud that at least she'd gone one round and had something to show for it.

Although her dad and uncle rarely saw each other after their failed boxing match, they managed to trade plenty of insults over the next thirty years.

"You know, Cal, come to think of it, there was a Hunter's Moon that night too, after your mother and I dropped Ray off at his house before heading out West to California."

From the side window, Will stared at the passing fields, then leaned forward to open the glove compartment. He pulled out the manual for his one-year-old Cadillac and flipped through the pages without studying any of them.

"Sure wish I could drive again. Properly. Save on this wear-and-tear."

"Properly? What are you implying, Pops?"

"You know very well."

"Tra-la, tra-la."

"Not to mention the gas! You've got to keep her under sixty, Cal."

"I do know that," she said, switching the radio on and then off, when all she could find was static.

"This business of aging is for the birds." Will returned the manual to its slot inside the glove box and tossed up his hands. "Oh, well. It's tough to grow old, but it sure as hell beats the alternative."

Once again, Callie pictured her dad in his forties, stepping lively in the middle of that so-called boxing ring overlooking Lake Shetek, sparring with his brother. And she saw him in winter, scooping Tequila up and tucking the little Chihuahua inside his storm coat, ready to scoot to the edge of a long patch of ice and slide its entire length, sure-footed, bespectacled, grinning and doffing his hat like a young Franklin Roosevelt.

"Pops, even though I'm on the road to knowing it all," Cal said with a smirk, "well, speaking metaphorically, of course, there are still a lot of fish to catch. That one big northern is waiting for us somewhere in the shallows."

"Or the deep," said Will. "Depending on the season."

"Anyhow, don't forget, Dad, you're the only one who knows how to start the 10-horse and keep 'er running."

"We'll see, Cal. We shall see. At least I can still imagine the bigger picture. Only . . . I'm not in it as much as I used to be."

"What do you mean?" Callie frowned, unwilling to sense the inevitable, the foreboding significance of Will's comment.

"Just that. The world. Options. That great wide picture—like Cinerama. There was a time when I could imagine myself heading off in any direction. Any old path I chose, wherever an idea took me. Even applied for the position of state treasurer one year, though a man has never occupied that seat. Heck, I gave it a go anyhow." Will lowered his head in order to peer upward through the windshield; he pointed at a small flock of birds on the wing. "High hopes. Right up there with the skylarks." He settled back against the headrest. "Not so much anymore."

"You'll never be anywhere other than in the big picture, Dad. Always and forever more."

"Well, now, don't you sound like a preacher. Or Ed Poe—except you're taking liberties with his words; I believe the line reads, 'Quoth the Raven, "Nevermore." ' Actually, you speak like your mother, Cal. She talks quite a game."

"That's where I got it—from Mom: 'Always and forever more.' Much better than 'Nevermore.' And you know what else she'd say: 'Buck up, now. Get on with ya.'"

Will's smile broadened on the good side of his face as he fished for a toothpick from the inside pocket of his suit coat. "Yup, that's my Emily."

"Just keep on dancin', Pops."

"What's that?" He cupped an ear.

"Keep on dancing! And keep on rowing. That's what you always say."

"As long as I'm able, Callie girl, just as long as I'm able. At least, I've had a lot of wonderful years, especially in these great outdoors. And I had a good run as auditor. Oh, there were a few bumps along the way, back there in Maywood County. But all in all, it was a pretty good run."

2

The Honeybees of this World

One can no more approach people without love
than one can approach bees without care.
—Leo Tolstoy

AS A YOUNG GIRL, Callie often visited the Maywood County Court-house on a Saturday, whenever her father had some catch-up work to do. Dressed in a tee shirt and pedal pushers, she carried a paper bag filled with sandwiches, plus two greening apples from the root cellar in the basement of their house on Norwood Avenue.

Cal opened the garage door and wheeled out her black and white Hopalong Cassidy bicycle with the jeweled, dual pistol holsters mounted on the crossbar, white-wall tires, and a wire basket attached to the han-dlebars. Inside this basket, Tequila, with her leash tied to the handlebar, hunkered down on a folded towel next to the brown paper sack, while Callie cruised the streets and bounced along the curbs and sidewalks on fat tires. Plastic handle grip streamers flowed in the wind.

Cal slowed down when she came upon Mr. Lambert walking slowly toward Main Street. Mr. and Mrs. Lambert and their daughter Laura—the new girl in school—had recently moved into a boxcar near the dump, north of Masterton. Unlike the other men in town, Mr. Lambert never tipped his hat. Why? Because he never wore one. But he did nod at Cal each time she noticed him. And he tried to smile.

Arriving at the courthouse, Callie and her Chihuahua skipped up the steps and paused at the entry of the Romanesque building: Walking through that stone arch made her feel as though she were entering a palace. She crossed the heavy leather and chain link treads, bounded up several more steps and into the first large room on the left—Will Lindstrom's Auditor's Office. Knowing precisely where to turn, the little dog always led the way.

While Tequila sat on Will's lap, resting her tiny front paws on the desk's edge, Callie took off to explore the insides of Masterton's most regal building, beginning with the basement filled with desks, a solid counter, and Maywood County's extension offices. She never stayed long in that part of the courthouse, for it smelled of pesticides and cigarette smoke, with no fresh air wafting through.

During his thirty years as county agent, Ernest Obermeier chain-smoked. After a time, his ashen face turned a ghostly white and he began to cough. Whenever he laughed at Will Lindstrom's stories and jokes, a strange rattle rippled through his lungs, as if gobs of fluid wanted to come up and out of his mouth. Finally, he could no longer play his tuba with the town band in the park on Saturday nights, or glide along Main Street with Flossie, his prancing Pomeranian. Ernest died at age sixty.

Back on the main floor, Cal placed a hand on the spiral newel post that shone as bright as a wet oak leaf gleaming in the sun, and traipsed up the grand staircase to the courtroom. Each of the wide wooden steps was worn to a cream color, especially in the centers, scuffed and dented from over sixty years of farm boots, wingtips, loafers, pumps, white bucks, wedgies, and saddle shoes.

With no one else around, Callie circled the broad courtroom in her sneakers, running her fingers along the light wooden railings and chair backs. She stood for a moment, facing the judge's bench, studying the two portraits that hung high upon the wall: George Washington and

John Fremont. From the jury platform, she admired Fremont's dark hair and beard and those keen eyes that seemed to focus upon the entire room filled with empty seats.

Cal sat down in the shiny leather chair behind the judge's bench, swiveled round and round, and then relaxed for a moment against its deep burgundy back, her bare forearms on the chair's smooth arms. Chewing a wad of Blackjack gum, she thought of what her third grade teacher had taught the class about this Mr. Fremont—that he was a great American leader who not only laid the foundation for the West, but had also surveyed these parts of Minnesota, along with Joseph Nicollet.

"Isn't it marvelous, children," said Miss Wigg, "that these explorers called the region we live in The Great Oasis? And Mr. Fremont dubbed a small body of water near Lake Shetek after himself, and named Lake Benton after his father-in-law."

How fun that would be, thought Callie, to go around the countryside and name a bunch of lakes after her own family—Lake William and Lake Emily. Lake Liz, after her sister. No, maybe it would sound better to say Lake Elizabeth.

She'd locate a large body of water filled with geese and ducks for her Granddad Vic, and one with arrowheads dotting the shore for cousin Jenny.

As for Uncle Ray, Aunt Eloise, and Grandma Julia, she'd check out the sloughs. Not the real muddy, stinky ones, though—except, maybe for her aunt. Ones with cattails and shrill redwing blackbirds and meadowlarks would be nice for the others, especially Grandma Julia who used to play piano and sing like a kazoo. And sometimes, she gave Callie a dime, along with wintergreen lifesavers and Yucatan chewing gum. Yet she could never extend that spirit of generosity to Cal's mother. And so a slough would have to do.

As for herself—Callandra Mae Lindstrom—she'd find a big lake loaded with turtles and great blue herons and northern pike, where lush green moss, attached to submerged rocks, waved like long hair in a gentle breeze. A lake that flowed into a lovely stream lined with linden trees.

And that stream would link up with the longest, widest river around, a river that eventually flowed into the sea.

Callie loved third grade, sitting at her desk, listening to Miss Wigg talk about the natural world around Masterton, including Lake Shetek and the surrounding prairieland.

"This beautiful body of water," she'd say, with a piece of chalk in one hand and her pointer in the other, tracing along the image tacked to a bulletin board, "is the headwaters basin for the Des Moines River."

To Callie, the shape of Lake Shetek looked like a steer crawling up to the sky with an arrow piercing its shoulder and a tear dripping from his eye.

"Does anyone know what the name Shetek means?" asked Miss Wigg, writing the word in large, fancy letters on the blackboard.

"Pelican!" shouted Bobby Keeler.

"That's right, Bobby, translated from the Ojibway language—pelican. I just love watching those birds fly in, don't you? Such long beaks! And how they fill up their throat pouches? Don't you wonder, children, what's inside those pouches and how far they can stretch before ripping?"

Miss Wigg, with rosy cheeks and a broad smile, leaned against her desk while her students shuddered and giggled. "What other birds do you see on our lakes?"

Callie raised her hand and described a slow single file of Canada geese that swam past her grandparents' dock at Tepeeotah. And she told about how one of the goslings had veered off on its own to follow an insect and grab a weed, then scurried back into line after a loud bark from mama or papa goose.

Miss Wigg laughed and smoothed back her hair. "What does that tell you? Children must mind their parents."

She talked about Buttermilk Run near Breezy Point, and Armstrong Slough, edged with cattails and floating pondweed; Beaver Creek, meandering through the wooded valley, home to squirrels and racoons; Slaughter Slough and Bloody Lake, where settlers rushed to escape or submerge themselves, trying to take cover during the 1862 Indian Massacre.

"And now," said Miss Wigg, "Bloody Lake is a lovely body of water where tadpoles dart about in spring."

Seated in the leather chair behind the judge's bench, Callie looked around the courtroom, remembering how Miss Wigg had nearly lost her teaching position after telling the students how upset she was about the big fight between what she referred to as "agriculture aggressors," who were greedy for more and more land, and those individuals she called "conservationists," who wished to preserve the natural world.

"I want you to know, children," she said, "that here where we live, in southwestern Minnesota, existed one of the greatest stands of timber and lakes and sloughs for all kinds of wildlife—a natural breeding ground for waterfowl. Let us pause now to remember Bear Lake, Rush Lake, and Crooked Lake, all a part of the Great Oasis."

After reading aloud Robert Frost's poem, "Driving Through the Woods on a Snowy Evening," she told her students, "It is important for all of us, especially for our youth, to hear songbirds and observe every kind of animal without having to go to a zoo. We must be able to wander through beautiful woods and glory in their inhabitants."

The Bear Lake timber Miss Wigg referred to had been cut down, and six thousand acres of lakes and wetlands were drained and destroyed after decades of court cases and a final ruling by the Minnesota Supreme Court. One of the local farmers, a Swedish immigrant and a key player in all that destruction, ended up owning 2,200 of those acres. When Callie learned that he had died in 1958, she wasn't sorry.

"The Native Americans suffered the most when the Great Oasis passed away in 1912," said Miss Wigg, who had tried and failed to get a petition going to reclaim it. For a long time, she coped with disgruntled farmers and townspeople flinging mud at her windows in the middle of the night, and tossing stacks of huge branches on top of her car. Someone even dumped a bushel of dead carp in her driveway.

Getting up from the judge's swivel chair, Callie wondered how Mr. Fremont and Mr. Nicollet would have reacted to all that destruction.

Through the tall courtroom windows, she watched Grant Van Vulsa, the town drayman, drive his horse down Main Street. Then she looked up at the leafy treetops swaying in the summer wind, massive elms that stood guard over the finest building in the whole of Maywood County. According to her neighbor lady, Julie, who spoke French, the courthouse was "... our own *élégant Palais de Justice* that introduces Masterton's Main Street to the world with *dignité, grandeur*, and courtliness." Little did Callie know that some years later, this elegant building she was standing in and where her father had an office would also be destroyed.

She returned to Judge Carlson's bench and raised the dark mahogany gavel high above her head. The sounds of this wooden hammer blasting against its block reminded Cal of the time she blew up her granddad's shotgun shell with a ball peen hammer. At three short intervals, she banged the gavel three times, totaling her age. The pounding reverberated throughout the courtroom: Because it was a weekend, no one heard the noise or came rushing through the wide door. No one heard Callie pounding the gavel, except her father; he had become accustomed to his daughter's Saturday rituals.

Next to the rear exit of the courtroom, Callie tossed her stale chewing gum into a large brass spittoon sitting on the floor; she glanced inside at the dark spittle lining the bottom. The odor of chewing tobacco and cigar butts co-mingled with the cheesy smells of old law books and stacks of paper shelved in a small anteroom that served as a library. She inched up the narrow back steps leading to the cupola and clock tower, tried to open the leprechaun-like door, but found it locked, as usual.

After retracing her steps back through the courtroom and sliding down the glossy banister to the main floor, Cal slipped in and out of the washroom tucked off to one side, beneath the staircase. The tiny room was filled with the strong scent of liquid soap seeping into the basin from the leaky brass peg of a tarnished dispenser mounted on the wall. If that translucent soap, tinged a bluish-green, could etch everything it touched, Callie wondered, what would it do to her hands?

At the sight of her pal returned to the auditor's office, Tequila jumped up and down, a regular pup on a pogo stick. Will asked Callie how her court proceedings went and listened attentively as she told about her decisions to reclaim the Great Oasis, and to sentence their neighbor, Ruby Ryan, to a year in jail for the harsh ways she treated her husband and children.

"You have a couple of good cases there, Callie."

Will fished a pair of dimes from his pocket and sent his daughter skipping back into the hallway for bottles of soda pop.

Over the noon hour, they told stories—some true, others invented—and talked about a dream trip to California. Will leaned back in his swivel chair, away from the large desk stacked with ledgers and statute books, stretched his arms toward the high, crenellated ceiling, and laced his fingers together at the back of his head, which, to Callie, made his elbows look like the half-open wings of a great blue heron standing at the end of their dock on Lake Shetek, cooling off in a hot summer wind.

Perched high upon the dark green counter top, Cal tapped her heels against the cabinet doors, sipped Grape Nehi, and tossed bits of bread and liverwurst down to Tequila.

After lunch, Will pulled a toothpick from his vest pocket and walked to the washroom with the little dog at his heels.

Back at work, he sat bent over his desk, wearing rimless spectacles, the toothpick clamped in one corner of his mouth, and carefully began filling in columns on a fresh page of the massive accounting book with thin, birdlike numbers drawn with an extra fine-tipped nib dipped in black ink.

Before pedaling back home with Tequila, Callie read aloud several lines from one of the large books: "Pursuant to Minnesota Statutes, the administrator's office is required to collect. . . ."

Bored by those words, she closed the volume and peeked inside the office vault with its long table, a manual adding machine at one end, and floor-to-ceiling shelves filled with ancient ledgers that smelled like musty grass and dried vanilla; in many of those books the original black ink had turned to sepia.

"Bye, Pops," she said, on her way out with Tequila tucked under one arm.

Callie's father, hand poised above a ledger, looked up over his glasses, and waved with pen in hand. "So long, Skeeziks. See you at suppertime."

NOW RELAXED in the passenger seat, riding along toward Richland Center, Will examined his toothpick, maneuvered the wooden sliver to the opposite corner of his mouth, and kept it there for a time.

"Are you out of pipe tobacco?" asked Callie, her hands at ten and two on the steering wheel.

"Uh-huh."

"Shall we stop to buy some?"

"Not necessary."

"It'll be good to get back home to Mom. And Liz and Brian and the kids. Let them know what we found in Rockford. Or didn't find!"

"I wonder how *they* would have reacted to Hannah and Nellie," he said, referring to his elderly cousins who lived not far from the Swedish Cemetery. "Especially Nellie. Sure didn't figure on her being so against our uncle all these years. She's what you'd call a . . . um . . . what's that word?"

"A homophobe. I think we both know how the rest of our family would have reacted. I can just hear Mom say, 'Now see here, Nellie, Uncle Amer had feelings, too, same as you and me. Just because he was different, with dreams of his own, doesn't make him any less of a human being.'"

"Sounds like Emily. Yes, that's precisely what she would have said."

"And deserving of a marker. She'd say that, too. 'Uncle Amer deserves a tombstone.'"

"Could be. I don't know. Guess everybody should have one. At least, he wasn't tossed into some potter's field out there in Montana. Such an untimely death—murdered by those no-goods! It always struck me, even when I was a kid and he left to go homesteading, that if Amer had stayed on with us, he might have lived to be an old man. He could have played his violin for years to come, kept playing with the Hadley Buttermakers for as long as he could pitch a baseball."

"He had to follow his dream, Pops."

"I know, but the acreage we farmed back then was so rich, hard to beat raising crops down there in the southwest. We had it all! Hadley's not far from Buffalo Ridge, you know, smack dab in the center of Maywood County, surrounded by prairie grass and cornfields. You can't beat that, along with Lake Summit and all those sloughs for hunting. What more could a fellow want?"

"What I said still goes, Dad. Amer had to chance it out West even though things were stacked against him—especially those tough men that couldn't accept him for who he was."

"If it weren't for those damned Carmichael brothers . . ."

"I know. Too many folks rail against what they don't understand. Ada Berg, for instance. Remember her?

"Of course."

"She never murdered anybody, but she sure criticized people. Even made fun of her son. Came close to killing his spirit. Shoot, she might have for all I know."

"Remind me."

"He'd done really well in college, straight A's, but had trouble with the little things in life. Don't you recall how she used to bitch about all the stuff he couldn't do? Practical things like taking out the garbage after it had piled up in a corner, keeping appointments, checking the oil level in his car and air in the tires, didn't know how to fix a door hinge, and on and on."

"What was that she said about him?"

"'An educated fool. That's all he is,' she'd say, 'Tommy is nothin' but an educated fool! All he cares about is books, books, and more books. You should see how he stacks 'em all up in the attic! I told him there ain't no room in the house proper for all that stuff, so ya gotta put 'em up there. Get 'em out of my way! Educated fool! He don't even know how to pound a nail into a hunk a wood.'

"Ada spewed those words with a most scornful look on her stupid face—smug old battle-axe! Imagine, putting her own kid down simply because he surpassed the family in what she called, 'Liberal arts smarts farts.'"

"I prefer the phrase without that last word, Cal. Pretty crude . . . sounds like jealousy to me—old Auntie Ada could have used a little schooling herself."

"Jealousy, prejudice, control: They'll never go away. Poor Uncle Amer. It must have been horrible to see him dead when you and Granddad went out there."

"Never got over it; witnessing him like that left quite an impression on me at sixteen. All Amer wanted was to make good on his land claim and build a life in Montana. Hell, during my lifetime, I've seen so much crap aimed at folks who are working hard to get ahead."

"I know," said Callie. "Road-blocks plunked down smack dab in front of those of us trying to make our mark."

She thought about what her ex-husband had told friends and family shortly after they were married—words she'd found amusing at the time, like when her mother used to tell her, "Oh, Ducky, don't make waves." Only later did she realize the true implication of Jim's comments after someone had said during the reception, "That Cal. She's a feisty one."

"Don't worry," he replied, rubbing his fingernails against the lapel of his tweed jacket, "whenever she gets too smart for her own britches, I'll set her straight, whip her into shape."

Callie thought he was joking, that he was actually proud of her fun-loving spirit and the so-called masculine stuff she knew how to do: toss a football, dig for worms and catch fish, play softball, swim out to the middle of the bay and back, row a boat. As a young girl, reading *Treasure Island*, she imagined herself as the cabin boy, just like Jim Hawkins, sitting in an apple barrel aboard ship, eavesdropping on the pirates. She'd thrilled at the idea of stowing away on Captain Cook's barque, the Endeavour. As a very little girl, she begged to meet and play with Sinbad, Dog of the Seven Seas, after seeing him in a short movie.

Home alone one snowy afternoon, and feeling the need for a little exercise, Callie rearranged the living room furniture. As soon as Jim walked in and noticed what she had done, he flew into a rage, chastising her for failing to ask permission. He flung open the sliding door and, while the wind and snow blew in, he shoved the new sofa out into a drift. Eyes wide, mouth agape, Callie froze, wondering if she would be next.

As the years passed, Cal's enthusiasm for life began to derail. The more she spoke up, stating her own opinions about various issues, and the more creative she tried to be, digging her heels in to hold on to her true self, the greater her husband's escalation of preventive measures: He declared that her talents were minimal, her ideas off track, her self-esteem too high. At gatherings, he would take charge, announcing, "Callie and I think this way . . . Callie and I think that way."

Sometimes, when they went fishing together, Jim ordered Cal to sit at the center of the boat. Then he kept a constant eye on her bobber. After a while, when he turned away, she stuck her tongue out at him and inched her way back to the bow.

Finally, as the months passed, he insisted on knowing where she was at all times.

All of that happened little by little, until one Friday evening, when Callie returned home from shopping, Jim yanked the door open and screamed at her for being fifteen minutes late for a dinner he'd prepared. He stabbed the over-done T-bone steak with a long fork and pitched it into the sink, topped up his glass of scotch, tossed Cal's barking sheltie onto the lawn, along with her car keys, kicked the door shut, and chased her through the house, raging at length, until he lost his voice.

Cal escaped, found her keys and her dog, and drove through the countryside, hoping that enough time would go by for Jim to pass out so that she could return home and be safe. Eventually, she stopped crying and felt angry that the old religious take on marriage still existed, muddling around in the brains of those who agreed that, no matter what, women should obey their husbands. That belief should have dissolved years ago, she told herself—deleted from the church records.

And then she focused on her parents, whose marriage made her feel happy, yet lonely; lonely for the kind of companionship she'd always witnessed between them. She envied their marriage, and that of her sister Liz and brother-in-law Brian. Spending time with family, in their homes, was like finding a protective cove during a storm: They were havens of order and peace where she could restore her mind and spirit: tell jokes, state her own opinions, laugh at her father's stories, try out her mother's old recipes, receive warm hugs.

Sometimes, Callie wished that she could return to the place of her youth, especially one day when she witnessed a young filly separated from its mother, and saw how, standing alone, the little horse cried out with trembling lips, while the mare whinnied from a distance.

The next morning, when Jim awakened to find Cal seated at the kitchen table, searching the yellow pages for an attorney, he gave her a quick hug and said, "I'm sorry about last night, Callie-Cal. It'll never happen again." Then he left for the farmer's market to buy a batch of yellow gladiolas.

Sometime later, though, it did happen again. And then again...and again . . .

But you finally made it out of that quagmire—the deadliest part— Cal reminded herself while humming a tune along with the clicking rhythm of tires on pavement. Like a choir director, she waved a hand high above the steering wheel.

"Now there's a simple melody," said Will, re-examining his toothpick. "What's it called?"

" 'I Did It My Way,' " she sang, looking to her dad who winked and nodded knowingly.

A cluster of pine trees and spruce offered up splashes of green just off the highway near Richland Center. Cal lowered her window in order to smell the fresh air. From the tops of those trees flew several broad-winged hawks in search of a meal among some of the smaller birds gathered in nearby fields. Callie honked the car's horn through a count of three.

This time, Will did not question her. Instead, he watched the hawks scatter, leaving the smaller birds to enjoy their lunch of leftover grain.

After leaving Rockford the previous afternoon, Callie and Will had driven through Beloit and Janesville toward Madison, Wisconsin. Rather than head for Eau Claire, Will suggested highway 14 toward Black Earth, Spring Green, La Crosse, and all sights in between, including the Kickapoo River Valley. Later, they would drive along the Mississippi River before reaching Saint Paul and continuing westward to Long Lake.

"That way," he said, "we can soak up all of those great views."

And so they would: the colorful fall leaves; farmland and small towns; lakes with waterfowl preparing to fly south along the steadily marching rivers.

"Seeing all of this reminds me of Uncle Amer."

"I know, Dad, what you said back there in the cemetery—that he'll be remembered whenever we see or hear the things that he loved."

Will pointed at several Canada geese gathered on a small lake, their necks as long as axe handles. And in a nearby field, a young calf, born late in the season, stood alongside its mother.

"We talked for a long time with the McKammans, back there in Montana," said Will. "You know, friends that took care of Amer just before he died. When he told them that he wasn't a religious man, Mrs. McKamman reminded him of the newborn calf he had saved—stayed up all night to make sure it would pull through. And she talked about how he'd play his violin and dance evenings. 'I'll always picture your uncle and Radge,' she said, 'dancing together at the edge of their day's work.'

"At sixteen, I couldn't understand why the Carmichaels had it in for him so, why they'd want to kill him. And Mrs. McKamman talked about the evil in this world, how some folks think it's their right, their duty, even, to bring down and destroy what they don't understand—anything, anyone that's different. 'They are the ignorant dregs of the earth,' she said. 'Beauty and truth inside the soul of another, unlike their own, are threats to be eliminated like troublesome honeybees.'

"Those were Mrs. McKamman's own words. 'Why if it weren't for the honeybees of this world . . .'"

Will removed the toothpick from the corner of his mouth and tucked it back into his breast pocket. "As I said, Cal, the image of Amer's unmarked plot is bothering me again. And seeing that old dog near the gas station outside of Spring Green . . . I don't know. Left me feeling a bit out of kilter. Doesn't take much these days to broadside me."

"It'll be all right, Dad." Callie tapped her fingers lightly at the center of the steering wheel to the three-quarter rhythm of their favorite dance tune. "We'll get things figured out, *mio babbino*."

"I see you're not wearing much fingernail polish these days."

Cal smiled and waved a hand. "Too many fish to clean!"

DOGS AND CEMETERIES AND PEOPLE. Start, stop, start, stop. Lives, like automobiles, run on and on 'til they're out of gas. Like the life of Radge. And Tequila. And now that old dog between the motel and gas station. It's curious to imagine what kind of existence anybody gets born into and how most everyone and everything on this earth either struggles or dances—or manages somehow to do both—in order to make it through to the end.

Callie thought about the deaths of her grandparents and the remaining time her father would have left, and if he'd ever see his brother again. She pondered Uncle Amer's life and the lives of folks from around Masterton, who, during her own growing up years, made such vivid impressions on her with their efforts to figure out who they were, what they wished to become, how they suited up in order to be somebody, their names written across store fronts, clinics, and law offices, on the side of a truck, above a dairy, on mailboxes, and now on tombstones.

As a young girl, although she wasn't sure of what all it entailed, Callie had learned that some of the so-called up-and-coming couples in town belonged to what they called a "Key Club." As a result of further eavesdropping, she pictured a drunken party and a bunch of house keys placed in a large bowl. If one of the men drew his own, he had to put it back and try again. Sometimes, a man knew precisely which key he wished to pluck from the glass receptacle.

Cal concluded that no one is ever finished growing up until it's time to leave this earth for good. And then who knows? Some spirits might decide to lift off and dart around the places and people they loved (or hated) in life, give 'em a little nudge—a wispy shadow, slight movements seen from the corner of an eye, the shifting of a windowpane, a sudden puff of air in the still of night, a creaking door, the burst of a flame amid hot coals, sweet notes flitting through the trees. If spirits exercise their ways and means, then yes, they'll be there.

While driving along the highway, recalling that doddering dog's driver prancing around his car to the music in his head, Callie began to hum the song about Mr. Bo Jangles and how he danced—remembering how her dad used to sashay around the house, hitching a shoulder to catchy tunes—and how Mr. Bo Jangles traveled everywhere with his dog and how, one day, his dog up and died.

Like the one she tried to save one cold and bleak winter, during the final year of her marriage to Jim. She recalled what happened that Sunday as if it were an unforgettable scene from a movie. As if the main character up there on that wintry screen were someone other than Cal. Which, in a way was true, because when things got rough, Callandra Mae Lindstrom was able to step outside of herself.

3

Gone to the Dogs

If a dog will not come to you after he has looked you in the face,
you should go home and examine your conscience.
—*Woodrow Wilson*

"I'M NOT GOING TO RESCUE YOU if you go down, Callie. He's most likely dead anyway."

It was first light on a cold Monday morning. The instant Callie cracked open the lakeside door, a blast of icy wind chased dust balls and sheets of paper across the hardwood floor. The frigid gust tipped over a faded snapshot of Cal and her husband, Jim.

"Who needs you," she growled back at him.

"You're a damned fool," he countered. "An idiot. Why don't you think for a change? Stay put. Besides, you'll be late for work."

"This is more important."

Lately, wherever Callie went, whatever she did, Jim cast a mean word after her. As a result, in order to survive his daily doses of cruelty, she had started to become someone she didn't much care for. In fact, hated. Like a dog who expects to be kicked, she turned and curled her lip at him before rushing out of the door, down the steps, and across the snow-glutted yard. She grabbed the iron railing and slipped along the icy concrete cuts of a snow-packed hill. By the time Cal reached the rocky shoreline and brushed away flakes from the seat of her pants, she'd cooled off, simmered down.

The temperature hovered at five below zero, plus wind chill—unusually cold for March. Nippy inside the house, too.

Callie grabbed a long stick from the woodpile and jabbed it ahead of her as she stepped onto the frozen bay. If the stick went through the ice, she'd have to find an alternate path, sections still thick enough to bear her weight. Once she'd made it across the slab closest to land, she'd be safer. But because there'd been enough mild days and pelting rain to begin the rotting process, one never knew for sure which parts of the lake were weak and honeycombed and which were safe enough to trek across. The fact that Callie was slender, yet strong enough to hoist herself back onto an ice shelf in case she fell through, might also help to keep her from drowning.

At least there were no rivulets trickling against the shoreline, forth and back, from beneath corroding edges of black ice. When that happens, the entire bay begins to pulsate, breathing, breathing, heaving under its own weight, causing ebbs and flows that litter an open body of water with shards of ice melting under a warm sun.

Paying attention to color (a deteriorating gray amidst the white) and consistency and the solid versus hollow or slushy sounds of her stick tapping against that great block of ice were all Callie had to go on as she inched towards her destination: a dark, furry, lifeless lump in the middle of the bay. Had the animal survived the piercingly cold, windy hours of the long night? Or had he frozen to death?

Callie first noticed the black and white dog around noon on a Sunday, running up and down the long stretch of West Arm Bay, where she and Jim were renting a cottage. She had watched him for a while, pleased to witness such exuberant play in a Sheltie, who appeared to be herding dead leaves fluttering across the surface between Skogsberg and

Fagerness Points. Perhaps he was just getting his exercise after being cooped up all morning.

Cal hummed a tune and went about her business, trying her hand at painting with watercolors, which she loved to do as a girl: vivid green palm trees and a red sail in the far distance on an azure sea. Now and then, she looked up and out of the window at the colorless, frozen bay.

By mid-afternoon, the dog was still running. Only now he seemed confused, as if searching for someone or something that was nowhere to be found.

Dressed in a thermal jacket, Callie hiked down to the shore and called out to the animal, tried to coax him in. But he veered off, sweeping along the ice until she thought he'd run his heart out.

Scanning the far shoreline with binoculars, she focused on a cluster of people at the other end of the bay. Some stood rigid, wringing their mittened hands, while others pushed a yellow and blue inflatable ahead of them. The dog skittered in the opposite direction each time they drew near.

Callie jogged back up the hill, grabbed her car keys, jumped in, pumped the gas pedal until the sluggishly cold engine ground to a start, and drove around the lake. After several turns on narrow streets, she located the neighborhood where a rescue team had gathered. One woman was crying. Her husband, also grief-stricken, had his arm around her shoulders.

"We're supposed to be dog-sitting," said the woman whose husband was equally concerned. "His name is Nick. We've been trying to catch him all day."

Callie joined in, calling the dog's name over and over while two men from the fire department scooted around behind their raft. The ice, extending out from a deep cove, was less stable on this side of the bay.

"It's impossible," said one, shaking his head, about to give up. "We don't dare chase after him on foot much less on a machine."

"Even if we did," said the other, "he'd take off again. He's definitely disoriented, probably looking for his home, family, something familiar."

Home for Nick was on a small lake in northern Minnesota, not here on this massive body of water west of Minneapolis, where gigantic houses sprawled across most of the land. And his humans were on vacation.

Although the outcome remained uncertain, there was something beautiful about Nick skimming over the ice as if sailing on a stiff breeze, ignoring peoples' desperate commands to "Stop! Sit! Stay! Come!" Although he didn't know where he was or where he was going, he was free.

Callie returned home, saddened by their failure to catch Nick, but heartened by the actions of caring people—especially such compassionate men; a novelty of late, she thought, wending her way back home and down, once again, to her own shoreline. How long could that dog run before he collapsed? Before his heart gave out?

At dusk, Nick was still running, except at a much slower pace and stopping often to gaze about and lick at the pads of his feet. Then, as night fell, he lay down on the ice, in the open, with his back to a bitter north wind.

Callie kept vigil from an upstairs window, squinting into the darkness until she could no longer see what looked like a small, dark boulder in the middle of that broad, olive drab and white expanse. Reluctantly, she went to bed, imagining the slow death of this exhausted animal.

The last thing her husband said to her was, "You wasted a whole day on that damn dog. How stupid was that?"

Wracking her brain for words recently memorized and added to her own verbal arsenal, she shouted, "You're nothing but a loggerheaded shard-borne scut!"

Sneering, Jim turned on his heels. "Where'd you get that?"

"Shakespeare."

"Ha! You and Shakespeare? What a laugh! Bet you don't even know what those words mean."

"Fat-kidneyed barnacle," muttered Callie, for once getting in the last word without feeling the sting of a slap across her face.

First thing Monday morning, after a restless night, Cal set out on her somewhat treacherous hike across the bay, determined but cautious, with Jim's words, "I'm not going to rescue you if you go down," running through her mind like a needle stuck in the groove of a vinyl record. She was determined not to go down. But if that did happen, she'd try to break ice and kick her legs until she could raise herself up and out—that is, unless hypothermia set in first.

She thought of her aunt Lilly, who'd died that way when she was just a young girl, gone down in Lake Wilson while skating too near a bridge. Callie hoped her mother wouldn't have to receive similar news all these years later. Although Emily had witnessed her sister's plunge well over sixty-five years ago, Callie knew she'd never get over a second drowning in the family. At least I don't have to scoot around any bridges, she thought, where the ice is always thin.

From a distance, Cal saw no movement in the dark mound of a dog. No sign of life. It didn't surprise her. How could any being, even one with a triple coat, survive such a night without shelter?

She could hardly bear to admit that Jim had probably been right. Yet, even though Nick might be dead, she couldn't leave him lying out there on the ice. At that moment, she realized how unprepared she was, having left the house wearing only a light jacket. No hat, a pair of thin gloves, and nothing to wrap around the little dog. Perhaps her husband was watching out for them after all, waiting with a warm blanket, ready to mourn with her, or to celebrate. She wished for that, but couldn't count on it. Such thoughts and gestures had become increasingly foreign to Jim—at home, yet not at work. Once, she'd asked him why he could never treat her and her family as well as he treated his students and colleagues. His reply: "Because I get paid for that!"

As Callie approached the Sheltie, she saw his head move slightly. Then he focused his eyes on her and made an effort to stand, but wasn't able. She tried to pick him up and couldn't. The warmth of Nick's body had melted the ice enough to refreeze onto long strands of belly hair, as well as on the gauntlet-like feathers beneath his forelegs. Nick was stuck.

With nothing to cut him free, Callie set to work peeling him away several fibers and layers at a time.

"Good boy, Nicky. You'll be fine," she crooned to a dog she'd never met until now, all the while tugging at his fur—some by the roots, which must have hurt him terribly. Yet, he never snapped at her or even whimpered. He just went limp and rested his muzzle on the ice. "We'll make it, Nick. We're gonna make it."

Then Callie remembered the car keys in her jacket pocket and used them to saw forth and back, first at the long strands the length of his legs, then at the belly fur. She sawed and pulled and peeled and when they were finished, they'd left behind several black and white clumps, which would eventually go down with the clutching ice as soon as spring nudged aside the long, cold winter. She snatched Nick up before he could bolt again (although he seemed to have little inclination), bundled him inside her jacket, and started for home along her proven path.

Above the sounds of her own labored breathing, Callie heard cries from along the shoreline some distance behind her, "Have you seen a little dog?"

"Yes, I have him!" she shouted back. "Follow me!"

Although she knew these were the dog-sitters, Callie was reluctant to stop until she had Nick safely inside her own home.

She'd given the dog a rub down and filled a bowl with water by the time the couple rushed across the last stretch of bay, up the hillside, and into the house. Exhausted and elated that Nick was alive, the woman cried and laughed at the same time. So did her husband who turned to embrace his wife. Then he hugged Callie. Having grown accustomed to living with a man concerned only for himself and his workplace, it amazed Cal to meet one with such empathy, such warm feelings for another. And for Nick. She closed the lakeside door, still feeling the kind touch from this stranger, and then stood next to the couple while they took turns cuddling the dog.

Jim, whom Nick had warily approached, then shied away from, was on his way out the back door. It didn't surprise Callie that Nick would go nowhere near her husband. Often, when their own dog (now deceased) entered the house, his tail dropped to the floor and he cast sidelong glances at Jim as he slinked off to a different room.

With his hand on the doorknob, Jim turned briefly. "You were lucky, Callie," he said with a snort. "A lucky fool." Then he left.

"We want to pay you," said the woman after Jim had gone.

"Yes, yes," said the man, reaching for his wallet.

Callie refused the offer of a reward. For a bit of time the three of them watched in silence as Nick lapped up the water in his bowl and pranced around the living room, stopping long enough to lick Cal's hand and look up into her face.

Two days later, the receptionist at the school where Callie taught music summoned her to the office.

"There's a surprise for you," she said in a sing-song voice. "Just delivered."

As Cal approached the main office, she saw a splash of red towering above the counter, a color and shapes rarely seen during northern winters.

The receptionist, standing next to the red roses, was wearing a you-devil-you grin.

"A dozen," she said. "I counted them. And I peeked at the card: 'TO CALLIE, WITH LOVE, FROM NICK.' Who's Nick?"

Callie remembered the bay ice and said in a voice shaky with emotion, "The beginning of something fine."

4

Flowers Don't Talk Back

Deep in their roots, all flowers keep the light.
—Theodore Roethke

STILL UNCERTAIN about how and when she could get her own life back, Cal figured if Nick could make it, then so could she. Remembering that proverb in Dana's book, she repeated it to herself: "Every dog must have his day, and mine will come by and by."

True, there had been some good moments with Jim, especially early on—trips to Lake Superior where they'd traipsed along the shoreline, gathering cloth bags full of smooth round stones, which Callie had saved, kept in a large basket on the hearth. They'd roasted hotdogs above the St. Croix River, on the Wisconsin side, read poetry aloud, tossed a football back and forth, waded in the cool water, and explored small caves as night fell—caves carved centuries ago into the lower parts of cliffs that rose high above the easy-flowing river.

Afterward, they sat on a pebbly shore watching the full moon turn from misty orange to pale cream as it rose higher in the sky. Callie pointed out the lady's profile, as she had tried to do on other occasions. But Jim could never see it—not even on a clear night like that.

JIM LOVED FLOWERS. On a Saturday morning, home from the local farmers' market, he stepped inside, embracing tall stalks of gladiolas, some of them yellow, Callie's favorite color. He'd also bought a tiny glass vase for the lilies of the valley that pushed through the earth next to the foundation of their cottage. While mowing the lawn, he never failed to leave an occasional wild daisy and volunteer violet standing inches above the cut grass: He called them "eye candy."

Eventually, Callie realized Jim's preference for things that spoke silent languages. As long as she kept still, stifling her thoughts and opinions, she would be treated as one of the flowers. Fortunately, there was a second acceptable language: the printed word. She had grown to love great prose and poetry, which Jim often read aloud to her—Hemingway, Yeats, Steinbeck. Later, he quoted from *Tropic of Cancer* by Henry Miller, whose remarks about women Callie found unsettling. She grabbed the novel and read these words: "There's something perverse about women. . . they're all masochists at heart."

Cal tossed the book aside. "What the hell!"

"One can find answers to everything in great literature," said Jim.

And then there was music.

Callie's life was already steeped in classical compositions, her piano and teaching skills. After she had met Jim, he introduced her to jazz; the voices of Ella Fitzgerald, Sarah Vaughn, Mel Torme; the keyboard sounds of Dave Brubeck; Stan Getz's saxophone; the Hot Club styles of Stéphane Grappelli and Django Reinhardt. He had even bought tickets for a Grappelli concert at Orchestra Hall, where that sonorous violin prompted such a sense of gaiety and well-being that Callie and her husband had, for a few moments, held hands.

But all of that happened long ago. Much of the good in her life with Jim had faded, overridden by the threats and abuse she could never forget. And later, Cal would wonder how she had ever endured those days, months, and years of insults and humiliation, the isolation from friends and family. Her friends finally stayed away: When Callie refused to turn her back on family, however, she paid the price. It was when she argued fiercely against being reduced to increasing degrees of nothingness, that the slapping and shoving began.

There was the night Jim came home smelling of strange perfume. His response to Callie's questions was flinging a book of poems at her (the one they used to read together), striking her between the eyes.

"You hurt me!" she cried, covering her face with her hands.

"I wish I'd blinded you," he shouted and walked out, leaving Callie to remember his words—in some ways, more lethal than bullets—for the rest of her life.

The softest place she had ever landed was in a huge snowdrift just outside their house. There she lay, for the third time in as many winters, sinking down, down, while the backdoor to her home clicked on lock. After the first of these landings, which shocked her, she became adept at giving herself over to the comforting snow—the soft, soothing crystalline snow that enveloped her. She didn't cry. Never cry outside in winter, her mother used to say, or you'll come down with pneumonia. Callie lay there for a long while, melting into the drift, remembering when she used to make snow angels. Only this time, she could barely move her arms or legs. She could only tilt her head back and look up at the sliver of a moon and the deep, starlit sky, while the cold seeped through her woolen sweater and slacks, reminding her that she was still alive. Cal tried to remember if her mother ever told her not to cry in summer.

As she tried to figure out how to get back in from the cold, her thoughts drifted down to the bay and how one day in spring it is blocked by ice and the next day it is completely free and flowing and the wind ripples across the surface and a hundred gulls and ducks scoot in, calling, partying.

You are free too, she told herself. Something inside you loosens up and you run along the shore and step into the freezing cold water so you can remember the winter and how it was and now isn't going to be for much longer and you get to live for another summer.

A push and a shove, the slamming of the door, a click of the lock, a snowdrift's embrace. Touch leaves memory. And words leave images—some lovely, others sliced to bits and full of scars from all those word swords. Scabbard upon scabbard of lethal word swords.

How could Jim give her both the gift of a leather briefcase for her piano books and sheet music, and a rage-filled night; a bouquet of yellow flowers and a shove into a freezing snowdrift? According to some people, including her mother-in-law, if Callie wanted to marry and keep a husband, she'd have to subdue herself and submit to his way of thinking and doing.

Bossy words like "Wives, obey your husbands," poured out of pastors' mouths during wedding ceremonies Callie attended as a girl, a teen, a young adult.

In the dark, lying deep in the drift, and growing colder and colder, she still couldn't do it—give up who she was, who she might become.

"Now, how the hell do I keep on rowing," she muttered, turning her head from side to side, "against three feet of this stuff?" From her mattress of snow, Callie eased herself up to a sitting position and focused on the two leafless maple trees and the one giant evergreen that graced their backyard.

The cracking and growling of shifting bay ice echoed in the quiet. A pair of Canadas flew low overhead, towards the snowy peak of the garage. Wind whistled through their wing feathers.

Callie gathered a double handful of white crystals and packed them into a hard ball, which she threw at the door. It was a feeble toss because her arms and bare hands were freezing cold. Yet with the impact of her snowball against that cheap aluminum storm door, she would have the last words:

Callandra Mae Lindstrom is not about to go down for keeps.

Come spring, she would figure out how to get away from a man who brought home yellow flowers and spared the violets and wild daisies rising in the summer grass, yet shoved a coatless human being into a snow bank and locked the door on her.

"Well," she muttered to the bare trees, "I guess it's because flowers never talk back."

And yet one evening, while "The Christmas Waltz" played on the radio, Jim took Cal in his arms and danced her around the living room, trying to hitch his shoulders in rhythm to their triple steps. For the umpteenth time, Callie fell back on the only definition of the word 'hope' that mattered to her—"the pinning of a possibility." Still she wondered how many more times she could latch onto it before *that* pin broke, stabbing closer to the heart. Because when you give up on hope and toss it aside, you have to figure out another way to endure.

A friend once asked Callie, "Why on earth did you marry the guy? Why do you stay with him?"

"Who knows?" she'd answered. "Why does anyone do anything? I guess, at the beginning, it was how he called me 'Callie-Cal' when we were out on the lakes fishing; except, now that I think of it, he always kept a close eye on my bobber, as well as his own.

"I loved the way he read poetry aloud, especially 'The Song of Wandering Aengus,' making me believe that I was the 'glimmering girl with apple blossom in her hair.' He kissed my lips and took my hand and off we went for a hike along a trout stream in Montana. Here was a man who loved music, verse, flowers, and, supposedly, the moon. He made it sound as though that's how he would live his life. And love me in return. It had to end, though, because I couldn't count on that last part."

"Wasn't it one of Rudyard Kipling's characters who said that men who begin to quote poetry are going to flit? Like swans before they die?" asked her friend Cindy.

Cal laughed. "Could be. Anyhow, I decided to become my own 'wandering aengus' and pluck those apples all by myself."

Cindy then told about a discovery that had nearly brought *her* down. She had found photos and love letters exchanged between her husband and a much younger woman—a girl, really.

"After reading a few of them, I forced myself from the clutches of the chair, that fly-catcher armchair next to the fireplace, grabbed a shot glass from the kitchen cupboard, ran out to the garage, and poured an ounce of gasoline into that glass."

Standing in front of her fireplace, Cindy, tall and slender with shoulder-length red hair, toasted the truth, along with her decision to file for divorce, and slammed the glass against the bricks, just above the burning heap of letters and graphic photos. The flames exploded up the chimney, sounding like a thousand ravens taking wing.

"You are no more," Cindy told those ashes.

Callie still had that little glass vase that held lilies of the valley growing next to the house where she and Jim used to live. But like all of the other gifts, lovely as they were, they could never make up for the bruises and hostile words, the confusion and deep sadness that would take such a long while to overcome.

"If I could hold forever one really fun place and time," she'd told her friend, "it would be Queen's Bluff on a hot summer's day, high above the St. Croix River."

Unaware that rattlesnakes could exist in the north, and carrying bags of fried chicken, she and Jim had climbed that bluff in shorts and sneakers. He snapped Callie's picture while she lounged in the tall grass, a smile on her lips, her smooth skin and dark brown hair, thick as a lamb's coat, glowing in the afternoon sunshine.

"I still have that photo somewhere," she said, "in a box of keepsakes. We sat with our feet dangling over the edge of the cliff and ate our take-out chicken, tossing the bones into a ravine below. There we were, right up there in the clear blue sky. Oh, we had so much fun that day.

"You know, I'd always hoped things would get better for us, that we could find our way back to earlier times."

"Believe me," said Cindy, "hope can be a mean thing. Sometimes, it keeps us in a place longer than we should stay."

Callie glanced across the room at her hope chest, a gift built of cedar, given in anticipation of her marriage, once filled with lace doilies and tablecloths, cream-colored pillowcases and sheets made of silk, white china teacups and saucers decorated with spring violets, a pink negligée and slippers, miniature pillows. All those things had been used up and worn out long ago; now the chest was loaded with books, sheet music, fishing tackle, and albums bulging with snapshots, including family members and the out-of-doors. Callie especially liked the one of her dog Piper taken at dusk when he was racing the length of a moonbeam pouring down the center of their ice-covered bay. The only image remaining of her husband was the one taken at the top of Queen's Bluff, overlooking the St. Croix.

In the first year of their marriage, Jim had written a poem for Cal, entitled "*Savoir.*" At the time, she had failed to recognize the warning in it. Years later, while sorting through her hope chest and a shoebox of treasures tucked away on a closet shelf, she found the half sheet of yellowed typing paper with these faded lines:

"*Little wise girl/knows me more than I/She holds me from myself/when I scream black wrath/or shatter the night.*"

What had made Jim like this? After all, during most of their nine years together, she had sometimes tried to change who she was in order to please him. Wouldn't that stop the abuse? Wouldn't it? But no matter how hard she'd tried to be a different person, someone supposedly more to his liking, none of it had worked. It would be during the third trimester of their marriage that Callie, with her sister Liz's aid and encouragement, could muster the energy and fortitude to get out—to save what was left of her self.

All other resources had proven useless: When she asked for help from her mother-in-law, a gospel-greedy enthusiast, the woman's walk-away reply was, "Go see a priest." Callie wasn't even Catholic.

"I thought you had relatives who were," said her friend.

"An aunt, but that was a long time ago. She had arranged for Mom to borrow a coffee urn from the church basement to use for grandma's funeral—that's as close as I ever got."

"Well, *I* went to see our local priest for some counseling," said Cindy. "I was desperate. But one session was all I could handle. That old guy sat on the other side of his desk and told me I'd have to change my attitude, that I was too aggressive. 'It doesn't work,' he said. 'It's detrimental to a marriage if a woman behaves in too forward a fashion. Wives need to be more docile and obey their husbands.' I left his office thinking the hell with that shit. It's the '80s for God's sake and they're still trying to stick us into that ancient morass? Besides, priests have no personal experience. As far as I'm concerned seeking marital counseling from one of them is like asking advice of a deaf-mute who can't read lips."

"Maybe if the priest had been younger...."

Cindy curled her lip. "Ha! Maybe we'd be better off finding a book on self-help, if there *is* one."

"I never thought of that," said Cal.

When she had begged two of Jim's teaching colleagues for help, they answered, "Sorry, he's our friend. We don't want to get involved." And they never spoke to her again.

When she confided in Doctor Carlson during a routine physical, explaining Jim's alcoholic explosions aimed at her with increasing violence, the doctor replied, "Just go home and be a more loving wife."

And *that* she could no longer figure out how to do and still be true to herself.

Cal was beginning to feel like a poppy in dry season, one that produced only a blossom or two and then dropped its petals before anyone could take notice.

Beyond those three attempts for help in order to hold on and survive, she kept quiet, not wanting her own family to know the details. Not just yet. After all, divorce still carried a stigma. And she wanted to show her parents, who had sensed something unsettling in this man early on, that she would hang in there—hope being the key word.

With that intent, she recalled those summer swallows who rebuilt their nests filled with eggs and nestlings ripped out by storms, over and over again. Yet, they knew when their time was running short with fall in the wings. They knew when to stop and fly away south.

Then there was that injured Canada goose hunted by a hawk. Unable to fly, he managed to hobble across the ice field and find cover.

The golden line her father had provided long ago became her mantra: "Keep on rowing, Callie girl, you just keep on a-rowing."

Thankfully, it was Nick, that tenacious little Sheltie, racing along the bay ice, then hunkering down for survival throughout the bitter night, who surfaced in Callie's mind, nudging aside the grief and confusion, encouraging her to get up and out of that snowdrift, making her feel more whole again with the memory of having helped to save his life.

Some months later, another dog would save *her* life.

5

Food for the Spirit

Dogs are better than human beings
because they know but do not tell.
— Emily Dickinson

MYRIAD STORIES TELL of canines saving peoples' lives by barking non-stop in the middle of the night when a fire breaks out or an intruder breaks in. Dogs protect children, tuck in babies, and look out for their masters. They watch over strangers in distress, such as the dog who helped to keep alive the imprisoned Saint Roch, a 14th century ascetic, by bringing him scraps of bread each morning.

For Callie, it wasn't nourishment for the body that was meted out by a certain farm dog who appeared in a country cemetery one afternoon, but food for a fractured spirit.

SEVERAL MONTHS after her miscarriage and immediate separation from Jim, Callie drove far into the countryside to an old and mostly forgotten cemetery called Windy Hill. Feeling closer to the unattended dead than to the living, she'd parked between the edge of a cornfield and the last row of tilted tombstones. After stepping slowly from her car, she stood clutching the door-frame for several minutes, looking first to the willow tree at one corner of the graveyard, then to the little brook that ran nearby.

As a young girl, she pranced through groves, measured trees by wrapping her arms around their trunks, and climbed them, especially the giant willow behind her family's home in Masterton. She trailed along creeks and waded in them and built dams with her childhood friends, watching their barricades of mud, leaves, clay, twigs, and stones hold for a time before trickling leaks gained in size and strength to flush away the dams. Flowing water and trees, after all, translated into a part of who Callie was—Lindstrom: the linden tree and the stream.

But this day, the weeping willow and the percolating brook did nothing for her, and so she lay down on the ground and listened to the brittle, sun-dried grass whisper in her ear, all the while feeling as if she were rowing a boat with only one oar and would never be able to stop turning in circles.

Jim had kicked her when she was down. It would be impossible to forget that booted foot swinging hard at her mid-section while she lay sprawled on the floor.

Callie rolled onto her stomach and heaved great sobs into her folded arms. Her pregnancy hadn't even made it past the first trimester. She would never know the sensation of her own water breaking, signaling the impending birth of a baby, being able to welcome new life into the light.

Just this morning, Callie had received the official divorce papers and an order of protection that would put a definitive end to the so-called "rights of other."

"He can't hurt you any more," said her lawyer, extending the brown manila envelope. Of all the people she had turned to during the last years, it was her sister, Liz, and this attorney who would eventually help to save her. No more "Sorry. He's our friend," "Go see a priest," "Just go home and be a more loving wife." Jim's Christian mother, his teacher colleagues, and Dr. Carlson could all go to blazes as far as Callie was concerned.

Her own mother and dad, who never heard about the lurid details until much later, guessed at Callie's on-going struggles. "You're made of strong stuff," said Emily. "We're here for you whenever you need us."

The marriage Callie had hoped for, had tried to change for, was finished. Embarrassment over its failure no longer figured in. She would be like the lady in the moon, looking far into the distance, seeing more clearly.

Just as in a scene from a movie, there would be no going back. On screen, a woman stepped out from a tiny elevator into an enchanting Buddhist-like valley surrounded by lush fields. Gently sloping hills cascaded far into the distance. An abrupt noise—that of a gigantic engine—broke the meditative silence. The woman turned to look behind her and saw gushers of toxins spraying everything in its path, up, down, sideways, spraying trees and squirrels, frogs and toads and turtles, Monarch butterflies and birds of every species, including flocks of swallows, those happy little birds that flitted about, built nests, looked after their young. Dripping with liquid poison everything began to die. All of the birds fell from the sky. And the last of the robed monks walked as though they were about to fall on their faces, lurching, lurching forward.

The massive truck barreled along with its huge tank full of sloshing chemicals, chasing after the woman who raced toward a distant valley overhung with natural mist. She managed to outrun the devil, realizing once and for all that she could never go back from where she had come.

For Callie, the pendulum finally hung still and could no longer swing back to knock her down again. Sometimes, she felt as though she were rowing and rowing, lost at sea with no horizon in sight.

One night, before falling asleep, she mustered an image. Although enshrouded in mist, it left her feeling more anchored than she had in months: "We just keep on rowing, don't we, Callie-girl?" From his boat's center seat, Will let go one oar and pointed at a sandy shoreline in the distance. "Better things are waiting."

Callie drifted into a dream where she was fishing with the women in her family, women who had never fished in their lives, except for

Grandma Julia. Four red and white bobbers danced on the surface. Callie stood at the end of the dock with her mother Emily. Grandma Dahl, enormous and in the unlikeliest of positions, perched next to Liz atop a huge boulder, swinging a long cane pole. Grandma Julia sat in an old wooden boat, manipulating her sleek double rod with a lower unit that fed out the line, and an upper reel that took it back in.

Callie cast her own line in a long, high arc, planting her bobber perfectly nestled among the rest, yet a trifle out of the way. Nodding their heads in approval, Cal's mother and sister and two grandmothers murmured words of encouragement. Then they all settled down to fish.

According to an Ojibwe legend of Leech Lake, many moons ago, an evil spirit captured a maiden and carried her away to a great dry plain. He left her there for a long while, and returned to his wigwam built of solid rock.

Confined to this place of loneliness and destitution, the maiden was visited by an emissary of Hiawatha, leader of the Iroquois. He gave her a strange black stone and taught her how to make it into a spear. Then he showed her where to strike it against the boulders of the great plain.

As soon as the maiden struck the rock, a gusher of water flowed over the dry plain and filled all of the space, allowing her to climb higher and higher up the boulders until she reached the top.

The rising waters imprisoned the evil spirit in his wigwam until the end of time.

As for the maiden, she escaped in a birch bark canoe that had floated out to her from shore.

Lying on the cemetery grass, Callie dried her tears and let a range of memories ripple through her mind like an easy stream, beginning with a favorite line from Puccini's *Madama Butterfly*: "I gave my tears to the earth, and it returns me flowers!" Now, thank heaven, she thought, there'll be no more blasting by a wind that continually blew my petals away.

And she remembered the arrowheads given as gifts to her and her cousin Jenny when they were young girls visiting Belle Kittleson at her tavern near Tepeeotah on Lake Shetek. She still had her prized black arrowhead tucked away on a wad of cotton inside a small box. Once she returned home, she would take that piece of stone out of its box and place it in a spot where she could see it every day for the rest of her life.

How long would it take to arrive at a place that pointed her in the right direction? Like the Indian maiden, Cal could sure use a canoe that would take her there, into those big waters where anything was possible.

Callie knew she must get up off the ground, retrace her steps to the car, and drive back home. But for now, she simply felt too hollow inside, too exhausted to do anything other than lie among the tombstones, a place she found strangely comforting—a place where she could let every thought that wanted in to meander through her mind.

She remembered her Grandpa Dahl who died before Callie turned five. He had the look of a man old before his time—a man who'd stood in long lines for long hours during the Depression, dressed in his rumpled best, only to find there were no jobs. And if there was a job, there'd be little or no pay at the end of his shift. Yet he returned the next day. And the next. Because anything was better than giving up. That's the look he had, her grandfather.

And then she thought of the pioneer women who'd lost their children to cholera or typhoid fever—or to a miscarriage—and had no one to talk to but a sheltering tree bowing over the burial sites at the top of a hill.

For Callie, despite the abuse which had become a predictable way of life, it was unsettling to be on her own and vulnerable in ways she had not yet experienced—a single woman approaching middle-age, responsible for every aspect of daily living. There was so much she didn't know, so many things Jim had always managed. Would she ever be able to recharge a car battery, add motor oil when the level was down, change a tire? Could she work her way through the aisles of a hardware store to pick out the necessary tools she'd need to fix things? Or was she just another 'educated fool?'

Already, she was making progress. She'd managed to pull the sump pump from its watery hole in the basement floor of her cottage in order to figure out, without getting electrocuted, why the damned thing had stopped working. Of course, there were precautions to consider like first unplugging the electrical cord.

Later on, she summoned the wherewithal to search out and deal with an execrable odor emanating up the cellar steps: This last bit of progress, however, came about only after an embarrassing exchange with a man from the city offices.

It all started with summer floods overworking the sump pump. Off and on for two days Callie wielded a broom, ushering pools of water toward the drain. Each time the pump started up, though, its attached out-take hose squirted and gushed like a row of vertical fountains, re-flooding the floor with the water Cal had swept down the drain.

"Always keep a roll of duct tape handy," said Will, standing next to her on the third day, patching the flexible black hose.

A week later, she swept and swept when the hefty water softener threw up all over the cement floor; no amount of cycle adjustment stopped the water from rising in its reservoir.

"The poor thing seems to be suffering from an esophageal ailment," Callie told her sister, who went along to help pick out a replacement for the stout old workhorse that had made queer but familiar noises for months.

The new softener, from a line of slender models, took up one third the space of the previous one. This trendy, silent successor looked anorexic by comparison, reminding Cal of Jim's new girlfriend, spotted together at the grocery store last week. Yet, not only did the new water softener do her thing, she could even tell time.

As a source of entertainment, Piper watched Callie descend, then fly back up from the basement, a place she abhorred. Since the age of five, she regarded basements as dark and dank, full of spooks and evil spirits. Because cellars had always been quarters to get in and out of as quickly as possible, Cal took the steps two at a time on the ascent, which caused Piper to leap up, bark, and prance around in circles, his toenails tap-tap-tapping on the hardwood floor.

When a dreadful smell rose from down below, Callie started to worry. Piper detected it first, sniffing from the top step, then quickly backing away and retreating to his cushiony pad in the living room. Then Callie caught a whiff of the foul scent drifting into the kitchen. As she opened the entrance to the cellar, she was hit with the full force of the stench. When she approached the sump hole, a large mass and the reek from it took her breath away. She gagged. "What *is* that stuff?" she cried out to the rafters. "Shouldn't sump holes have covers over them? Shouldn't there be a neater arrangement than this?" she shouted at the open pit with a drunken pump tipping to one side. The fat, ribbed hose with slits and wads of duct tape that clung to it like barnacles rose up three feet and passed overhead into a hole in the wall to the outdoors.

In a panic, Callie rushed back upstairs to phone the city. "Help! There's a sewage backup in my basement!"

Piper followed her outside. Together, they sat on the back steps waiting for the man.

"I OPENED A FEW of the man hole covers along your street," said the officer from public works. "She's flowing real nice, just like she should."

Callie had never before heard anyone refer to a river of sewage as "she." A boat, yes. A car, yes. A water softener, for fun. Even a country. But sewer water?

At least he was polite.

Once down the basement, however, the man narrowed his eyes and looked at Callie in a strange, accusatory way.

"This here is the sump hole. Not even connected to the sewer line," he said. "It's just a water drain."

After a long pause and a lingering search of Callie's face for some clue as to her stability, he added, "I wouldn't know how this stuff got in there."

His expression and tone of voice had changed, as if Cal had done something weird in her own basement sump hole. As though she'd trumped up a reason for having a man stop by. As if she were desperate.

"I live here by myself," she explained in a strong voice. She meant to appear normal and in charge. "I'm perfectly capable of taking care of what needs to be done." She crossed her arms for emphasis and said, "There's nobody here who would play a trick like this—unless someone broke in and did it: I've got a wacky next-door neighbor."

Callie shook her head and made a chirping sound from the corner of her mouth, the way her father did when he was stymied.

Was she losing her mind? Was she demented like Grandma Julia who, at age eighty-eight, had defecated in a corner of her bedroom?

"Well," said the city officer, "you've got a real mess on your hands; that's all gotta be scooped out." He turned abruptly, and trudged up the steps to the front door. "You'll want to wear a mask and rubber gloves. Thick ones. Be sure to pour plenty of bleach in that sump hole." The man hustled down the sidewalk and into his car.

Callie raised a hand as if to call after him. Instead, she let the man go, lowered her arm, and slumped back down on the steps with Piper by her side, feeling as desperate as a mouse in winter, reduced to nibbling a sliver of soap.

Alone with her catastrophe, she understood: There'd be no alternative but to deal with it by herself; she had survived far worse than this.

Within minutes, she began plotting to eliminate the cause of that putrid scent, which wafted through the entire house, making Cal's gastric juices rise from her stomach into her mouth, as though she were being enveloped by the stench of a pig farm in August.

"I can do this," she grumbled. Rising from the steps, she went in search of supplies.

Piper waited outside.

What looked like feces and toilet tissue floating in the sump hole turned out to be the rank, decomposed bodies of several red squirrels.

"They might have been frantic, searching for a way out," she told her mother over the phone, "or maybe they were playing and one followed the others into the hole."

After all, they lived there, too. That is, until a large family of them began rolling acorns along the ductwork overhead. Callie and Piper were living below a bowling alley for squirrels and no amount of ramming a broom handle against the living room ceiling or pounding on the walls or a mad barking dog changed things—except for bits of plaster raining down onto the carpet and Piper working himself into such a frenzy that he clamped the end of his bushy tail between his teeth and turned in blurry circles, until the sofa intervened.

The bowling stopped briefly in appreciation of a dog gone berserk and a crazed woman who thumped and shrieked, "Get the hell out of here!"

At Will's suggestion, Callie purchased a live trap at the hardware store and taught herself how to use it. She also climbed a ladder to seal up the hole near the roof.

"Do you need any help?" her dad had asked.

"No thanks, Pops. I think I've got it figured out."

That evening, the quietest in weeks, Cal went to bed with a volume of Emerson's Essays and read the one entitled "Self-Reliance." She was fascinated by the phrases she'd underlined when she was in college. They meant such different things to her now. And phrases that weren't marked grabbed her attention, new material for this stage in her life. She was no longer "pinched in a corner. . ." And she certainly would not be "ashamed of that divine idea which each of us represents." Although Emerson wrote from a masculine point of view, Callie learned to add an "s" each time she encountered a "he": "She walks abreast with her days . . . with the exercise of self-trust, new powers shall appear."

Emerson was right. Callie was learning to keep her wits about her while living on her own. She remembered to turn on the porch light before nightfall so she wouldn't have to find her way to the door in the dark after going to a movie or a concert, wondering what creatures might be lurking in the shrubs or behind the massive maple trees. She watched the swarms of lake coot swimming in tight black clusters, ensuring their own survival with a rest during migration. A loner in those flocks was picked off by an eagle or pulled under by a giant carp, unless they were sharp-eyed and knew the exact moment to dive deep and resurface in the huddle. There is safety in numbers in the animal world: Massive numbers of emperor penguins and tens of thousands of monarch butterflies know how to stay close and warm within their own communities.

For the first time in a long while, Callie was that loner. The next thing she'd have to figure out was how not to be picked off. How to be a loner and not be lonely.

She envied the birds that swam past her dock in pairs, mallards and Canadas, male and female, looking out for each other. But then, there would be that single loon, a lone duck, a goose, or a white pelican, which seemed to get along just fine, skiing onto the bay's surface, searching for food, splashing a bath, paddling along in the sunlight.

I may no longer have a companion, she thought, or the friends we'd made, but at least, I still have my family, including Piper. She gave thanks to the fates. Despite his efforts, Jim never succeeded in keeping her away from family. Although she often took a beating for it, she would never let it happen.

More than ever, Cal believed that her parents would always be a part of her; their careful nurturing would remain to help counter the negative. She thought of a favorite line from Ibsen: "I almost think we're all of us Ghosts. . . It's not only what we have invited from our father and mother that walks in us . . ."

So that's what her parents meant when they said, "Just keep on rowing, Cal. We'll be there. Even when we're gone, we'll always be there for you."

Callie remembered being ten, out selling Christmas cards for Girl Scouts. Pedaling her bike through town in a sudden downpour, she skidded, tipped over, and saw the boxes of cards break open and fly from her basket into a muddy, rain-filled gutter. Soaking wet, she gathered them up and rode home sobbing.

Her mother bought all twelve boxes.

There were plenty of people in Callie's past, who had endured rough times and whose stories she knew: Auntie Sarah, who cloaked her existence with laughter, simplicity, and denial in order to make it through to the end; Lucie Moulin, a Parisian girl linked to Selmer Johnson from Masterton; Camille Baudin, who lost her parents to the Nazis; Laura Lambert, a childhood friend who loved cats, but grew up in a household without laughter.

Cal remembered shrieking with delight at five, while her Grandpa Dahl twirled her in circles, face up, like on a ride at the county fair, faster and faster until her legs floated straight out into the blurry world. And how, before bed, she'd say, "Grandma, show me your teeth." The kindly, heavy-set woman who came to visit once or twice a year shoved both uppers and lowers forward with her tongue.

At night, Grandma Dahl's dentures floated in a fancy cut glass bowl covered by a glass lid. Callie imagined those teeth swimming around in water with tiny fish, opening and closing, talking away, sending word bubbles up to the surface. The next morning the teeth would fix themselves back inside her grandmother's mouth so she could eat breakfast and tell Callie more stories. Callie loved spending the day in Grandma Dahl's kitchen, baking bread, devouring potato lefse, and rolling Swedish meatballs between the palms of her hands.

These recipes, and dozens more, Grandma Dahl handed down to her daughter, Emily. And from Emily to Liz and Callie.

But Cal no longer needed those instructions, accumulated over the years, written out on index cards by her mother and grandmother. Now, she knew them by heart. "A dollop of butter" and "A pinch of salt," no longer confounded her.

Emily, quiet and observant, sat down one evening to a meal her daughter had prepared. "You got a good scald on this, Callie." And when she laughed, her face was a party.

Simple successes, in and of themselves, meant headway, another step toward self-reliance. Sometimes, though, when a soul is down and desperate, fate steps in. Help appears, as if out of nowhere. Along a hard way, someone or something arrives unexpectedly. Which is precisely what happened to Callie that fall afternoon in the country cemetery.

Lying on the grass with her forehead still resting on folded arms, Cal felt a nudge against the back of her head and heard a soft snorting sound. She looked up to see a large brown dog, who without hesitation sat down beside her. Callie looked around for another human. Seeing no one else, she balanced on an elbow and reached up to touch the dog's shoulder. Posed like a sentinel, he looked at Cal full in the face. She stared back, convinced that there are things a dog knows—things a dog understands. Finally, she laid on her back, alternately gazing at the deep blue sky and at the animal. Soon, he stretched out beside her.

Lulled by the dog's warmth and measured breathing, Callie fell sound asleep while the wind rushed among the headstones and through the weeping branches of the willow tree. And while she slept, that dog never left her side.

Much later, when she awoke, the dog opened his eyes, too. And when she sat up, he sat up, sensing that it was time for both of them to leave—all without a word from either of them.

At the very least, that animal had kept her on this side of life, had given her the calm and the courage to stand up. She thought of coaxing him to come home with her. But he stood apart and watched her with a different look in his eyes. Callie understood that his purpose had been completed. While she lingered by the open car door, the dog trotted away, down the narrow gravel road, stopping once to turn and look back at her before disappearing into the tall grass.

For a moment, Callie watched that wide stretch of grass roll with the wind, undulating like waves on a lake when winter gives way to spring. A surge of confidence came over her—one that she hadn't sensed in a very long time.

IT IS TRUE that winter water rolls sluggishly for many days before it solidifies. And it takes longer for ripples to fan outward on a smooth ice-ready surface as the last ducks of summer splash about and shore boulders grow crusty with crystals. But many mornings, at dawn, mist rises from the logy surface like dancing ghosts escaped from the clutches of that final freeze. For lake water remembers the summer and sends its emissaries up and out to waltz for a spell before they slip away to wait in the wings for another season—a warm, promising time that will help to make things right with the world.

For Callie, recalling all she had endured was like looking at the first round of a sunrise. She could stare at the inching disc with a pomegranate blush for only so long. Once that ball rose above the trees, glaring and hot and threatening to blind her, she had to turn away.

Callie sensed that she and Jim were finished the night he refused to see the lady in the moon. Her profile was perfectly clear to Cal, but Jim said that he couldn't see it. "And besides," he added with a smirk, "everyone knows it's a man in the moon." He turned away, eager to get back to the house and Monday night football, leaving Callie alone, feeling like a skinny little teal flying solo into a north wind.

Tonight, she couldn't help wondering if the lady in the moon had a dog.

6

The Story of Miquette

Heaven goes by favor; if it went by merit,
you would stay out and your dog would go in.
—Mark Twain

CRADLING TEQUILA IN HER ARMS, Callandra Mae Lindstrom, as a young girl, sat down on the curb in front of Danny Hendrickson's home. The house, freshly painted a golden yellow with white trim, had lilac bushes growing on either side of the railed steps leading up to the front door.

Callie placed her Chihuahua on a patch of grass next to the curb on Norwood Avenue, ran her skates back and forth along the gutter, and looked across the street at her own family's house built in the 1940s— white with green shutters and a green and white awning above the wide picture window. Several red maples lined the boulevard. A stout blue spruce, barely taller than Callie, grew on the right, next to the garage.

She waved at her mother Emily who had stepped out onto the front yard to water the geraniums growing inside their new wooden wheel- barrow—a green and white planter designed by Callie's father, Will.

Then she bent over to check the tightness of her roller skates strapped to sturdy shoes, and waited for her friend to fly back on his.

Nearly every afternoon, Danny lassoed Rover, his Golden Retriever, shouted "*Allez! Allez, le chien!*" and got towed around the south side of Masterton. The second time he did this, Danny's strap-on skates peeled away from his tennis shoes, causing him to stumble, somersault, and crash to the sidewalk. Rover rushed back to lick Danny's bloody knees and stay with him until Callie arrived. After witnessing the accident, she helped her friend back to his house and into the bathroom where they washed the wounds and applied Mercurochrome and Band-Aids. That's when Callie realized that she'd have to wear her saddle shoes if she wanted to roller skate around town safely, with Tequila bringing up the rear.

Now, from several blocks away, she spotted Rover galloping in her direction and Danny hanging on to the rope, knees bent, roller skates aimed straight ahead. Within minutes, the clicking sounds grew louder and louder, until he and his dog closed the distance and pulled up next to Cal.

Callie stood and petted Rover, who was panting and prancing about, eyes aglow, ready for another round. Tequila turned to growl and nip at his chest fur.

Julie Hendrickson, Danny's mother, stepped out the front door, carrying a large tray with a pitcher of Kool Aid, two paper cups, a heap of ginger cookies, chunks of sausage meat for the dogs, and a glass of red wine for herself. Then they all moved to the picnic table beneath a maple tree in the backyard where they talked of summer vacation, how entering fourth grade in September seemed an eternity away with the whole summer ahead of them. And they discussed the personalities and history of their dogs, Tequila and Rover.

Julie took a sip from her wine glass and said, "Speaking of doggies, Cal, would you like to hear about the life of Miquette?" She turned to her son who was sitting on the grass next to Rover. "Danny already knows this story, don't you?"

Resting his head against his dog's side, Danny smiled and nodded.

"Who's Miquette?" asked Callie.

"A little girl pup that lived in France, shortly after the Second World War."

"Did she speak French?"

"Well, yes, as a matter of fact she did. Instead of saying 'Bow-wow,' she'd say 'Ouah-ouah.'"

Callie laughed, set Tequila in front of her on the picnic table, and fed her a piece of sausage meat. "Was she your dog?"

"Not really. She actually belonged to my father, Papa Jouvet, who worked at one of those big movie theatres on the main avenue in Paris. That's where Miquette lived, where she called home; the address inscribed on her doggie tag was *Cinéma Marignan, avenue des Champs-Elysées.*"

MIQUETTE, A LIVELY RAT TERRIER, was the daughter of Folette, each named after a character from an old French comedy about a constrained young woman who yearns to follow her dream and become a movie actress—against her mother's wishes.

Homeless and starving, after being neglected and ousted by the man who once owned her, Folette came to live at the *Marignan* movie theatre, where she gave birth to Miquette and two other puppies.

Monsieur Jouvet, who worked at the *Marignan*, found other homes for Miquette's siblings, and provided mother and daughter with a cozy corner inside the theatre.

"Miquette was very sweet," said Julie. "As a young pup, she made every effort to sit and roll over, shake hands and speak, while Folette barked her head off, as if trying to control the actions of her daughter.

"One day, the mother died, leaving Miquette to stay on alone. The years passed. Every morning, the young terrier sauntered around inside the theatre, oversaw the sweeping and scrubbing of aisles, the cleaning of seats, and followed my papa upstairs to the space where he organized and set up film reels.

"The chef from a neighboring restaurant prepared two meals a day for Miquette."

"Oh, wow," said Callie. "Lucky dog."

"*Mais oui.*" Julie took another sip from her wine glass. "She dined well."

Many afternoons, the sturdy little dog strolled the *Champs-Elysées*, entering every store where she was welcomed, known by all, and awarded with pieces of baguette and sausage meat. In each shop, she would speak, sit up on her haunches, and perform backward flips.

Sometimes, she crossed the bustling, wide, tree-lined avenue. Without fail, the policemen stopped traffic so she could trot safely across to whatever destination piqued her interest. In exchange, the police officers were given free seats at the movie theatre.

"Papa Jouvet adored Miquette," said Julie. "He brought her home from time to time, but we never took her on vacation with us. Instead, a friend who lived in Normandy cared for her during the month we were gone on holiday. She was so happy there—you can imagine—running free through wheat fields and along sand beaches. Then back to the stone cottage."

In order to arrive at that house, Miquette, along with her temporary master, descended into the Paris subway, rode the *métro*, exited at *la Gare Saint-Lazare,* and boarded a train that would deliver them to the Norman countryside, a province recovering from World War II and the Nazi Occupation.

"One day, another friend asked Papa if he would keep *Herr*, his German Shepherd, because that particular summer he was unable to take the dog on vacation."

"And did he?" asked Callie.

"Of course. Papa was a most generous man. However, from the outset, having to live with *Herr* wasn't to Miquette's liking.

"At first, the impressive shepherd remained fairly neutral, demonstrating little inherent aggression, coming across as alert, proud, and posturing, his hind quarters low to the floor, slinking about to check out all rooms before parading down the *Champs-Elysées*. Eventually, he began to growl at Miquette, giving her the evil eye, standing between her and her food dish. Finally, *Herr* barricaded the theatre door to prevent her from stepping out onto the avenue.

"Soon after, Miquette disappeared."

"Oh, no!" Callie reached for Tequila and gave her a hug.

"My papa felt so bad, panic-stricken. He and his co-workers searched every nook and cranny of the movie theatre, hustled up and down both sides of the long avenue, stopped at each of the stores and restaurants, alerted the police, placed a '*Chien Perdu*' sign in front of the *Marignan*, taped other 'lost dog' posters on street lamps, stop signs, and store fronts. And they questioned passersby."

Inside the theatre, *Herr* Shepherd remained calm and silent, taking over the wine-colored velvet chair that had belonged to Miquette.

Late that afternoon, the theatre staff was notified about the discovery of a terrier found perched on a seat inside one of the train cars at *la Gare Saint-Lazare*. The tag on her collar listed her name and place of residence: *Miquette, Cinéma Marignan, avenue des Champs-Elysées, Paris.*

"My father rushed over to the largest, busiest train station in the city—one and a half miles away. And there was Miquette, sitting inside the train, looking out of the window from her seat. Papa gathered her up in his arms, and brought her back to her rightful place inside the movie theatre."

"What about that German Shepherd?" asked Callie.

"*Herr?* Oh, my father immediately found someone else to care for him. After all, Miquette deserved to be free and happy, and shouldn't have to put up with an animal she was afraid of and might do her harm.

"So that's why she got on the train."

"That's right. She was desperate to find that country house where she'd spent so many happy moments with her temporary master. She had yet to locate the right train, but avoiding the subway, Miquette figured out how to get to the appropriate station—on foot, above ground. That sweet and gifted girl followed a route she had never before taken."

7

Fleet as a Summer Swallow

THE earth keeps some vibration going
There in your heart, and that is you.
—Fiddler Jones,
Spoon River Anthology, *Edgar Lee Masters*

THAT IT TOOK less time for a dog, than for many humans, to take action in order to escape a threatening situation struck Callie now that she'd been there. Although, during her early years while growing up in Masterton, Cal hadn't witnessed brutality, she understood, to a degree, why Miquette had to get away. And yet, she laughed at what she thought was a funny story, picturing the rat terrier seated on a train, gazing out of the window, as if she were going on holiday. Now Callie got it: Miquette was desperate, seated all alone, quivering, staring out of the window, eager for the train to leave the station.

Remembering Miquette, along with the country dog who stayed by her side that fall day in the cemetery, Callie knew that if she could get through these next months, she would make it for good—even when the snow began to fly and she wasn't to cry anymore.

"A penny for your thoughts, Cal." Will eased sideways against his seatbelt for a quick glance at the speedometer. "You're pretty quiet, kiddo. Not tired of driving, are you?"

"Oh, no, I'm all right, Dad."

Will reached over to squeeze the back of Callie's neck, lightly, the way he did when she was a girl. "You're better than all right, aren't you, Cal? All settled in your own place, you and Piper."

"We are!" Callie flapped her elbows out from the steering wheel. "I finally got my wings back. And Piper is some watchdog."

She talked about how her young Sheltie stood at attention near the edge of their dock, barking at the white and red bobber dancing on lake ripples.

"Whenever we're down there, he insists that a fish take the worm, demands action, just as he does when we go out in the rowboat. When I tell him that the line is weak, the bobber old, and the worms are worn out and lazy from too many days in the ice cream bucket—although I've changed the dirt and added water—that dog just keeps on panting and won't give up. I tell him, 'I hope I can deliver, Piper, catch something.' Then he throws me a look and goes back to staring at the bobber."

"I've had plenty of hunting dogs in my time," said Will, "but never a fisher dog."

Callie laughed and swept her hair back from her forehead. " 'When the wind's out of the east,' I tell him, 'the fish bite the least.' But he just goes on waiting and watching, yipping, convinced that something will snag the hook—eventually."

One afternoon in late spring, sitting next to Piper, her legs dangling over lake water from the end plank, Callie looked up to admire the fresh new leaves hanging from the ancient maple tree and the skinny, lime-green weeping willow branches. She turned to study the straight sections of dock leading back to shore, and listened to the brash call of a blue jay.

Piper kept watching the bobber and grew frantic when it disappeared. Cal reeled in a big sunny while the herder of fish pranced around in circles, toenails clicking against the dock boards.

Once, when Callie removed the bobber so she could feel the light nibbles while raising and lowering the rod, she caught a prized fish. Piper grabbed the crappie as it dangled from the end of the line. Somehow avoiding the stingers, he wrapped his jaws around it, and wouldn't let go. Together, he and Cal dashed up the steps to the cottage.

"Did he help clean it?" asked Will.

"Nope, but he ate some, fried."

"His reward, eh?"

"Yup."

Callie told her father about skating on the lake last winter, below her "new" little cottage on the hill above Cook's Bay. For the first time in ages, she'd felt fleet as a swallow, skimming across weed beds and pan fish frozen beneath a surface as smooth as polished granite.

It felt strange to be gliding over fishing holes where patches of milfoil swayed and grasses swirled like long hair in sun-dappled summer water. In winter, when the air smelled of ozone, everything froze mid-sway, including the random gape-mouthed crappie or sunfish that lay close to the surface, encased in ice, one clear eye open to the sky.

With Piper running alongside, she had unbuttoned her coat and held it open like a sail as the wind blew her gently across the ice. Not having felt so free in such a long while, Cal stayed out until after dark, racing along the moonbeam that poured down the length of the bay.

She didn't mention that that night was a happier replay of one long ago, when she and Jim were still together, living in a different cottage on a different bay with a different dog.

The ice was like polished granite then, too. And there were weed beds and little fish frozen beneath the surface. Callie had even held her coat out for wings. But there was nothing gentle about the wind that night. From behind, it blew with gale force along the hardened water, insisting that she skate forever, sail away, disappear into the ether. *Do not turn around*, the wind seemed to say. *Do not go back. Keep skating!*

A resolute friend, that wind.

Callie did not want to leave the lake then, but the darkening sky came down fast and her old sheltie dropped to the ice at shorter intervals to gnaw at the fur frozen between his toes. Conditions deteriorated by the minute as the sleety storm moved in, followed by heavy snow. When the drifts piled up, the skating would be over, unless she took a shovel down the next day. Though, who could clear enough weighty snow to skate free like that?

The moment Cal turned towards home that night, the gale sucked her breath away and stung her face with needles of sleet. Squinting and shielding her eyes with gloved hands, she beat her way back to the giant maple standing near the shore—a concave ancient, having lost a third of itself to a wild summer storm that hurled every kind of trick, including a ton of hail, forcing a family of raccoons to scurry for cover. With the sound of a speeding train, the wind peeled shingles from rooftops, twisted tree trunks, ripped away branches.

Small plants dotting the hillside managed to survive.

When the heavens cleared and the lake sparkled with sunshine, nature seemed to mock accusing looks directed skyward with "Who, me?"

Callie had always admired that old tree still towering over shallow waters. Although its remaining branches still reached for the sky, Cal often wondered about the deeply injured trunk and how its sap could go on flowing. Each spring, when she expected the tree to be dead at last, new leaf buds swelled and unfurled as vigorously as all of the other maples in the neighborhood.

The same summer, just before that section of tree went down, a massive tribe of black Helldivers clustered together like large magnet shavings upon the bouncing waves, alternately bucking the crests of whitecaps and disappearing in the troughs. Like miniature schooners that must remain at sea so as not to crack up on the rocks, those Grebes rode out the storm as one.

Short of breath and with jerky strides on a surface where whitecaps once rolled, Cal pressed on, remembering the grounded goose she had seen the week before, limping and struggling for cover beyond the dangling strings of a willow tree.

She'd noticed the lump of it growing larger as it inched its way toward shore along the slick and bumpy surface of the bay. Like the last living thing on a northern lake in winter, where life plays hide and seek in a blocked and frozen world, the injured Canada goose tottered on webbed feet, sweeping the ice with the tip of its long wing. Startlingly white against a black neck and head, the bird's cheek band wrapped under her throat like the chinstrap on a helmet. She halted and stretched her body, aware that something was materializing overhead.

Against the overcast sky, a hawk, winging tight circles, opened its hooked beak and plunged toward the goose. Stretching her curved neck upward, the goose pecked at the hawk, which swooped away on a current, then circled while the goose plodded on, watchful, gauging the next attack. Over and over, like dive-bomber and ground artillery, the hawk executed his arch maneuvers against the hobbling bird who parried with her long bill.

How much longer could she defend herself? When would she give up and collapse on the ice, food for the hawk? Would she fight to the end?

Although she must have been exhausted, the goose, showing no signs of flagging energy, remained committed to her own survival after a grueling hour of battle.

It was the hawk that finally quit—stopped diving. And then, as if to pay homage, he flew one last broad circle high above the goose before gliding away over trees etched into the horizon, until the speck of him disappeared.

As for the goose, the day was still hers after fighting for it with a strength beyond understanding. She paused when a brown leaf skittered past her across the ice. Then, as if there'd been no other interruption, she resumed her clumsy shuffle along the last uneven stretch of frozen lake, settling in for a rest under bent cattails and last summer's grass beaten down by the snowstorm, invisible with the darkness of night.

Callie forged ahead on her skates, watching for the dim porch light that guided her home on those black nights that dropped early. Reaching land, she clamored over ice teeth clamped down hard on boulders along the shoreline, reached the giant maple tree, and leaned against its storm-injured trunk before edging up the hill to a lonely house.

By the time she returned—barely ahead of the storm's front end—and lumbered through the door on her blades, the wind and foul weather descended full force. So did the voice from hell.

These days, although her "new" cabin is empty, except for her prancing Piper, it is not a lonely house. At the far end of the living room are her piano, family photos, and books, including Emerson's Essays. New friends and family come often to visit. And the pile of wood for her fireplace remains high—logs cut and stacked by Will Lindstrom, the summer sawyer of Pine River.

"THIS IS QUITE A BRIDGE," said Will as they drove across the Kickapoo River near Readstown, a pleasant Wisconsin village off Highway 14. "Talk about long! It's like passing through a steel truss box."

Callie slowed to a crawl so she could check out the beams and the water below—green and fast-flowing with mud banks and pine trees lining the river's edge. Any place with water grabbed Cal's attention, bringing back memories of their time on Lake Shetek, Leech Lake, Pine River, and the rushing mountain streams of the far west.

Her family had stopped near one of those mountain rivers during a trip to California. Although Callie was only six, she remembered the relief of escaping their stuffy black Pontiac, grateful for a break after hours and hours on the road. Cool, clean air, and the scent of laurel along the forest floor perked her up like a wilted flower snapping to. She skipped and frolicked like a fawn into the woods, across a pine needle carpet, up to the cascading river.

While Emily and Liz unpacked the picnic basket, Will and Callie waded and splashed in a stream that felt as cold as Lake Superior. When she giggled over the size of her father's pale white feet compared with her own, tanned by the August sun, he replied, "You can laugh all you want, Callie girl. They provide me with an excellent under-standing."

Perched on a large gray rock, Cal and her dad watched the mist rise from frothy waters that rolled and tumbled over stones and swirled around large boulders.

She balked when her parents said it was time to get back on the road. Reluctant to leave that mountain stream, she lagged behind for a last look, memorizing their place on that gray boulder and the never-ending flow of cold, clear water. A small pine tree stood apart from the rest.

If only they could have stayed longer, she thought, adding another link to her father—another lake, another river to figure into his years. And now, into hers.

While driving along the outskirts of Readstown, Callie glanced over at her dad, whose surgical scar left a deep depression between his cheekbone and jaw line. Although he was receiving treatment, it was just a matter of time before a new batch of malignant melanoma cells would start to take over. When Will turned to smile at her, she thought of what her mother Emily used to reel off: "Smile and the world smiles with you. Cry and you cry alone."

Callie recalled the fathers of her childhood friends. Even as a little girl in Masterton, she knew her daddy was different from all the rest. Most of the men were good to their kids, just not around much to teach them things, like how to dance the waltz and row a boat, how to catch and clean fish, memorize the names of waterfowl, go for a long walk (including their three-day hike) in the countryside, just for the love of it.

A couple of the dads were drunks, slurring their words, and embarrassing their children. One man, in particular, stuck in Callie's mind, for he had sparked fear in her when she was a young girl lacking in understanding and sufficient vocabulary to describe the situation. All she could come up with, regarding her friend Muriel's father, was, "Mr. Kraus is really creepy."

One afternoon, when the girls were nine or ten years old, jabbering and giggling as young girls do, Callie noticed Mr. Kraus standing in the hallway, peering at them through the partially opened bedroom door. Without a word, he edged in, closed the door, and sat down on the bed next to his daughter. He placed an arm around her shoulders, and began running his other hand up and down the inside of her thigh, turning his head to peer and smile at Callie. Cal looked on, flabbergasted. She knew that kind of behavior was not normal. During those few minutes, the expression on Muriel's face changed from one of concern to that of a consecrated saint—white to rose, an innocent half-smile, wide eyes staring at the cross above her dresser.

After Mr. Kraus left the room, there was only silence between the girls and the stiff posture and set jaw of a child who couldn't look at her friend any longer. She gazed down at the floor, at her small pink rug. After a few minutes, Cal left, never to return.

Sometimes, Muriel came to Callie's home or they met at the movie theater for a Saturday matinee and then played together in the park—but not without some constraint. Neither one spoke about what had happened that day. Yet, Callie wondered if Mr. Kraus touched other girls like that. Would he have done it to her if she had returned? How many more times was it happening to Muriel? Whenever Cal talked about the Friday night boxing matches she watched with her own dad and the times they spent fishing together on Lake Shetek, Muriel just glanced at her with a frown, a confused look, and then turned away.

Years later, Callie thought of Muriel and her father when she visited a relative named Sarah. Although she was her father's cousin, everyone in the family called her Auntie Sarah. She was a small, fragile-looking woman with freakish hands. Although her deformity isolated her within her own family, she always found something to laugh about. Even in middle-age and beyond, she seemed more like an arrested adolescent, giggling over silly things like a tube of melted Tangee lipstick left on the porch railing in the hot sun, and shrill Mrs. Swenson belting out lyrics, slightly off pitch, above the Lutheran congregation during a Sunday morning battle of hymns. To be around Sarah, you'd have thought she was among the happiest people in the world.

Sarah had just turned nineteen when her mother died. An only child, she stayed on with her father, who insisted that she remain at home, keep house, and take care of him: He repeatedly told her that she was unfit for this world.

In 1959, Auntie Sarah and Uncle Hugo came to Masterton for a visit. Callie was fifteen and finally able to put words to what she'd observed. But such words remained secrets, not meant to be spoken out loud. In public, grownup mouths clamped in thin lines, eyes averted. In private, they whispered about shameful goings-on, controlling parents, impropriety.

Callie's mother once asked, "What right does anyone have to determine who is fit or unfit for this world?"

It was a question without an answer in the 1950s—and before then, when girls were expected to do as they were told.

While Cal was making plans for a week's vacation in Florida, her sister Liz suggested, "Why not look in on Auntie Sarah. She's in a nursing home in Winter Haven, you know. Only a couple of hours from where you'll be staying."

"Oh, wow, it's been a long time," said Callie. "Lots of weird memories. But yeah, I'll go."

8

Skipping the High Notes

Hence my long years of solitude at the home of my father,
Trying to get myself back,
And to turn my sorrow into a supremer self.
—Mary McNeely,
Spoon River Anthology, *by Edgar Lee Masters*

THEY WERE LIKE TWO GIRLS sitting on a dock, perched at the edge of Auntie Sarah's bed, legs dangling, devouring the chocolate vanilla creams Callie had brought as a gift. Surprised and delighted to see a long-lost relative, Sarah giggled, butted shoulders with Cal, and plucked another chocolate from the box.

On a Saturday in March, Callie parked her rental car near the Sunrise Center in Winter Haven. She had made the hour and a half trip from Bradenton to visit her father's eighty-eight year old cousin, whom the family hadn't seen in years. Driving in Florida for the first time, Callie was heartened when she happened easily upon the nursing home at the edge of town.

Between the parking lot and sprawling brick building, a small square drew her in with its ornate benches, waving palms, a lush fountain surrounded by Birds of Paradise fluttering on a breeze, and Poinsettias as enormous as shrubs. Before Callie reached the entrance to the nursing home, a blast of chilly wind blew the fountain's waterspouts off course, dousing her with a heavy mist.

Once inside, she stood for a moment to dry her face against the sleeve of her light jacket, and to watch the graceful movements of so many colored fish—orange, yellow, red, blue, purple—swimming about in a large aquarium.

With her thoughts collected, she went in search of Sarah.

Locating room 302B took nearly as long as the drive to Winter Haven. No matter which way she turned or how often she asked directions of scurrying aides, Callie could not find her way to Auntie's room. Through wing after wing she wandered, frustrated and nauseated by the smells of so many old and sick people in such close quarters. She threaded her way through hallways lined with once vital women (and a few men) sagging listlessly in their wheelchairs. She stepped around buckets of mops in gray water and rolling carts with breakfast trays stacked topsy-turvy, spilling over with runny oatmeal and wedges of soggy toast.

After many turns, dead-ends, and backtracking, Callie finally found Sarah's room. She knocked at the partially opened door and peeked in to see Auntie sitting on the edge of her bed, looking disheveled, as if she'd dressed in the dark, the buttons of her nubby green cardigan out of alignment. When Callie called her name and stepped into the room, Sarah looked puzzled at first. Then squealing with delight, she laughed with a whoop, eased herself down from the bed, and gave Cal a big hug and a sound kiss on the cheek.

"Everyone from up north sends their love," said Callie, surprised at Auntie's youthful demeanor. "Mom and Dad said to . . ."

"I love to be loved," said Sarah with a giggle that rippled as if from the throat of a songbird. "I didn't fall in love. I fell on the floor instead."

Silence.

"You're supposed to laugh there."

Callie smiled. "Mom and Dad said to be sure . . ."

"You look just like your mother," interrupted Sarah, touching Callie's face with those hands. "How are Emily and Will? Are you still living at home?"

"Oh, no. I've been on my own for a long time. Anyway, Mom said to tell you that . . ."

"You know, after my Mother died, Daddy...why, he told me 'your place is here at home.' Oh, I wanted to go to Rockford in the worst way, learn to be a secretary, but he made me stay right there in Belvidere with him. He worried about me, you know."

Sarah spoke like a young girl while holding out her flipper-thumbed hands, the sight of which used to frighten Callie as a child—especially after she'd overheard Uncle Hugo say that his daughter was unfit for the world with such hands.

"Besides," she added, her squinty, laughing eyes focused sharply on Callie's, "somebody had to do the cooking and cleaning!" Her voice ended on a high note and another giggle.

For as long as Callie could remember, Auntie Sarah was always going around with that mole-eyed smile and high-pitched laugh even though she seemed to have had little in life to make her truly happy. With no siblings, she'd grown up around stodgy adults, spending her days collecting buttons, playing the piano, sitting on a blanket in the shade of a willow tree, cuddling her little dog, and growing to look as old as her elders.

After decades of waiting on her father and his brother Hjalmer, whose wife had also died, Sarah lived alone for a time in a rooming house in south Winter Haven. She used to write Callie's parents long letters about her favorite television programs: *The Lawrence Welk Show, Animal Kingdom, The Wide World of Travel, Name that Tune.* And while she never tended a garden of her own, she wrote about the flowers that grew up in her neighborhood as if they were her personal acquaintances: charming Bougainvillea, fascinating Purple Roses, lovely Mariel Hibiscus, Passion Flowers. Once, she filled an entire page with details about Angels' Trumpets and Devils' Trumpets and how the first hung downward as if playing towards earth from Heaven and how the second pointed upward, trumpeting to the skies from a place called Hell.

As an adolescent, Callie scoffed at those letters. "Auntie needs to get a life," she'd announce to her parents.

"Now, now," Emily would say. "Mustn't be critical."

"Well, all she writes about are lame television programs and flowers, flowers, flowers. *And* her stupid button collection."

"That's enough, Callie! Someday, you'll understand."

Once, when Auntie Sarah and her father visited from Illinois, Sarah spent time sifting through Emily's boxes of buttons while Callie looked on, intrigued. Sarah had no workable thumbs—just tiny flippers hanging limp and useless as dewclaws. With the first two unusually long fingers on either hand, she sorted and picked through hundreds of buttons, homing in on pink pearlies, green and blue love knots, brass anchors, mother-of-pearl, black glass. These treasures she wired onto pieces of cardboard and squirreled away in her small suitcase.

Like Callie's grandmother, Sarah could play any composition on the piano—only with eight fingers—eight magical fingers reaching across the octaves to create complicated chords and arpeggios that rippled and flowed like easy ocean waves. She had no need for scores or fingering notations.

If Auntie Sarah could play like that, thought Callie, why couldn't she do other things? Like type and take shorthand. Why had her father used those hands as an excuse to keep her at home when she could easily make it on her own?

Just last summer, Cal had observed a pair of lake swallows teaching their young to fly up and into an easterly. All but one of the tiny birds clustered together, flitting anxiously up and down on the blue boat canopy, until they were confident enough to launch themselves out over the water. Nudged from the nest by its parents, the reluctant little bird finally took off. He had to fly or starve.

"So, I cooked and cleaned," Sarah continued, "and I forgot all about secretary school. I stayed at home and took care of Daddy and Uncle until they passed away."

Just then, Sarah's roommate spun her wheelchair around the curtain. "I'm going to play bingo," she announced, surprised to see company. "That one there," she nodded in Sarah's direction, "is lucky she can walk."

"That's true," said Callie.

"Would you like to go for Bingo, too?" she asked Sarah after the elderly woman had wheeled herself out of the door and into the hallway.

"No, I stay in my room unless I feel like playing piano or the organ. I even take my meals here."

"You don't go to the dining room?"

"Nope, I stay put. My roommate is ninety-two and she yammers all the time. Never get any peace and quiet, so I eat right where I'm sitting while old jabber-box there is gone for a while." She swung her legs out and back against the side of the bed.

"After Daddy and Uncle Hjalmer died, I got used to living alone, playing my piano. Why, I even had an audience for my music!"

Sarah spoke of turning on her piano light and beginning to play.

"From the corner of my left eye," she said, "I noticed a slight movement. A small-bodied, long-leggèd spider had dropped an inch or two from inside the white glass shade and hung vibrating from its thin strand of web. I kept playing for 'spidey,' my audience."

Sarah described how it was lulled into stillness by the soft, slow movements of one of her songs, then how it spun in circles to the bombastic chords of another. When the light bulb got too hot for Spidey, she switched it off and ended her concert.

"The next day, when I returned to the keys, lo and behold, my fan was still there, waiting for an encore. We did that together for some time.

"And then one day, he was gone."

Callie studied Sarah's living quarters. Near her single crank-up bed, a sagging arm chair and modest chest of drawers huddled together in a corner, covered with stacks of newspapers, blouses and sweaters, framed pictures, books, and a small television set. A row of pasteboard boxes filled with *National Geographic* magazines and *Reader's Digest Condensed Books* lined the floor between Sarah's bed and the window. An off-white divider curtain made the place feel like the cluttered half of a hospital room. The thought of spending entire days—years of days—sitting on this bed, in this crowded, stuffy enclosure, made Callie want to flee—charge past the aquarium, out the door to her rental car and back to the ocean.

Auntie Sarah pulled a lace handkerchief from the rolled cuff of her threadbare cardigan and dabbed at her nose. "I miss my little place. I had to give up everything when I came here: Mother's good dishes and silver; my piano; most of my button collection." She tossed her hands in the air. "When you get old, that's what you do. Doctor said I should come here, but it's not home to me."

She talked about her dizzy spells and the colon cancer surgery she'd had at age eighty. She explained how she still found blood in her stools, which frightened her, but the doctor didn't think she was strong enough for another operation.

"Mother had two strokes, you know," she said, savoring the last piece of chocolate from the box Callie had brought. "She was only forty-eight when she died. I was just out of high school and Daddy wouldn't hear of it when I said I wanted to go for secretary training. Just imagine—I never saw a pay check in my life."

Then, she leaned head-to-head with Callie, and said, "And I never received a proposal of marriage."

"Really? You never dated? What did you do for fun?"

"Oh, Daddy and I got around. We visited relatives in Loves Park and Winnebago—Aunt Lil and Uncle Jack; they lived above their general store in Monroe Center, you know. Poor Lil, she was so heavy and crippled up with the arthritis, she couldn't get out of bed. Their girl, Tessie, took care of her until Lil passed away."

"I remember Tess," said Callie. "She finally left Monroe Center and got married."

"A man from Chicago," said Aunt Sarah. "He was a nice man, I think. Anyhow, in later years, Daddy and I came down to Fort Meyers on a vacation trip with Uncle Hjalmer and Aunt Sadie. I got such a kick out of them. Uncle liked to talk, you know, and Aunt Sadie would say, 'Hjalmer, if you want to go on jawin', you can just stop the car and go argue with that cow over there.'"

Sarah shook with laughter at the memory of sassy aunt Sadie. Then, in a subdued voice, she said, "Daddy liked it so much here in Florida that we left Illinois for good." She reached for a worn photo album on the nightstand and handed it to Callie. "These are all I have left."

Cal opened the black cover embossed with a golden palm tree and the words *Souvenir of Florida*. Some of the black corner tabs had come unglued. Brittle pages held black and white snapshots from the 1940s and '50s, mostly of people Callie didn't know or relatives she barely recognized: Aunt Sadie in a black swimsuit whose skirt failed to camouflage her massive body; skinny Uncle Hjalmer in a one-piece reminiscent of the 1930s; Sarah's father, posing like a muscle man in tight black trunks with a white belt cinched below his navel.

Of all the pictures, only two were of Sarah: one as a young girl in a sun dress and Dutch boy haircut, standing under a willow tree next to Tag, her white Spitz; and the other, a middle-aged Sarah in an oversized print house dress and sturdy black shoes. In this photo, she was standing next to her father, who, looking younger than his daughter and rather racy for the 1950s, was dressed in sandals, tight pants, a see-through mesh shirt, and a shell necklace.

Toward the end of the album, it was obvious that Sarah had carefully arranged those pictures that meant the most to her: Illinois apple trees loaded with blossoms; Sarah with her dog Tag, seated on little chairs of a spring afternoon, enjoying a tea party under the flowering crab, surrounded by lilac shrubs, hydrangeas, gladiolas, and chrysanthemums— all in black and white.

"What a sweet little dog," said Callie.

"She was." Sarah glanced at the photograph and held a hand to her cheek. "Every evening, after going potty, Tag would look up at the night sky—at the stars and the moon—sit staring for a long time, as if she wanted to go up there."

The last photo was of her father as an elderly man, tanned, sporting a thick white crew cut, sitting on a bench along some quiet, shady street in Fort Meyers.

"Sarah," asked Callie, "did you ever have any boyfriends?"

"Oh, yes, when I was twenty, there was one young man I especially liked. We went to the picture shows and to the park for long walks. I liked him a lot."

"And?"

"Well, it was the strangest thing. Daddy took him fishing one afternoon—just a kind gesture, mind you—and I never saw him again."

"You don't mean ... did he ... ?"

Sarah burst out laughing. "No, nothing like that. I caught glimpses of him around Belvidere and at church, but he wasn't friendly like before. He never called again."

"What happened?"

"I don't know for sure. He eventually married a girl from Loves Park."

Sarah looked down at her hands. "Daddy said I'd never get married."

"Why not?"

"Well, because I talk all the time!" She yipped and flung her arms outward. "Somebody has to talk! You can't just sit around and look at each other."

Callie laughed and applauded.

Sarah was quiet for a moment, then smiled at a memory: "Oh, we had a lot of fun together. That young man, he had such a sense of humor. Used to make me laugh. We made each other laugh a lot."

"Did you ever meet another?"

"Oh no. There was never anyone else. I stayed at home."

"Maybe you should have gone to Rockford and become a typist."

Sarah suddenly became agitated, as if Callie had gone too far. "I told you," she said firmly, "my place was at home. Daddy needed me. He needed a wife. After Aunt Sadie passed away, Uncle Hjalmer moved in with us and I took care of him too. I took care of Daddy and Uncle until they died."

Sarah fell quiet and turned away. For a long moment, she stared through her window at the dark brick wall opposite her room.

Callie might have missed those four words the way Sarah had tucked them in among her other thoughts. 'Daddy needed a wife.'

She stared at the back of Auntie's head, at the little bald spots among the patches of matted gray hair, and reached out to touch her shoulder. But Sarah quickly turned back with a warning look, and held up a hand.

"Daddy and Mother are buried in Belvedere," she said, "and that's where I'll go when I pass. It's all taken care of."

The smells of weak coffee, canned green beans, and hamburger patties drifted in from lunch carts rolling through the hallway, making Callie even more queasy. It seemed impossible, sitting in room 302B of the Sunrise Center Nursing Home, that she was even in Florida. But there she sat, within driving distance of the beaches where relatives frolicked back in the 1950s. Where Auntie Sarah had lived a life of someone else's choosing.

"You know," said Sarah, "for a while, after Aunt Lil died, I didn't think Tessie would ever get away. She had to take care of Uncle Jack for such a long time. But she had a right to get married. After all, they did!"

"Well, so did *you*—have the right."

With an icy stare, Sarah cast a final warning. "I *told* you. *I* was needed at home." While Sarah picked at her food, Callie paged slowly through the photo album, studying each picture with new eyes: Uncle Hjalmer and Aunt Sadie, Uncle Hugo and Auntie Sarah.

"I hope you can stay longer." Sarah set her tray aside. "I don't get many visitors. You're all up in that Minnesota deep freeze!" She giggled and reached into one of the pasteboard boxes that lined the floor.

"Of course I can stay a while longer," said Callie, imagining a not-so-rapid departure from this little room, realizing that she'd likely never see Auntie again.

"Here," said Sarah. "I want you to have this."

She presented Callie with a bent piece of yellowed cardboard on which she had wired a dozen brightly colored buttons. "The last of my collection," she said.

Surprised, Callie remembered her mother's words from long ago: "Some day, you'll understand."

"Oh, thank you," she said, embracing Auntie Sarah. "I will treasure these."

When she stood up, Sarah took a few steps and began swaying backwards. She grabbed the curtain that divided the room in half.

"Are you all right?" asked Callie.

"Oh, yes. I'm fine. It's just a case of the staggers, when you don't know if you are going to stand or fall down. Or if you're coming or going."

ARM IN ARM, the two women ambled down to the community wing where Bingo cards lay neatly stacked on long tables, and blue, white, and red chips nestled together in their plastic containers. Sarah sat down at the piano and placed her hands over the keys. Like swift birds, those eight fingers flew over the octaves while she sang, "*A Pretty Girl is Like a Melody.*"

"I'm second soprano now," she declared, swiveling around on the piano stool. "It wasn't going so well as first soprano anymore. I told my doctor that I felt dizzy at choir practice and you know what he told me? He said, 'Well, Sarah, you just keep on singing, only skip the high notes.'"

She laughed and laughed until the laugh lines ran like cockleshells from the corners of her eyes over her entire face.

"Here, see if you can guess this one," she said, circling back to the piano with a giggle.

9

Salute the Sun

Anyone entrusted with power will abuse it if not also animated
with the love of truth and virtue, no matter whether
he be a prince, or one of the people.
—Jean de La Fontaine

SOMETIMES CALLIE FELT LIKE CRYING for Auntie Sarah, sorry for all the times she had criticized her simple and unexamined life.

But then she remembered their long visit together, and Auntie's gift, and how the late afternoon sunshine slanted through a narrow window, spotlighting Sarah at the piano. Glancing back at Cal with impish eyes, she crooned a few notes without words, her slender hands commanding the keys.

"See if you can guess this one," she'd said.

"*You Are My Sunshine!*" cried Callie. And she chirped the lyrics along with Sarah.

Never again would she snigger at an elderly woman who spoke adoringly of ordinary things: a favorite television program; flowers, flowers, and more flowers; her button collection; a young man dating back to earlier times. Cal used to think of Auntie's voice as warbly and high-pitched, like that of a songstress from another century. But when Sarah sang for her in the nursing home that day, she sounded like a young girl, her voice sweet and lovely.

Once Sarah asked, "Did you ever have to give up a dream, Callie? When you were a girl?"

"I tried not to," she'd answered, pausing for a moment.

"There were a couple of teachers in Masterton who discouraged us girls from going on to college. Education for women: that was one dream a few people tried to squash, especially Mr. Pike, our English teacher. He'd yell at us, 'Keep still, you girls! Stop talking! Shut up! No more questions!' And then he'd turn from the chalkboard, pitch an eraser at us, and focus on the boys."

One day, during first hour, Mr. Pike created a sign that he hooked to a string and hung around Callie's neck, ordering her to wear it for the entire day. The sign, drawn in large black letters on heavy red construction paper, stood out against her back—against her white blouse:

I TALK TOO MUCH!

In addition, he forced her to grip a long, yellow pencil between her teeth. Then he linked up with all of her other teachers, instructing them to make sure she didn't remove either piece until the end of the day.

Hour after hour, Callie tried to hold herself together as she slipped through the hallways, sidled along rows of lockers and into the next classroom where, seated in her desk, she had to face the next teacher. As the day wore on, with more and more chastisements for trying to remove the pencil because her jaws were aching, her shoulders began to droop, and she felt too sad and tired, even, to be angry. All she could do was stare at her desktop, listen to another baritone voice, and wait for the next bell to ring.

During the last hour of the day, her physical education class was held on the basketball court, where fifty ninth-graders were supposed to learn how to dance. Their teacher, Mr. Ahrens, who was also a counselor, singled Callie out. After forcing her into the center of a circle made up of Cal's classmates, he gripped her shoulders in order to turn her around 360 degrees, and ordered all of the other students to read the sign aloud and take a lesson from it. That's when Callie broke down. Releasing the pencil from her mouth (without permission), and gushing a day's worth of pent-up tears, she crumbled to the floor.

Suddenly, from the back of the auditorium, a voice called out, "Stop humiliating that girl!"

Callie wasn't sure what that long word meant, but knew she had an ally in Mr. Erickson, the typing teacher. He strode down the aisle of the auditorium toward the steps leading up to the gym floor and motioned for Mr. Ahrens. While they talked, Callie stood up, ripped the sign from around her neck, and kicked the pencil across the court. Several girlfriends rushed to her side.

Mr. Ahrens ushered her to a spot next to the theater curtain, which hung in dark, heavy folds. He stood silent for a moment and then apologized. Cal looked up at him, said nothing, and escaped to the girls' locker room.

While taking cover for a moment in the shower stall, Callie recalled Mr. Erickson's words. Although she would have to look up the definition of 'humiliating,' which sounded a little like the words 'human being,' she was grateful that at the end of this nightmarish day, that one word came like a final punctuation mark from the mouth of one teacher bold enough to break the chain in order to show that he cared.

After returning home from school, Cal brought her personal dictionary, a tablet, and a blue pen out to the backyard. She looked up into the willow tree and waved at Sam Cat who gazed down at her from his perch on a high branch.

As soon as Callie sat down at the picnic table with Tequila by her side, a little red dragonfly landed on her sleeve. She watched him clean his first set of legs and salute the sun. Afterward, he stayed by her writing pad, all the while glowing bronze in the late afternoon light, while Cal jotted down the word 'humiliate," along with all of its definitions.

Then she picked up Tequila, her Chihuahua, and gave her a gentle hug.

"Shortly before my senior year," she had told Auntie Sarah, "Mr. Ahrens called me into his office to discuss my school records and future plans. 'If I were you, Callandra,' he said, brandishing a stack of deportment files with my name on them, 'I'd give it up. You're not college material.'"

"And what did you do?" asked Sarah.

"I didn't say a word, but my whole insides fired back at him: 'Go to blazes! I'll show you!'

"Thought I could trust him after he'd apologized three years earlier for what he'd done to me on the basketball court.

"And when I read *The Scarlet Letter* for the first time, it sank in, especially the meaning of the word 'stigma.' Although my only sin back in ninth grade (and onward) was talking too much, I had acquired a temporary stigma: yellow paint soaked into the corners of my lips from chips off the old pencil."

"What a numskull," said Sarah. "Well, don't take any wooden nickels. Some folks you can never trust. But here's one thing I've always been able to count on." And Sarah spun around, turning back to her piano.

MUSIC SUSTAINS A LIFE—guides it on into the next day. And the next. Auntie Sara got it. Uncle Amer had it. Even Grandma Julia made beautiful music—like notes from brilliant songbirds drifting about the cottage at Tepeeotah, and then peeling through screened windows from inside her little house in Masterton, flocking around a young Callie. The gift of music kept her dancing, even in later years, when she felt like giving up. She had hoped, back then, that there would come a time when she would no longer have to hide behind her piano.

And then there were books—with words that could make you laugh, think, bring out the best in you: "Life is better than death, I believe," wrote Alice Walker, "if only because it is less boring, and because it has fresh peaches in it."

10

Villages of the Dead

. . . the time of towns is tolled from the world by funeral chimes,
but in nature the universal hours are counted by succeeding
tribes of animals and plants and by growth of joy on joy . . .
—Ralph Waldo Emerson

" 'LIFE IS JUST A BOWL OF PEACHES,' " sang Callie, one hand on the steering wheel. After a quick look at herself in the rear view mirror, she finished the tune with a silly French accent: "Don't you take eet serious, babee, cuz life is waaay too meesterious."

She glanced at her dad who sat relaxed in his seat, smiling, eyes closed, shoulders wrapped in the late afternoon sunshine angling through the passenger window. He had removed his rust-colored suit jacket and necktie, and folded them neatly on the back seat. How little space those clothes took compared to the heap of starched crinolines Cal had hauled off to college—in a different car, of course.

Callie and Will left Readstown and the county seat of Viroqua behind. Fresh in their minds were the forested hills, lush coulees, and sandstone cliffs within the Kickapoo River valley, along with the faded King Midas Flour advertisement covering the entire end of an old wooden barn.

Callie had asked a gas station attendant in Viroqua if he knew what "Kickapoo" meant.

"One who goes there, then here," he answered, pointing away, then back again. "It's an Algonquin word. The Kickapoo manages to flow north, south, east, and west during its one hundred and twenty-five miles of passage. It's one of the oldest river systems in the world."

"And so it goes," said Will, nodding his head in all four directions. "Here, there, and everywhere."

The attendant laughed and started singing the Beatles' tune.

Within minutes of taking to the road again, Callie spotted a large turtle looming up from a shallow ditch next to the highway. He paused at the road's edge, his head held high. Cal drove slowly past it, then felt sickened as soon as she noticed in the rear-view mirror a black Silverado pickup swerve onto the shoulder in an effort to run over the turtle. The driver gunned his engine and sped on by with throbbing sounds of rap music streaming from the truck's open windows. He had missed crushing the turtle.

With no one else behind her, Callie backed up and stopped a few feet away from the large domed shell—rather lonely-looking just sitting there on the gravel with its head and legs tucked inside, and its tail clenched sideways into the shell.

"What's it doing crossing the road this time of year?" she asked, getting out of the car.

"Sometimes in early fall," said Will, "hatchlings dig up from their nests and go off in search of water."

Callie circled cautiously around the animal. "This is no hatchling, that's for sure."

Will detached his seatbelt in order to turn and watch what his daughter was going to do. "Be careful now, Cal. Watch out for more crazy drivers."

Callie inched up behind the massive turtle and placed her fingers beneath its wide chestnut brown carapace, midway between the front and back legs, which popped out like miniature elephant legs and began swimming wildly against the air, its dark toenails extended with pieces of brown grass clinging to them.

Cal checked for traffic before scooting across the highway. When she was a little girl, she'd watched her father save a small painted turtle as it tried to cross a busy street in Masterton. That one had only three little sausage legs dotted in red, a bit of a pointy tail, and a strong neck and head with stripes like ink lines drawn on yellow.

And then there was that big turtle who paid her a visit more than once, years ago on Lake Shetek.

The long neck and enormous head on this snapping turtle stretched around toward Callie, its intense, angled eyes directed at her face. The sharp, horny beak opened slightly below large pinhole nostrils, transitioning from a frown to a smile, as if it would speak. Instead, it tried to nip at Callie's left forearm, which she quickly drew closer to her side, only to feel a scratch from toenails along her right wrist. In spite of the struggle, she didn't let go, and continued to heft the reptile low to the pavement over to the other side, in the direction he was heading to begin with. She set him down on the pebbly shoulder and watched him scramble away without looking back; he tumbled down into the ditch, righted himself, and ploughed through long grass that led to a narrow creek.

Taking a deep breath, Callie wiped her hands on her jeans, and returned to the car. "At least he didn't get hit by that jerk in the truck."

"Way too many rotten types out there," said Will. "I've seen that kind of behavior time and again."

"Zero respect for wildlife," said Callie. "At least that turtle can hang in there a while longer." She pictured him once again—plunging into the ditch and making his way through the weeds without looking back.

In past years, she was always turning to look back: at a field of fresh clover near a sparkling stream where she and Jim had picnicked; at the cliffs they'd explored; across that boardwalk next to the sea; inside a motel room, before closing the door.

Callie drove on in silence, asking herself when she had stopped looking back so often, hoping for those pleasant repeats to help counter the negative, hanging onto wishes that would never come true.

When had she started edging over to exist in the moment? She thought of that process as incremental, like the old corn sheller on her aunt and uncle's farm. After the cobs got pulled from their crib, and the husks and chaff were stripped and tossed away, all that remained were the kernels—those shiny, yellow beads of matter.

And there was the time when she and her cousin Jen visited Belle Kittleson's tavern near Tepeeotah. Belle had given each one an arrowhead and had let them hold an ancient beaded bracelet she'd found near Slaughter Slough. And then she explained how turtles—those gentle innocents of Mother Earth—were considered by the Lakotah to be powerful symbols for women, to help them maintain their strength and endurance.

"They would place a beaded turtle," explained Bell, "inside the crib of a newborn girl."

"How come?" asked Jen.

"For protection; and a long life."

HAVING PASSED through the ornate wrought iron entrance of the Rockford Swedish cemetery just yesterday morning, a passel of thoughts stuck in Callie's mind—thoughts about family, including Auntie Sarah, now in her mid-nineties, whose remains, when the time came, would be transported from Winter Haven to the cemetery in Belvidere, where she would lie next to her parents for eternity.

Now, as a result of her own experiences, along with those of others, the realizations of abuse against girls, women, children, and animals led Callie back to the brown study of prejudice and murder that had ended Uncle Amer's life.

"Guess we should face it," Will had said. "*We* know a lot about him, but there'll come a time, with the next generations, when the memory of Amer will fall by the way."

"That's why there should be a marker. Before we left home for Rockford, you said you wanted to make sure there was one, 'so all who pass by will know that he mattered in this world.'"

"I know, I know. Being lowered into a cemetery isn't enough, is it? We've got to consider something more for him."

Visions of burial grounds—those villages of the dead, where Callie and her childhood friends used to wander—brought up all sorts of macabre images, frightening notions of death and what a body must look like after years and years beneath the ground. She and her girlfriends had read about how, in some southern states, like Georgia, a string was often tied to the finger or toe of a supposèd dead person (before the era of embalming), then strung up through a hole in the slab and connected to a bell hanging from the headstone—just in case.

"Imagine," said her friend Judy, "when the wind blows. What a sound that would make! Hundreds of bells all tinkling at the same time!"

"And here come the relatives flooding over to the cemetery in the middle of the night," said Laura Lambert, "to see if their bells are ringing."

When Callie's friends talked like that, she pictured scores of bodies suddenly coming to life, banging at the inside lids of their coffins, signaling, getting dug up, flipping out of their containers, dancing, running back to town along the main road in long strides, clawing at the air with long fingernails as the wind blew through their long gray hair—long, brittle, streaming gray hair—all on their way to a fresh peach stand.

As girls, adopting cemeteries for playgrounds, Callie regarded the breezy hilltop burial ground north of Masterton as a strange little town high above Beaver Creek. Narrow, bumpy paths, lined with ornate façades, led to miniature buildings sculpted from beige and gray stones standing in *bas relief*. Chiseled anchors and beveled crosses, worn round and smooth, posed as eternal reminders of townsfolk who clamored through life to make their marks—stout monuments that would take eons to crumble. After that, would anyone be left to remember? Or care?

Interspersed among those larger headstones lay rows of modest, flat granite slabs, some flush to the ground, while others, in the century-old section, lay deep-set and tilting into the earth.

Buried in the far northeast corner, near a scrawny oak tree that had outlived its time, Callie's grandparents, Vic and Julia Lindstrom, had been laid to rest. One evening in late summer, Will and his family shuffled through acorns and short brown grass to stand before the graves of his parents, their dark granite marker shining in the last rays of sunlight.

The glowing colors reminded Callie of her granddad's gunstocks as he sat polishing them in the firelight inside their cottage, and her grandmother's gold-rimmed teeth as she sang and played her upright in the next room.

After a time, the surface of Vic and Julia's marker grew dull, permanently etched in yellow-green. As the years passed, so grew the lichens.

Yellow had always been Callie's favorite color ever since she was a tiny girl aware enough to focus on a single page in her children's book, *Little Black Sambo*. Time and again, she returned to that ring of tigers, head-to-tail, running circles around a tree so fast they deliquesced into butter—the richest, most deliciously colored butter she'd ever seen. If only she could pull it from the page, how wonderfully scrumptious it would taste, melted on warm toast, hot biscuits, and sweet corn. From that moment on, Cal was partial to the color yellow, the color of lemons and canted sunglow, mustard and harvest moons, bananas, dandelions, Van Gogh's sunflowers, steaming corn bread, and real butter. Not the fake stuff that came out in the 1950s. Called oleomargarine, it was nothing but white goo in plastic bags with built-in buttons filled with dye that you pressed and kneaded into the white mass until it turned a dull yellow. When her father, as a young man, worked at the creamery in Hadley, he'd tease the farmers about delivering their filled cream cans, collecting their money, then going into town to buy bags of oleomargarine.

He'd ask them, "How on earth can you go back to the farm and look your cows in the eye?"

Now, of course, those herds are long gone. And so are the farmers that milked them, and their wives with their buttery cakes and golden pies. Those folks are planted near Callie's grandparents on the wind-blown hill overlooking the fallow fields.

Surveying that village of tombstones whenever she returned to Masterton, Callie remembered how obvious it was that all men and women were not equal, even in death. Many of the markers lay humble, barely visible, without a trace of anyone stopping by, unless the deceased happened to have been veterans of war. And there were lots of those, resulting from the two great wars, wars that were supposed to end all wars. But then came Korea and Viet Nam and whatever other skirmishes in between that might have barely made the headlines.

Every year, veterans of foreign wars hobbled through the cemetery, placing crinkly red paper poppies and miniature stars and stripes stapled to wooden sticks into the ground next to select tombstones. All of that colorful decoration made obvious the many unadorned gravesites of men, alongside their wives or parents, who had not "served their country," for whatever reason, and had long ago run out of relatives and friends who could be counted on to plant flowers next to their stones and edge away encroaching sod in preparation for the annual Memorial Day celebrations.

Alvin Posthuma, the elderly veteran who loved literature and played Taps on his trumpet every year, always stood close to where he now lies. Inscribed on his tombstone is a quote from Truman Capote: "What is death but an offering to time and eternity?"

Callie's mother used to gather lilacs for relatives, for the graves of forgotten neighbors, and for the "boys" she and Will knew who had been killed overseas. A lot of mothers did that—cradled armloads of lilacs on their way up to the cemetery.

The colossal *bas-relief* stone anchor, towering above all others in that village of the dead, belonged to a man named Herbert Horn. Word had it that he once worked for the OSS (Office of Strategic Services) under Roosevelt, spent winters in the south of France, and had an authentic painting by Cezanne hanging on his bedroom wall. And he had strange gadgets lying around his house: secret maps disguised as playing cards, a compass hidden in a brass button, a small camera in the shape of a matchbox, coins with swivel blades, and a pencil containing a tiny dagger. After all that intrigue, why he left Washington D. C. and chose Masterton, Minnesota to live out the rest of his life had everyone talking for years about the notion of *in cognito*. His *bas-relief* stone anchor was the key monument for summer games.

After playing hide-and-seek around Herbert Horn, Callie and her friends launched themselves over the split rail fence for Jack-and-Jill rolls downhill through sun-baked tallgrass and into the creek where painted turtles hunkered along the edges. If only the dead could have heard their shrieks as the girls tumbled and splashed in the fast-flowing water. After those heavy spring rains, the river might have roiled them along into the Des Moines and all the way to the mighty Mississippi.

Maybe some of the dead did hear the children, in a fashion—especially those who'd reluctantly quit this earth, leaving their strong, life-loving spirits somewhere up on that grassy knoll, among the oak trees and cottonwoods. What if they drifted back into town to hanker over a juicy burger and butterscotch malt at the Hub Café? What if they tried to elbow people? Some still haunted the living, wreaking havoc on them. Thelma Christensen's spirit, to name one, might very likely have turned into a hellion.

Thelma, whose husband Everett had taken up with Ruby Ryan, got so wired from the Dale Carnegie classes held weekly in the basement of the Methodist Church, that it wouldn't have surprised Callie if she had held on to some of that pluck in the great beyond. Surely, any woman who could bring herself to shout in public, "I never want to see that dirty low-down bloated toady pig ever again!" must have taken plenty of that with her to the grave. Into the grave and out again.

Most of the elderly townspeople Callie knew as a child were still neighbors, lying close to one another beneath the sod north of Masterton. All, that is, except for the Catholics who established their own burial grounds south of town—Saint Agnes'. Inside the entrance to their village of the dead towered an iron Jesus nailed to a cross with metal teardrops stuck to his forlorn face, and a ring of thorns hammered onto the crown of his longhaired skull. Once, when Callie asked why several makeshift crosses were stuck in the ground outside the fenced-in cemetery, her mother explained that those markers belonged to people who lived their lives contrary to the church's teachings.

"Such as?"

"Oh, gamblers and others of ill repute."

Later on, Callie found out that individuals historically cast out included not only gamblers, but heretics, hookers, homosexuals, thieves, divorcees, manifest sinners, abortion-seekers, and suicides. And long ago, denied especially by the French clergy were artists, actors, and writers, like Molière—and more recently, the singer Edith Piaf. All heretics.

As a pre-teen, Callie asked her dad what a heretic was.

"A freethinker," he answered.

"Well, what's so bad about that?"

"Damned if I know."

Besides St. Agnes' and the Hilltop cemetery, older burial grounds outside of Masterton captivated Callie and her friends who often tramped through the one east of town. Occasionally, they biked out there late at night, in hot summer or frigid fall, especially after trick-or-treating, still dressed in their Halloween costumes of smelly rubber monster masks, white bed sheets, and black-and-white glow-in-the-dark skeleton outfits from Buckles' Five-and-Dime.

Frightened by the notion of ringing bells, unsettled spirits, and evil lurking in the dark of night, and spooked by the decaying smells rising from ancient graves, the girls shivered while keeping a look-out for headlights, determined to remain in the inky darkness of the country cemetery until at least three cars had passed by. At first glow of high beams bending around the turns in the gravel road, they scrambled to drape themselves over the tallest headstones they could climb and remain still as statues. Afterward, they boasted about how they sure as hell scared the bejesus out of those drivers—even the men.

"Did you hear their tires spit stones?"

"I wish we could have seen their faces."

"Ho, boy! I'll bet we scared them shitless."

Bored by mid-summer, Callie and her friends wandered about one of the cemeteries, reading aloud the names of those who had once walked among the living, recalling the personalities of young and old souls they had met up with in town. Leaning against the handlebars, they straddled their blue and red and yellow bikes, studying the tombstones and sharing stories about the locals, some of whom were still living back then: Knute Bentson, who had to sell his family farm and move to town; Rudy Larson, who got by with murder; Olaf Berg and Clem Leaser, who established a precursor to the sidewalk café; Hilda McNamarra Johnson, a gifted soprano; Pinky Wisdorf, who regularly chewed his mustache thanks to an underslung jaw; Ruby Ryan, a fun lady for some, a trollop to others; Marbella Kinmore, owner of the most fashionable clothing store in Maywood County; and Mr. and Mrs. Lambert, survivors of the Warsaw Ghetto.

As a grown up, Callie easily remembered those long-ago citizens of Masterton, the high- or low-pitched, gruff or whiny sounds of their voices, how they ambled, limped, edged, marched, pranced, staggered, and click-clacked down Main Street.

And then there was that little girl who spun around like a Skittles Top, bumping into everybody along her path, until her mother strapped a harness and leash on her.

Aiming daily for the bar with a hurried limp, helped along by a turtle-like swing of the head, Knute Bentson, for health reasons, had sold his farm west of Masterton, hired an auctioneer, and moved into town, driving a pickup truck loaded with pasteboard boxes filled with the last of his possessions. From then on, he traded the open air of his

Maywood County farmland for a stool inside the smoke-filled Lounge 59, next door to the library. Displayed at his funeral (and for a brief time at his gravesite) was a one-man timber saw with a Holstein cow and a bright red barn painted on its wide, toothy blade.

Another farmer, Rudy Larson, lay between two of his wives in the cemetery near Hadley. (Wife number three, who supposedly died of natural causes, had left instructions to be buried next to her first husband in Ames, Iowa.)

Everyone in town spoke of how Mr. Larson had likely murdered those first two wives, but no one could prove it. Lena, dressed in a nightgown, had been caught up in the power take-off at three o'clock on a winter's morning.

Months before, the PTO had been hooked up to a tractor for powering Rudy's hay elevator.

"All it takes," explained one of the locals, "for a person to get grabbed up by an open power take-off shaft is a single thread of clothing or a strand of loose hair. Lena's entire body was broken, almost unrecognizable."

Some years later, Olga, the second wife, disappeared and was never found. One farmer said he could hear loud voices and a scream coming from near a drainage ditch in the middle of the night. Another swore that he had seen Rudy hauling several large garbage bags into a landfill some distance from his own fields.

After each death or disappearance, Mr. Larson tearfully presented a rational explanation to the court and to the local sheriff. Since no body was recovered the second time around, he was allowed to return home, a fresh widower.

Even though people started referring to him as "Killer Larson," a number of available women soon lined up at his farmhouse door. Mesmerized by his seductive brown eyes and strong, long-fingered hands, they offered him velvet cakes, banana cream pies, and trays of freshly baked chocolate chip cookies. One elderly woman even went so far as to send away for a new wig—blond—and invited Rudy Larson to accompany her to a Sadie Hawkins dance at the sale barn in Masterton.

"Sure beats dancing with Walter Magnus," she told a friend between shrieks of laughter. "Walt may be wealthy, but that long yellow beard stinks to high heaven. Just like his pig farm. After one go 'round on the dance floor, it took forever to get that awful smell out of my blouse, not to mention my hair! Horses and cows ain't so bad. But pigs! Damn hard to get close to a bearded pig farmer! I'll go with "Killer Larson" any time, thank you very much."

Whenever someone complained to Walter Magnus about the far-reaching stench drifting outward in all directions from his pig farm, he replied without hesitation, "Smells like roses to me."

Callie and her family actually did meet a pair of pigs who smelled like roses—Potbellies that their mother's friend Alice kept as pets on her property near San Diego. Although they lived outside, Cochie and Porcie, full-grown, had access to Alice's entire house through a basement door. All they had to do was step inside, trot up the staircase, and tap their middle-toes along the entry floor.

One evening, while eating at a seafood restaurant, Alice clapped a hand against the side of her face. "Oh, my God, I forgot to barricade the kitchen and bungee-cord the refrigerator!"

Whenever she went out, Alice cordoned off that room with a half sheet of smudged plywood held in place by an old spare tire from her Ford Explorer.

After dinner, back at the house, Callie and family followed Alice into her kitchen and discovered the refrigerator door hanging wide open and the lower vegetable drawers tugged all the way out. Shreds of lettuce, chunks of cucumber, an unopened jar of mayonnaise, and strips from a large head of cabbage were strewn around the floor.

Cochie and Porcie lay snoozing in a corner on their pile of perfumed quilts with a couple of carrots next to them.

Callie thought they were clever and cute.

Back in Masterton, at the noon hour of many a summer's day, Olaf Berg and Clem Leaser hauled their chairs out onto the sidewalk in front of the hardware store, where they ate bologna sandwiches, petted Old Nell, Clem's Chesapeake, and entertained local children with magic tricks: a coin found behind an ear, a dollar bill shaped like a bow tie, a gum wrapper folded into a tiny sailboat, moveable goose feet created with a long circle of string entwined around Clem Leaser's scarred and swollen fingers.

Clem liked to tell the story of how devoted Old Nell was to hunting.

"We were out at Big Slough," he said, "and lo and behold, this dog o' mine took a detour with a Canvasback in her jaws, and gave birth to seven pups on top of a rat house. One of 'em rolled off into the water and some guy come along in his duck boat and saved it." Clem reached out to pat the top of Old Nell's head. "We found homes for all seven, didn't we?" She looked up at him with a grin.

Olaf Berg, his head the size of a bull, his voice the pitch of a calf, used to ask the neighborhood kids if they liked to fish.

"Yah," they answered in chorus.

"And do you have plenty of worms?" he'd inquire, lips pulled back to show off his butter tooth.

"Yah, dug a bunch this morning."

"Well then, be sure to keep them fresh and moist. Best to hold 'em in your mouths like spaghetti and pull one out at a time as needed. Don't swallow them or you'll run out of bait!"

The kids, some gagging, others hollering, "Yuck!" lowered their heads and fled down the street. Yet, the next day, they could hardly wait to rush over to Olaf Berg seated in his folding chair, grinning and winking, nibbling on another bologna sandwich.

During her youth, Hilda McNamarra, a blue-eyed strawberry blond, wanted more than anything to sing opera and play a violin. At eighteen, she left her family's farm east of Masterton to attend college, and in her sophomore year, succumbed to the advances of a vocal teacher who had no intentions of leaving his wife.

Months later, Hilda and her baby boy returned to the farm, pretending that the child had been orphaned when shirttail relatives on her mother's side—a young couple—had died in a car crash somewhere deep in the hinterlands of Texas.

Hilda eventually married Mr. Johnson, an elderly farmer near Pipestone, moved in along with her son Tubby, cooked five meals a day, fed the chickens, gathered eggs, tended an acre of garden, kept house, and tried to teach her son how to play the violin. Every Sunday afternoon, she sat patiently at the piano while Tubby stood behind her, scritch-scratching the bow across the strings, intentionally running the tip of it through his mother's graying bouffant, which she wore all poofed up like Marie Antoinette's. Whenever Hilda brushed her hair, she saved the wads of "rats" to incorporate into her daily do. For, as she often said, "You never know when I might be asked to make an appearance."

At age thirty, having received no invitations to perform, and dissatisfied in marriage, Hilda took to her bed, claiming that she had fallen ill and could no longer walk. As months turned into years, the hired cook reported telltale signs of movement, such as a hairbrush in a different spot on the dresser, a reorganized stack of books on the radiator, a crumpled lace hanky accidently dropped in the hallway just outside her door.

Early one morning, after nearly ten years, Hilda got out of bed and inched her way down the steps to resume her wifely duties—but only in the kitchen and in the henhouse, for her husband had recently passed away. She fired the cook, waved goodbye to Tubby who moved to Minneapolis, and in her fortieth year, was seen climbing a large oak tree located behind the machine shed, apparently just for the fun of it. From then on she could be seen doing a lot of fun things, especially in the company of a neighboring farmer who took frequent breaks from caring for his bed-ridden wife suffering from a bad heart.

As for Ruby Ryan, the town flirt—nearly every evening she could be heard cussing out her husband Carl inside their dark house with the windows flung open. Minutes later, she'd spike her way downtown to the Silver Star for gin martinis and Lucky Strike cigarettes.

Wealthy Judge Carlson got his kicks out of making fun of foreigners, especially *Herr Schmidt,* the Klein family's relative who visited from Cologne, Germany once a year. He'd paint the man as an idiot or a Nazi, when all Mr. Schmidt did was go about his business in a quiet and dignified manner, respectfully communing with the great out-of-doors.

"If I had my way," Judge Carlson seethed, "I'd send every Kraut, Spic, Kike, Jap, and Chink back where they came from. Pronto!"

"And how about the Frogs?" asked Will.

"Nah, the French were our allies. Ain't gonna say nothin' against 'em."

"Hmm, so well put. All I can say is that Mr. Schmidt is a fine man, too. The war has been over for some years now. Time to move on, Judge."

During his annual visits, *Herr Schmidt* hiked the country roads and rested in comfortable ditches padded with long grass, dry and toasty warm under a hot summer sun. Warblers and meadowlarks sang from wooden fence lines butting against fields, and from thin branches of volunteer shrubs pushing up along the slopes of the ditches. Cows gathered at the fence to watch the man nap.

"You'll find no better friends than these, Callie," her dad used to say about the lakes and land, the birds and animals, and gentlemen like Mr. Schmidt, a fellow rambler.

"It took me a long time, Cal, after the second big war, to stop thinking of all Germans as our enemy. With the Japs, it was harder, because of Pearl Harbor, and likely because I've never met any of them personally. But after getting to know *Herr Schmidt,* I understood that not everybody from Germany supported Hitler and the Nazi regime. In fact, although he wouldn't go into detail, Mr. Schmidt admitted that he tried to help the Allies and the French underground. Sometimes, we just don't know the whole story."

11

Remain Vertical,
Children of the Blood

. . . Oh straight line! Pure lance without a horseman,
how my spiral path dreams of your light!
— *Federico García Lorca*

KEY PARTS of that whole story got filled in by Julie Hendrickson, Danny-the-rollerskater's mother. She had already told Callie about her father's dog, Miquette, who lived in Paris after the war. Years later, when the story of her cousin Camille began floating around town, the history teacher at Masterton High School invited Julie to speak to his classes, including anyone else who wished to join them. Except for some math and science kids, students and teachers from all the other classrooms filed through the hallways and into the auditorium.

At two o'clock on a Friday afternoon, Julie Jouvet Hendrickson stood before a microphone placed at the edge of the raised basketball court, where years ago, Callie had been singled out with that sign on her back and the pencil between her teeth. Now the theater curtains and a white screen closed off the court.

Julie looked out over the young faces peering up at her from rows of seats. She smiled and waved at Callie and her parents who had returned to Masterton in order to attend this presentation, which Julie began with a favorite quote by Federico Garcia Lorca.

The lights were turned down and the first slide to show on the screen was of Camille Baudin standing in front of the white Basilica atop Montmartre.

"Camille," said Julie, "had returned to France twice throughout her middle years, but never once to this place on the hill overlooking Paris. It was here that my cousin and her parents struggled under the German Occupation between 1940 and 1944. For her final trip, in 1990, she invited me to go along. What I learned from this paramount journey, I am pleased to share with you this afternoon."

THE TWO WOMEN STOPPED to catch their breath.

"Oh, my dear," said Camille, "it feels terribly strange to be up here. I'm so glad you came along. The last time I was in Paris, I intentionally put off visiting this hill, where mama and papa. . . . To think it has been nearly fifty years."

Camille Baudin and her cousin, Julie, panted in the midsummer heat as they closed the distance between the last step and Sacred Heart cathedral. They had made it to the top of the butte—*Montmartre*—where the white basilica towered overhead. Feeling a bit like martyrs themselves after climbing the three hundred steps, they looked down from where they had come, down to the first tread, and beyond—at the panorama of Paris spread out far below.

Camille had suggested walking up from the base of the mount instead of riding the funicular, saying, "I wish to experience this part of our day without any confinement."

The wide square, called *La Place du Parvis*, was crammed with tourists, street mimes, and vendors. Real life statues in costume stood tall, anchored to their pillars: Bo Peep, Egyptian Mummy, and Silver Robot mesmerized the crowds with their disciplined stillness; then came the strange gyrations, slow bows, and mechanized kisses blown to strangers whenever a coin clinked into a cup on the pavers below.

Children, afraid at first, took cover behind their mamas' skirts, then became entranced at how long the human effigies could remain vertical—so still for so long against the gusts of wind and harsh noonday sun beating down upon them.

The metallic gold mummy, aglow in the sunshine, bowed slowly from his pedestal after a timid child tossed her coin into the cup and quickly retreated back to her parents.

In front of the low wall, African immigrants wound up tiny toys and set them in motion to march between brightly colored blankets covered with displays of large necklaces and handbags.

Massive clouds ballooned white against a deep sapphire sky, replicating the domes of *Sacré Coeur*.

Beckoned by the strains of old Paris street songs, Camille and Julie crossed the square, turned onto a narrow street, and paused in the shade of a chestnut tree. Clusters of tourists swayed in rhythm to "*La Vie en Rose*" performed by a violinist, who, according to Camille, had claimed the best niche on *la rue du Chevalier de la Barre*.

"Because," she added, "this was our spot."

While the elderly musician bowed his violin, he stared at Camille as if he knew her. Julie glanced at him, then looked back at her cousin, sensing some kind of connection, studying her features afresh: black hair with a touch of silver coming undone from a French roll coiffure, wispy strands working themselves loose from under the wide brim of a floppy black hat secured with a long stick pin; a paisley scarf draped loosely around the shoulders of a white blouse; her long, gauzy skirt rippling in the breeze.

Just then, Camille's dark eyes brimmed with tears.

"What's the matter?" asked Julie. "Is it the music? It's almost too beautiful, especially out here in the open air."

"I'm sorry," whispered Camille. "I wasn't expecting to feel this way. It's as if I were waiting for my parents to come back." She pointed at the niche in the wall behind the violinist. "You see, this was *our* place, where my father and mother came every day to make their music."

Julie could barely hear her cousin's voice above the song and sudden burst of wind stirring the leaves overhead.

"This is the very spot where they played during the war. It was so long ago, but now that I've returned, it's as if they should still be here. I can almost see them behind that man, their backs against the cement wall—papa with his faded cello, mama and her silver flute."

The violinist, somewhat younger than Camille, was dressed in colors of butter and cream: He wore fine gabardine slacks with a beige summer jacket, a dress shirt with a peach-colored necktie, tan shoes, and a Panama hat set at a jaunty angle. Tucking his violin firmly under his chin, the musician smiled dreamily as the mellow notes of *La Vie en Rose* sailed up through the trees and circled around *Montmartre* like wafting birds. Focusing on Camille until the end of the song, he nodded before acknowledging others who were dropping coins into his opened violin case.

"It was in 1940 when we had to start living under the German occupation," said Camille, leaning against the strong trunk of the chestnut tree whose bark was thick and furrowed like a giant cable with twisted strands. "I was only four years old; yet I remember it so clearly. But only in black and white. Never in color.

"We came here every day, to this very spot—mama in her long dark skirt and papa in his best trousers and a white shirt that was always a little gray with the collar quite frayed from the stubble on his neck and chin. I'll never forget all those mended holes on worn cuffs. When it was cold—and it seemed always to be cold—he wore the one black sweater that mama had knitted. As the war continued, that sweater got to be way too large for him."

Camille went on to explain how her father had been shot in the legs during the civil war in Spain when he had fought with the Republican forces against Franco's fascists.

"Somehow his friends managed to get him to Paris and that's where he met my mother, in 1936. I was born that same year.

"We lived in Chartres for a while, because Papa had to take therapy in the hospital there. Other than a bad limp, he was able to walk again. He was so handsome—strong and proud. Always tried to stand tall, no matter how he felt or what was happening."

Nearly the same age, Julie tried to picture her cousin as a child, along with her parents, here on *Montmartre*—how Camille had described her father's olive skin and dark brown eyes glowing with pleasure each morning as he and his wife gathered up their instruments and clasped hands to swing their little daughter between them as they strode the narrow streets.

"We walked here from our flat as if we were on our way to church." Camille's face turned dreamy. "I used to curl up in the folds of mama's skirt with a crust of bread. Sometimes I slept. Sometimes I danced. I knew that it pleased them to see how much I loved their music."

Lulled by the last strains of *La Mer*, Camille and Julie waited beneath the tree while a flow of tourists edged past. A steady breeze swept up from the park behind the basilica as the violinist began to play *Sous le ciel de Paris*, a lively tune.

"Would you mind, dear, if we went somewhere to sit down?" asked Camille.

"Not at all. How about the park over there, near the church?"

"Yes, that way we can still hear the music."

It was cool and tranquil in the park, not far from *Sacré Coeur*. The wind, easing through the branches, accompanied the faint sounds of the violin. Camille and Julie sat down on a wrought iron bench beneath a wooden arbor threaded with vines. Nearby, a young couple was sharing a sandwich and a bottle of wine.

"Those were terribly drab days back then," continued Camille, her eyes focused on the youthful pair. "We were always hungry and so cold. But I don't ever remember feeling discouraged; mama and papa didn't allow it. Often, as we walked toward our niche on damp mornings, the sewer odors steamed up from the grates along the streets. It was disgusting. There were those old block letters stenciled in yellow along the gutters that warned '*Défense de pisser.*' But no one seemed to pay any attention, especially the homeless men and the drunks. I always ran ahead of my parents and held my nose against that stench of urine."

Camille talked about the ragged men she saw sleeping at the edge of a street in the early morning. Everything about them was thin and scraggly: their bodies, their hair and whiskers, their homespun clothing. There they lay beneath the bare branches of trees that clacked against each other in the cold wind. And she told of the ravenous dogs that sniffed about the ground, licking up crumbs of old bread missed by the pigeons.

"Those dogs," she said, "they were like skeletons with sores and mangy patches of dull gray fur. They always steered clear of people, tilting their heads a certain way. You could see the mistrust in their eyes when they glanced back at you—they'd been kicked so much, especially when they tried to get too near a café or a grocery, it's a wonder they even had the energy to trot away.

"Nobody we knew ever had enough to eat during those war years. We managed to buy a little bread each day with a coin from papa's violin case. And sometimes we were given field rutabaga to boil when the gas was turned on at night. There was a neighbor in our flat who worked at a slaughterhouse. When pigs and cattle became scarce for the occupying troops, they'd started killing horses for food. When she could, our neighbor scooped the blood from the cement floor and put it into a small pot to bring back to our quarters. We dipped our bread in blood that coagulated into a gray paste when mama boiled it. Oh, that warm blood with a little salt—it was delicious."

Camille had an aunt, her mother's younger sister, who worked down in the city preparing food for German officers—foods her family rarely saw: vegetables, fruits, meat. Her mother and aunt worked out a plan where every few weeks Camille was to go to the back door at a certain time while her mother waited for her at the end of the alley.

"They'd coached me well, I must say. From a crack in the door, auntie handed me a big covered pail full of vegetables and maybe a piece of fruit or a chunk of meat. Then I was supposed to walk slowly back to where mama was hiding.

"But one night, a stern-looking Gestapo cornered me in the alley.

" 'What do you have in your pail, little girl?' he asked. I had to think fast and told him, 'Just scraps for my rabbit.' I hoped he would let me go. But instead he took the lid off my pail. I held my breath, certain that I would be arrested and auntie would be in terrible trouble. There, on top of the good food, auntie had thought to place gobs of rotten lettuce and dried turnip roots. The officer smiled a tight, thin-lipped smile, and sent me on my way, wishing my rabbit *bon appétit*."

Camille fell quiet, far away with her thoughts, holding her fingers to her mouth and nose as if to recapture those tastes and odors from long ago.

"I can still remember how it smelled in that alley," she said. "The fish and meat and onions. Even the rotted stuff made my stomach growl.

"Some days we didn't get many coins in the violin case. But Mama and Papa never complained. We went to the bistro anyway, near *la Place du Tertre*. Papa held me on his lap while we listened to the music. Django Reinhardt was very popular, performing at *La Normandie* down on the *Champs-Elysées*. But he liked to break away to the cafés up on the hill and around *Pigalle*. That's where he used to play his jazz guitar before the war.

"Once papa brought his violin to *Le Lapin Agile* on the *rue des Saules*." Camille turned on the bench and pointed in a direction past the wall. "It's just a few blocks that way. It was so beautiful how they played together. Gypsy music. We were most happy then, I think. All that music helped to make the war seem far away for a time. And it made us forget how hungry we were.

"The Nazis (papa called them '*les boches*' in private) passed by our . . ."

"What does that mean, '*les boches*?'" asked Julie.

"Blockheads. Short for *tête de caboche*, which is a head of cabbage. Everyone had insulting names for everyone else. They called the French 'crapauds.'"

"Meaning?"

"Frogs. They said that when a Frenchman laughed his adam's apple bulged from his neck like a frog. Also, frogs' legs were a delicacy before the war.

"Anyhow, those Krauts passed by our niche and some of them were sarcastic and threatening. But others seemed friendly and when they dropped coins into the violin case, mama and papa nodded in a stiff way, without smiling.

"Friends stopped by nearly every day and laughed and sang in low tones. But they didn't stay long. Sometimes they brought sweets and twirled me around by my arms with my face up, until *Sacré Coeur* and the chestnut trees and the sky and clouds turned into one big happy blur."

Camille explained that just before these friends left, they quickly whispered things in Spanish while her mother kept a look out.

"They passed notes. And sometimes, one of them tucked a large book into mama's bag. After a while, one or two nervous types, who seemed to be in a terrible hurry, stopped to exchange strange words that sounded like riddles. Then they took the book from my mother, and rushed away without dropping a coin into the case.

"And this," she added, "is the way our lives went until the last week of June, 1943."

Camille paused to take a sip of water from a small bottle that Julie had handed her. In disgust, she stared at the label and threw the glass bottle into a garbage bin next to the arbor.

Stunned by that abrupt action, Julie figured it must have been the label that had offended her cousin—Vichy.

Camille tucked her hands among the folds of her skirt and leaned back against the bench.

"Some nights, when I was supposed to be asleep, I heard mama, papa, and others talk about plans. And they talked about Jean.

"Jean Moulin was a close friend of my parents since 1940 when they lived in Chartres. He'd been elected prefect there just before the Germans came. When most of the townspeople evacuated, he stayed on.

Some of the officials tried to get him to sign a false statement, forcing him to side with the Vichy government, but he refused. They beat him and he had to go to hospital. Which is where papa met him while he was there for the treatment of his legs. When Jean came to see us at our flat, he brought me little presents. Can you believe it? I still have the cloth doll he gave to me one of the last times we saw him—all those decades ago.

"But mostly, there was serious talk and a lot of planning. When I got older, auntie told me many things about him. Later on, I discovered a great deal of information on my own. The man I once knew as Jean, who was almost like another father to me, had worked with Charles de Gaulle, organizing the smaller resistance groups into the Free French forces. He was called Max then.

"After he met with de Gaulle in London, he parachuted into occupied France and met with group leaders to unify the resistance movements. He was never in one place for more than a day or two.

"He was very confident. You know, the French have a way of describing someone like him—'*Il se sent bien dans sa peau*'—comfortable in his skin. He was one of those rare men who knew how to stay calm in the midst of danger. I remember his eyes—knowing eyes that seemed to hold everything he had seen and experienced, and he could convey it all back to others with a steady look. Jean had this direct gaze that just penetrated you when your eyes met his—sort of like Picasso's.

"He was very handsome with his black hair combed straight back. And he had full, sensuous lips—the complete opposite of *les boches* with those knife-edge mouths.

"When he wore a mustache, it seemed as though he had just come over from Hollywood, especially with that fedora angled over his right eye. I have seen pictures in books and they are just as I remember him, with that long black scarf slung around his neck. I used to tug at it when he left, trying to get him to stay longer. I think I must have been in love with him—as much as a seven-year-old girl could be."

Camille pulled the silk scarf from her neck and folded it neatly.

115

"I loved Jean next to papa and mama and auntie," she said after a pause. And then she leaned over and shouted, "Oh, Julie, I don't know about you, but I'm hungry!"

"Me, too. Seeing that couple over there, with their sandwiches and wine. . . ."

"I know of a café, not far from here."

They stood and stretched, then took a roundabout way to *La Place du Tertre* where a dozen artists worked at their easels, painting scenes of Montmartre and Paris monuments and sketching caricatures of tourists posed on folding chairs.

A short distance from the busy square, beneath a bright red awning, Camille and Julie joined others on the terrace, gathered at little round tables that seemed too small for anything more than two cups of coffee on saucers. Yet the waiter would soon manage to set down plates of *omelettes*, *salades*, wine, water, silverware, and napkins.

For an *apéritif*, they ordered *Lillet*, served in small wine glasses etched in red and blue; those lines created the image of a dancing woman in full skirts.

The café stood next to *Saint-Pierre de Montmartre* church and while the two women waited for their meal, Julie read aloud from the large plaque on the stone wall. The church, it said, was known as the Temple of Reason during the Revolution of 1789.

Camille snorted with laughter and shook her head.

"What is reason?" she asked. "Everyone on earth comes from such a different reality. It amazes me that anyone can get along. What is sane for one is irrational to another. What's outrageous to some is justifiable for others.

"From the beginning of the occupation, there were Nazi collaborators alongside citizens who gave German soldiers wrong directions and turned their backs on them at victory parades. I once saw a young boy throw snowballs at a couple of *boches*. It hardly ever snows in Paris and I imagine that he felt giddy as well as rebellious. He was tall enough that he might have been shot for doing that. Instead, they forced him to stand and peel potatoes nonstop for sixteen hours. He was one of the lucky ones.

" 'Remain vertical'—that was often said as a joke among my parents' friends. But it seemed more of a benediction. Each time Jean left our flat, he'd say, 'Courage. Hold tough, don't talk, remain vertical.' All in French, of course."

Actions, Camille explained, eventually became more militant. The Resistance sabotaged telephone lines and trains, defaced 'official' propaganda, and wrote counter-propaganda for print in underground newspapers. They gathered weapons, which were hard to come by, and created escape networks to help Jews and downed Allies. They became spies and wireless operators. Some even dared to shoot collaborators and Nazis at point blank.

"Mama told me about how even the men cried when the occupation armies goose-stepped down the *Champs-Elysées* in 1940. From then on, life was cold and dull, sprinkled with small acts of defiance that grew more and more powerful and organized. That's when Jean became Max."

Julie raised her glass to the memory of Max and thought of Camille's description of him: black hair and scarf, full lips, stunning eyes.

"By age eighteen, living in the United States," said Camille, clicking her glass of *Lillet* against Julie's, "I was obsessed with how the Resistance had worked during wartime. Many immigrants who arrived in France in the thirties brought their combat expertise with them—Poles, antifascists from Italy, Catalans after the fall of Barcelona, Spanish Republicans like my father. Even German anti-Nazis."

"I had no idea," said Julie, noticing how Camille turned to look toward the street where a variety people strolled past the cafe, some with leashed, happy-prancing dogs. "Hearing about that changes my view that all Germans were guilty."

"Well, yes. Plus an organization within the French Communist Party helped form the International Brigade that had fought against Franco in Spain. So you see, the structure was already in place in 1941 for the Immigrant Resistance Movement based here in Paris.

"Once, in our flat, I found a book that looked like those I told you about. You know, the ones that were slipped into mama's bag. I was curious and so I opened it. And there, encased in hollowed out pages, was a gun. That is when I began to worry. I am just a young girl, you understand, but at that moment, I became very afraid for my parents— for the safety of my parents.

"Papa spoke French nearly all of the time except at night when he tucked me into bed. Then he sang Spanish verses from a poem that Federico Lorca had written. Lorca was killed, you know, during the civil war in Spain. Who would have thought they'd assassinate poets?

"But in wartime, we soon learn that artists, writers, intellectuals, humanists are among the first to be destroyed—or at the very least threatened into submission."

Julie looked closely at Camille's dark eyes and black hair flecked with silver, and thought that she likely took after her father, inheriting his passion.

"In Andalucia," said Camille, "where the weeping of the guitars goes on all night, and there are cups of red wine and hot-blooded dancing, it is useless, it is impossible to silence the music."

Julie held up her Lillet glass once more and pointed at the red and blue image of the dancing woman in full skirts.

Camille smiled. "I feel it in my veins, Julie. The music and the poetry will never be silenced. They gave me that, my father and my mother."

The two women finished their simple salads and *omelettes*, mopped up the buttery oil and bits of egg with chunks of *baguette*, and downed the rest of their white wine.

Camille insisted on paying the bill. Julie left the tip.

Arm-in-arm, they *flanéd* past colorful shop windows and into the backstreets of Montmartre, where an occasional well-fed dog trotted with a purpose down the middle of a road.

"I was to stay with auntie for a few days," continued Camille, "while mama and papa went away. I didn't know then that the Gestapo in

Lyon had arrested Jean during a 'safe-house' meeting. Someone had betrayed him. He was taken to prison, beaten, and interrogated by Klaus Barbie and his henchmen. Because Jean carried in his head names and dates, places and activities for the unified resistance, they tortured him day after day until he went in and out of coma and became unrecognizable.

"Klaus Barbie, that savage Butcher of Lyon, responsible for the slaughter of thousands, including little children, broke nearly every bone in Jean's body. And still he lived, our Max.

"There was a witness, another prisoner, code-named Garnier, who had been head of the Phalanx network. He saw Jean lying on a bench in the interior courtyard of the prison. Garnier got a message through to a journalist who published it in an underground newspaper; it eventually surfaced, and I read that passage over and over again from a book I found years later: 'Max is in a pre-comatose state, his face tumefied. I was instructed to shave him, a macabre and curious order, and I wondered for what purpose.'"

Julie's eyes began to water.

"Oh, my dear," said Camille, reaching out to hold Julie's hands. "It broke my heart to read those words. Still, to this day.

"They brought Jean back to Gestapo headquarters here in the city and then mama and papa learned that he had been taken to the suburb of Neuilly, to a villa commandeered by Boemelburg, head of the Gestapo in Paris. One night, papa explained that he and mama had to leave for several days: Jean needed help.

"When my parents kissed me goodbye, I cried so hard. We had never been apart for longer than an hour or two. Papa hugged me and told me never to forget the music, to mind auntie, and that he and mama loved me very much. I remember the musky and lemon verbena scents from his face and neck as I clung to him. Then mama kissed me over and over, forced a smile, and followed papa with a little dance step before closing the door.

"I never saw them again. *Maman et papa.*"

Camille shivered in the warm breeze. Afternoon shadows had lengthened and soon it would be time to leave the butte of *Montmartre.*

"From then on, I stayed with auntie. She protected me from knowing too soon what had happened to my parents. And to Jean. After the Liberation, auntie married an American soldier who moved us to the United States. He was very nice—a warm and loving man. He and auntie adopted me when I was ten.

"As it turned out, mama and papa had intricate ties to the Resistance. They started out communicating information to wireless operators nicknamed '*pianistes*.' The circuit of the armed *Maquis* was called '*musicien*.' To secure their sets, the '*pianistes*' had to hide parts of their wireless transmitters with friends, including my parents. They could never transmit longer than a few minutes with the antenna out of a window because the German tracer vehicles were constantly cruising the streets to catch signals.

"Some of the tip money they earned from their music helped pay for replacement parts. And for guns. Eventually, they helped to blow up trains carrying *les boches.*"

"Your mother was part of that?" asked Julie.

"Yes. There were many women active in the Resistance.

"As soon as mama and papa learned of Jean's arrest, they left to meet up with their trusted friends in order to figure out a plan to save him. But they were all captured and imprisoned at Gestapo headquarters in Paris."

"Did they ever get to see Jean?" asked Julie.

"That we never knew. But we learned years later that he died on a train bound for Berlin. Jean had been tortured for so long that his heart finally gave out.

"Mama and papa remained in the prison here in Paris for several weeks and then were transported along with their friends to Berlin, where they were killed. Not one of them ever revealed any secrets." Camille took a deep breath and shook her head. "I just know they didn't."

Julie looked at her cousin full in the face. Seeing the certainty and devotion in her eyes, she was sure that Camille's parents had never betrayed the Resistance. Never sold out *la France* and what their country stood for: *liberté, fraternité,* égalité.

Camille sat up straight. " 'Courage, stay strong, don't talk.' Sadly, the last part of Jean's advice—'remain vertical'— could no longer happen for any of them. To this day, I can hardly bear to think of the tortures they endured. If I let my mind go there, I get physically ill, emotionally upset for days at a time. No, I must remember them the way they were when I was just a little girl.

"They'd written a letter to be given to me when auntie felt that I was ready to read and understand it—an encouraging letter full of love, telling me not to be sad for long, that what they had to do would make a difference. "We love you forever," they wrote. "*Pour toujours, notre chérie.*" They were convinced that because of their efforts, those of us still alive would have a happier life, that we wouldn't suffer as they had. This vision kept them going to the end.

"You know, Julie, I think back about the blood from that slaughter house. Those animals may have fed *les boches*, but some of their blood came our way. The blood of those like Jean and my parents never belonged to the enemy. It fed us. Silence was their response to the Gestapo Inquisition. Knowing how strong they were helps me get through the rough times. I am so proud of them.

"Now I work hard at my music, my life. I make every day count to ensure that they didn't give for nothing. Papa always said that music feeds the soul. I didn't need reminding, but I'm glad that he wrote it down in their letter to me. I wish they could have gone on to write millions of words and sing as many poems."

"In some ways," said Julie, pointing at her cousin, "they did. And still are."

The women sat quiet for a moment at the little outdoor table where they had stopped for pistachio ice cream and espressos. Although Camille seemed very tired, she smiled at Julie with clear eyes. Each gave a nod as they raised their porcelain cups to the memories, to the legacy, to the music.

They paid the waiter and retraced their steps past the ornate boutiques where merchants leaned comfortably against their doorframes, greeting passersby.

Back at *la rue du Chevalier de la Barre,* the elderly man had just stopped playing for the day and was polishing his violin with a small white cloth when Camille approached him. He looked up, surprised and happy. Suddenly he placed a finger at the corner of one eye and, in pantomime, slowly traced a line down his cheek as far as his mouth where he halted and drew a little smile upwards. Then he took up his violin, raised his bow to the strings, and said, "*Pour vous, madame, une dernière chanson.*"

He sang and played one final piece: *Un jour tu verras.* One day you will see.

Camille removed her black wide-brimmed hat, tossed it onto a bench, then slowly danced and sang, remembering the precious days she and her parents had spent together, happy, skipping down the streets hand in hand, singing and dancing love.

She graced the ending notes with a flourish, her scarf and gauzy skirt floating around her in the breeze. Facing each other, Camille and the violinist stood still for a long moment, like the human statues on the square in front of *Sacré Coeur.*

And then they bowed to one another.

Camille fished in her purse for a few francs, but the man shook his head, closed the violin case, and blew her a kiss as he walked away, down the tree-lined path.

12

Selmer's Sketch

When people die, everything that's good about them still exists.
They're just not around to remind us.
—*Clarence Johnson, brother of Selmer*

DRIVING AMONG THE ROLLING HILLS and streams near Coon Valley, Callie Lindstrom thought about Camille and her parents, and how grateful she was to have learned the details of that story from her neighbor Julie, back in Masterton.

When considering the hardships endured by the many people Cal had known throughout the years, her own struggles seemed minimal. The dignity with which most of them faced their troubles provided lessons for her, gave her the energy and wherewithal to ponder other lives—lives that would help to set her on an important learning track.

She was astounded, for instance, by the uncanny strength of Jean Moulin (Max), leader of the French Resistance. Captured by Klaus Barbie and tortured daily for months by members of the Gestapo, Jean never revealed any information that would have compromised others. His body, completely broken, but never his spirit, died at age forty-four.

Having read all she could find about this man, Callie was determined never to forget him. And some time in the future, she would visit Paris and stand by Jean Moulin's tomb inside the *Panthéon*.

Among the gravesites closer to home was Marbella Kinmore's. For decades, Marbella ran the Fashionette in Masterton, where nearly every woman in town shopped for a new dress or *peignoir*. And where Ruby Ryan, the town flirt, tried to engage Callie's dad.

At the funeral, while slowly passing by her casket, townsfolk could be heard whispering loudly, "Oh, my land!" and "Oh, my stars and garters!" for Marbella had gone from her usual strawberry red hair to a hay-colored gray. Yet, everyone could still smell that wonderful perfume emanating from her lovely dress and the coffin's satin lining.

Now, every year on Memorial Day, some admirer placed bottles of *Chanel No. 5* next to Marbella Kinmore's heart-shaped headstone. The clear glass bottles were empty, of course. Otherwise, somebody would be apt to swipe the expensive perfume. Callie could smell the sensual aroma when she got down on her knees, pulled out the stoppers, and sniffed.

"Mustn't touch, sweetie," her mother used to say about the trinkets and daffodils that decorated graves. "Bad luck comes to those who steal from the dead."

Callie was a little girl when Emily told her that, giving exception to the various doodads and vases of flowers that had tipped over. "You may upright those," she'd say.

Near the local cemetery's stone arch entry lay two more gravesites of interest to most everyone in Masterton and surrounding villages: brothers Clarence and Selmer Johnson, soldiers from World War II.

Clarence lost a leg somewhere in Europe, and Selmer returned from France shell-shocked and heartbroken. At the end of the war, having helped to liberate Paris, he met a girl named Lucie, an art student living in the Latin Quarter. After being together for just a few weeks, he proposed marriage with plans to bring her back to the family farm near Masterton.

But she said "*Non, je regrette,*" explaining that she had fallen in love with another—a man named *François.* Besides, having grown up in Paris, she was fairly certain that farm life, even in America, wouldn't suit her.

"I wonder how long she would have lasted at the Johnson place if she *had* come back with Selmer," said the town gossips. "Living down there in that damp hollow where they get no sunrises or sunsets, and nary a breeze, why, I sure can't picture a young Parisian gal planted there, biding her time. Can you?"

Within several years, Selmer (called a lunatic by some) became practically immobile from shell shock, until he started receiving treatment and taking tranquilizers prescribed by old Doc Dohms. Selmer and Clarence, with only one leg, sold the farm after the deaths of their parents, and moved to town. Neither one ever married.

From then on, throughout the warmer months during the 1950s, 60s, 70s, and 80s, the Johnson brothers hung out daily in front of the Maywood County Bank, Clarence leaning against the long brick ledge with his crutches propped beside him, and Selmer, tall and thin, standing at attention, head barely shaking, eyes straight ahead, blinking and blinking, squinting into the sunshine. Every day, they walked to their post in front of the bank, Clarence speeding along on crutches, swinging his stump, Selmer alternating between an old dancing gait and staggering forward as if battling the wind.

Joining the brothers were Norman Koost, retired high school math teacher, bent nearly in half from a spinal deformity, and Glen Lowe, born with Down's Syndrome, which everyone at the time called Mongolism.

Year after year, Selmer stood like the soldier he was with his arms taut at his sides, continuously rubbing his fingers together, except when he reached for his wallet to gaze at a piece of paper saved within. Even as a very old man, he carried the drawing Lucie had made of him in Paris, in 1944. Now and then, he'd carefully tug it from its slot in the soft, shiny, brown leather wallet he kept in his back pocket, unfold the creased paper that had grown limp as gauze, and show it around. He never revealed much of the story behind that sketch or boasted about it in any way. He simply said, "This was made for me by a girl I met in Paris. At the end of the war."

Throughout the decades, as more and more details surfaced about Selmer's time in France, especially in Paris, it didn't take long for folks in Masterton to piece together his story, embellishing and adding missing fragments that wanted to be told. People from all around southwestern Minnesota enhanced, gilded, embroidered, and bedizened a subject that consumed them for a time, primarily the women who dreamed of traveling to such an exotic place as Paris and falling in love with some handsome Frenchman who would whisper in their ears, "*Darling, je vous aime beaucoup.*"

Eventually, the townsfolk left off with Selmer, whose increasingly bland personality made it impossible to advance his part of the story. Instead, they began asking, "Who was that young girl—the one who sketched Selmer—and whatever do you suppose became of her?" As soon as someone found out her last name—*Moulin* (no relation to Jean)—speculation set in and more rumors circulated. Some people even went to the library, located next door to the Lounge 59 bar, to read up on Paris during the war and to see about an artist of that era by the name of Lucie Moulin. What really prompted the literary firestorm was the fact that the local priest, Father Joseph, had met Lucie's brother, also a priest, while visiting the Twin Cities. Father Paul told Father Joseph all about his sister and what eventually happened to her. To help matters along, several people in Masterton knew how to speak French, including Julie (Camille's cousin) who lived across from Callie and her family on Norwood Avenue.

If anyone from Hollywood had got wind of Masterton's intrigues and its collective effort to create Lucie's saga, well, they would have found a diamond mine.

"Oh, boy," said Pinky Wisdorf, chewing his mustache while parking his '58 Edsel in front of Masterton's movie theatre. Even the Edsel's grill seemed to say 'Ooh, Ah,' as Pinky pointed at the marquee. "Imagine Lucie and Selmer's story right up there on our big screen!"

Which is exactly what happened a few years later, starring the great French actress Simone Signoret. Foreign films were a rarity outside of Minneapolis and Saint Paul, but this one came to the prairie, despite objections from the Catholic Church and censure from the Legion of Decency, whose members compared it to *Love in the Afternoon*, condemned in 1957. Despite threats of excommunication, theater owner Marvin Slaybaugh went ahead with the showing.

Although there was only a brief mention of Selmer Johnson and the town of Masterton, hundreds upon hundreds of folks from the southern half of the state lined up to buy tickets. And even though the movie was quite different from what everyone was used to or expected (Westerns and "inoffensive" American love stories), many sat awestruck through "The Saga of Lucie Moulin" several times over, especially the women, because it was set in Paris and because the actor who played the part of François, Lucie's lover, happened to be one of the most romantic, seductive actors of the time. What would Selmer Johnson think, having lost out to Charles Boyer?

Some thirty years later, to commemorate the French bicentennial, a second version of Lucie's story hit the ultra big screen. Filmed on location, it never appeared in Masterton's movie theater or any other show house in southern Minnesota. Anyone who still remembered Selmer Johnson and the name of Lucie Moulin would have had to travel to the Twin Cities in order to see *"Ego Te Absolvo."*

Callie Lindstrom went to the Uptown Theatre and sat through the movie twice, remembering bits and pieces from her Catholic girlfriends, who had been forced to attend a session with Father Paul Moulin, a visiting priest from Minneapolis, who presented what he called a "Precautionary Morality Play." He had great influence over those young girls by relating the story of his sister who lived in Paris. Afterward, Callie's friends had been warned multiple times by Sister Thomasina, who constantly referred to "those nasty, filthy feet on a fly," that if they made wrong choices in life, they would end up like Lucie.

Callie had also eavesdropped on the women in her mother's 500 Club and heard things from the horses' mouths: Clarence and Selmer Johnson. She would never forget that tattered piece of paper tucked inside Selmer's worn, brown leather wallet—long, long ago, when he and his brother stood daily for hours, for years of hours, leaning against their ledge in front of the Maywood County Bank.

13

Ego Te Absolvo

This here's the saga of Lucie Moulin.
Figure it out, if you can.
—Herbert Horn, aged 89

July 14, 1989

JOSTLING CROWDS spill up from subway exits onto the Paris bou-
levards. Webs of white lights link boutiques and stores fronted by
burgeoning sidewalk cafés. *Steak-frites* sizzle on grills. *Crêpes suzettes*
sugar the air. Along the *Avenue des Champs-Elysées*, blue, white, and
red banners hang limp from street lamps in the still summer night.
Tricolor flags begin to sway as a slow snake dance funnels toward the
Arc de Triomphe where noisy revelers pour into narrow side streets on
their way to the Eiffel Tower.

Several streets away from this *fête*, Lucie Moulin stands before a third
floor window with inky night on the other side, eyes glaring back from
her reflection in the glass. A gray chenille robe draped heavily on her frail
body, she rocks forward to study that face in the window, inching closer
to those sunken cheeks and hollow eyes, that wide, grimacing mouth.

"*Qui est-ce?*" she mutters, flicking her fingers at the image, shuffling backwards. "Who is this? How mean of that horrid woman to hover about and scowl at me so. Go away! *Va-t'en!*"

Lucie begins to keen softly, rising to a wail from deep in her throat, and growing unbearably shrill for patients gathered in the far end of the room, forcing them to cover their ears. With claw-like fingers, she clutches and tugs at the short, patchy remains of gray hair and jerks her head around like a petulant rider reining in a confused horse.

"*Mau-vaise, hor-rible!*" she screams with each yank. "Ug-ly, hor-rid sin-ner!"

As quickly as she began, she stops and cocks an ear to the murmuring crowds below.

"*Ecoutez! Les moines sont arrivés,*" she cries with excitement, her laughter emanating in bursts. "The monks have arrived. They are chanting! Look everyone! The monks have arrived!

"Father Dubois! I must see Father Dubois!"

But the sound soon dies away near *la rue du Gros Caillou* as the crowds dwindle, having found their way to the Spectacle of Lights, leaving Lucie in silence within the gray walls of *l'Hôpital-Asile Sainte Jeanne.*

LUCIE HAD AWAKENED early on the morning of Bastille Day, July 14, 1989. It was also her sixty-fifth birthday, although she hadn't realized it. Outside of the asylum, no one remembered, except her brother.

"*Madame Moulin,*" said the attendant, "Father Paul is on the telephone, calling you all the way from America to wish you a happy birthday."

Lucie grudgingly took the phone and stared at the receiver for a moment before raising it tentatively to her ear. As she listened to Paul repeating, "*Allô? Allô,*" her eyes shifted from side to side.

"Don't waste your *mo-nay!*" she shouted and threw the phone against the wall. After the attendant succeeded in calming her down and feeding her some pills, Lucie spent the remainder of the day gazing between window bars, until the sky changed from soft blue to twilight above the high wall of the asylum and over the tops of the apartment buildings across the way. She stood there until those eyes in the glass staring back at her demanded a final account. At that moment, Lucie recalled the page she had torn from a religious magazine and hidden beneath her pillow. Because it was her holy card, she knew exactly what she must do.

The other patients, unusually quiet this evening, were seated in front of the television, enthralled by a re-run of the military parade that had rolled down the *Champs-Elysées* earlier in the day. Believing that war had returned to Paris, Lucie stayed far away from the T.V. How odd, though, was that clip-clopping of horses, their riders resplendent in unfamiliar uniforms. She blocked her ears against the rumbling of tanks and the loud whine of sleek aircraft sweeping above the *Arc de Triomphe*, spewing blue, white, and red smoke. She stole an extra long look at the close-ups of soldiers marching proudly down the avenue, followed by scores of jeeps. Those men appeared so different from the French soldiers of her war, World War II, when they mingled with the Allies.

The French especially loved Americans, the G.I.s of the 4th Infantry Division, who helped to liberate Paris from the Nazis in August of 1944. That was when Lucie met Selmer Johnson, a country boy from Midwestern America. He came to her apartment for several hours each day, whenever he could get away from his unit. At war's end, Selmer proposed marriage, wishing to take Lucie back to Minnesota with him. At first, she said yes. But then, after walking along the river Seine and sitting together at the wharf's edge, she felt uneasy. Selmer's body had begun to tremble. His lips quivered and tears rolled down his cheeks. When she touched his arm and asked him what was the matter, he froze, shook his head, remained silent. Minutes later, he returned to his old self, jumping up and dancing along the river to the distant sounds of an accordion.

It was while they were standing on *La Place de la Concorde*, when Lucie knew she couldn't marry Selmer; shots were fired from a window across the street, blasting holes into the cement wall next to steps leading from the square of harmony up to the *Tuileries* gardens. Several bodies lay on the sidewalk nearby, one of them crying for his mother. His body shaking, Selmer screamed and rubbed a fist against his cheek, biting the fleshy side of his hand.

That's when Lucie realized that her boyfriend was suffering from shell shock and couldn't stop weeping about the things he had witnessed and the friends who had struggled in their gruesome deaths during the battles. Although it seemed a weakness to Lucie and her friends, she ended up crying along with Selmer who told her that he felt like he was dying inside, yet ashamed and embarrassed by what was happening to him, along with what his superiors were saying—that he was a coward, lacking in moral fiber. After that lecture, he sensed that the enemy might not be the only ones who would shoot him.

Lucie guided Selmer away from *La Place de la Concorde* and back toward the river where they could gaze at the bridges and see *La Tour Eiffel* above that part of the city.

The next day, while Lucie continued to celebrate the end of the Nazi occupation, two of her friends died, shot near the square of harmony from the upper-floor windows of a tall building across *la rue de Rivoli*.

"I CANNOT LIVE through this again," she wailed, confused by the television spectacle she watched from the corner of her eye—the thousand blinking lights on the Eiffel Tower, the breezy dialogue between handsome and beautiful reporters leaning into the camera and into the imaginations of those who sat in the stifling room of the asylum, their mouths agape.

Lucie turned back to the window. Finally recognizing herself, she beat her chest with weak fists. "Sinful," she cried out. "Sinful, sinful child!"

A few patients slowly shifted their attention from the television screen to a space above it, then sideways to the nurse who rushed past them.

Exhausted from her long vigil of watching day turn into night, Lucie allowed the nurse to guide her away from the window and back to her room where she shed her robe and slippers and crept into bed, safe at last in her small enclosure. Like an exhausted child, she slipped beneath the covers, sliding her hands under the pillow to make sure her treasure was still there.

Caressing the worn piece of paper, she drifted into a restless sleep— a strange sleep where she dreamed remnants of herself.

1974

SLENDER, WITH THE GRACEFUL, erect carriage of a ballerina, Lucie appeared younger than her fifty years. Her actions, however, were deceiving. One had only to look carefully into her gray eyes and at the set of her mouth to detect a troubled spirit.

While François took his afternoon nap, Lucie sat at their tiny kitchen table re-reading old letters from her parents. Awash with admonitions, the sharp words shot up off the pages to give her a fresh jolt, just as they did when she was twenty and full of life, eager for adventure once the war was over. She colored her lips then, and pinched her cheeks when she ran out of rouge, wore a wide-brimmed magenta hat secured with a long stickpin. The young woman had taken up drawing in the studio of a middle-aged artist for whom she posed nude. Her short little bursts of laughter, sounding like bells, delighted friends as they gathered late at night on the terrace of *le Café des Ecoles*.

One afternoon, Lucie's father, provoked by his daughter's gaiety, by her flushed cheeks and raspberry red lips, by the rumors of her affair with an American G.I., by the nude sketches she'd brought home from the artist's studio, gripped her face with rough fingers and tried to rub away the color, shouting "*Putain!* You belong on the streets!"

"Oh, *ma chère fille*," soothed her mother, "your father only wants what is best for you."

"Please, *maman, papa*, consider what I want."

"What you want?" countered her father. "You made a sacred vow. And now you are nothing but a whore!"

"It distresses us to find that you have broken your promise," said her mother.

"How could you hold me to that?" Lucie sobbed. "I was merely a child."

"You and your brother promised the Church," said her father. "You made your promises to God. Paul has fulfilled his. But you . . ."

"I was just a little girl, Papa."

"It's not too late, *chérie*," said her mother, wiping the streaks of tears from Lucie's face. "There is still a place for you."

After days of relentless pleading and insistence by her parents, Lucie finally agreed to meet with Mother Superior. But the plan for her to enter the order of *Sainte Bénédicte* crumbled the day François Gladel came for a visit.

Seated at the table re-reading those old letters, it was if her parents had come back from the dead, had risen from their graves to invade her kitchen. Lucie felt herself shrink inside as they begged her to reconsider. Deeply troubling was the last sentence her father ever wrote to her: "Now, as you are no longer my daughter, go your way and be damned."

Paul's note she kept apart from the others. There was really no need. It just seemed proper because of what he knew and had never revealed to their parents. "It would kill them," he wrote, "if they ever found out about you and François. How could you do this to the family?"

Lucie gathered up the letters and locked them away in her desk as soon as she heard François moving about in their bedroom. She would let him find her sitting at an empty table, her right hand cradling her forehead.

François slowly entered the kitchen, barely refreshed from a nap, his face showing the yellow pallor of poor health. Tall, with thinning black hair and expressive dark eyes, he moved with an aristocratic ease that belied his weakened heart. Brusque motions had always been foreign to him, especially so since he'd become ill. He spent his days reading French and American classics, listening to Mozart and Debussy, and taking daily walks with Lucie. Only now, his walks along the Paris streets had become increasingly brief.

François approached Lucie, placed a cupped hand under her chin, and gently raised her face to his. He traced a finger down her aquiline nose and up along her high cheekbones. This time, he could not make her smile.

"You mustn't fret so, my darling," he said, kissing the top of her head. With tapered fingers, he smoothed her long ash-blond hair bound by a black ribbon. "It pains me to see you so unhappy."

"I can't help it." Lucie reached back to touch his hand.

"What is troubling you so?"

"Never mind. I'll be all right."

"Are you going to see Father Dubois again this afternoon?"

"Yes, of course. I am nearly ready."

"I don't understand why you must go every day. We are together once and for all. You should be happy, *chérie*. I am."

"Please, François, don't start."

"But *every* afternoon. If only you could . . ."

"I must!"

Lucie stood abruptly and gathered her handbag and a sweater. She was dressed in her usual outfit: black flats, silk stockings, a creamy camisole beneath a sheer lace blouse tucked into her slim black skirt. For years, she'd worn a camisole and lace to please François. But this morning, while dressing, she noticed how yellowed and frayed her clothing had become. I'll have to replace them, she thought, with more modest attire.

"I am sorry, François, please forgive me."

"There is nothing to forgive, my darling."

François took the black cardigan from Lucie's hand and draped it around her shoulders. He leaned down to kiss her pale neck. Lucie closed her eyes, inhaled the acrid smell of his skin touched with the faint scent of lemon verbena, and tried to remember how their life used to be.

"*Je t'aime, chéri.*" Lucie left the apartment to go to confession.

1969

LUCIE, AT AGE FORTY-FIVE, relished her strolls with François along the vibrant streets of Paris. One morning in early June, they walked arm in arm, taking care, as usual, to bypass the gate near *la Place de la Concorde*, and instead entered the *Tuileries* gardens opposite *la rue de Rivoli*.

Lucie avoided the "square of harmony" where end-of-the-war bullets killed citizens and gouged the cement walls, leaving large pockmarks as reminders of unbearable losses; two of her young friends had been gunned down at that exact spot while dancing, celebrating the liberation of Paris. A ricocheting bullet had nearly struck Lucie as she circled *la Place de la Concorde* during a wild jeep ride with friends.

"This way, *chéri*, she said. "Come, let us rest a moment."

Grateful for a respite, François carefully steered Lucie around a cluster of iron chairs chained near the Tuileries fountain, not far from the Louvre. He gave the attendant two francs for the privilege of sitting in the park where they basked in the sunshine and watched children play at the perimeter of the round pool, poking at their toy sailboats with long sticks. Nursemaids lifted robust babies from their carriages and cradled them in their arms.

An elegantly dressed couple strolled past the Tuileries pool, each holding a long leash with a dachshund attached to it.

"I see the dogs are flying low this year," remarked François. "That pair must have grown up under an armoir."

After a time, heartened by the presence of children and prancing dogs, Lucie and François left the gardens, sauntering arm-in-arm toward the river. A breeze swept through the leaves of chestnut trees towering above the *bouquinistes*. Lucie paused to browse among these bookstalls, glancing at old lithographs and ancient volumes, some moldering after years of exposure to the summer heat reflecting off sidewalks. François waited for Lucie near the *Quai du Louvre*.

Standing next to the railing, he pointed at the tip of the larger island in the middle of the Seine River. "It is like the prow of a great ship, *n'est-ce pas?*"

"You say that each time we come here." Lucie laughed and waved at the passengers floating beneath the bridge in a sightseeing boat. Several of the tourists waved back, delight radiating from their upturned faces.

Crossing the *Pont Neuf* onto *l'Ile-de-la-Cité*, Lucie and François headed straight for the *Marché aux Fleurs* where they lingered among great bunches of flowers balancing on stands and burgeoning from large pails, their blossoms of pink and lavender, crimson, yellow, blue, and gold decorating the sidewalk.

Behind *Notre Dame* cathedral, they spotted their favorite resting place—a wrought iron bench with curved wooden slats. Just as they approached the seat, a young couple rushed over to claim it first.

"Do you feel strong enough to go on, François?"

"Yes, I'm actually feeling quite well today." He gazed tenderly at Lucie and took her arm. "My heart seems to be beating as it should."

Lucie smiled and pressed her cheek against his shoulder as they crossed the bridge onto *l'Ile St-Louis,* the smaller of the two islands, where they stopped for ice cream. Afterward, attracted by an array of colorful *Quimper* pottery in the window, they stepped inside a little shop called *Antiquités Bretonnes*, where they browsed for a few minutes before taking a taxi back to their apartment.

"It was a lovely day, *mon cher,* but I'm afraid we overdid it," said Lucie, noticing how François' body sagged and his face lacked the healthy color that comes with exercise.

She turned back the bed covers, helped him in as she might a child, and sat next to him until he fell asleep. Then she left for *Saint-Roch*, her parish church.

As she ascended the stone steps, Lucie drew her black shawl over her head. Once inside, she bathed her fingers in holy water, crossed herself, and genuflected before tiptoeing up to the chancel, where she genuflected again, this time more deeply. She gripped the tall back of a wooden chair, and then sat briefly before kneeling on the little caned stool in front of her. Lucie always chose a chair closest to the altar.

On Sundays, she placed more than she could afford in the collection basket. The way the long-handled container slipped and darted among rows reminded Lucie of the rhythmic advance and retreat of a large-headed snake. Whereas the other parishioners quickly tossed in their offerings, Lucie gripped the *pannier* as if she were loath to let it go, and slowly added her franc notes to the existing pile of coins, never noticing the puzzled frowns on those faces surrounding her. She eventually let go, edged forward onto the kneeling bench, and clutched her rosary, calculating the distance on worn beads until she reached the dangling silver crucifix.

At this time in her life, Lucie confessed twice weekly through the wicker mesh of the confessional into the large leathery ear of Father Dubois, a robust, elderly priest whose acerbic tone broadcast a constant reminder of how she had fallen away and how she had disappointed, not only her family, but the clergy and nuns of *Saint Roch*.

"Such a fine family, *les Moulin*," repeated Father Dubois. "You must always consider your brother who works tirelessly in America for the one true faith—the Holy Roman Catholic Church. Let Father Paul be your strength, your foundation, your guiding light."

After each confession, Lucy rose with stooped shoulders and brimming eyes as Father Dubois quickly made a sign of the cross and uttered in monotone, "*Ego te absolvo.*" Instead of offering calm departures, those three words pierced Lucie's heart, reminding her of how irretrievably she had fallen from grace. She could never go in peace no matter how many times Father said, "I absolve you of your sins."

The muscles in her body quivered, as she stood inside the dark confessional, grasping the wooden ledge worn smooth by thousands of desperate hands. It is good to feel pain, she thought, leaving the dim enclosure and making her way toward the nave. It is right to feel the pain of all who entered there before me. She turned to look back at the confessional with a sad smile, imagining the ornate, vertical box as a coffin—her own shadowy coffin, etched for decades by the breaths of those whispering their sins through the grating. Each time she glanced back, the three words she had dutifully parroted as a child resounded in her head: "I AM SIN."

"I . . . am . . . sin," Lucie repeated as she dropped several coins, metal against metal, into the slotted box next to a stack of fresh white candles. She gathered a pair whose clacking sounds echoed softly inside this section of the vaulted stone church. While lighting her candles from the flames of those already burning, she felt their powerful warmth as she planted hers alongside the rest. Streams of wax trickled down the forest of tapers as they bent in the heat. Stepping closer, Lucie leaned over the conflagration as if she would singe herself. When the heat became too intense she inched away, but not before burning a little spot on the tip of her nose. She thought of Saint Ebba and her sisterhood of nuns who, in twelfth century Scotland, cut off their noses and upper lips with a razor in order to maintain their chastity by appearing repulsive to the advancing Viking pirates. These raiders were so enraged and appalled by the maimed faces, they burned the entire monastery to the ground, including the holy virgins who perished in the flames—"spotless victims to their heavenly spouse, the lover and rewarder of chaste souls."

It would be so easy, thought Lucie, reaching out to touch the flames, as if they were part of a beautiful mass of nephrite jade.

She bowed her head over the flames rising from mounds of white lava, until the glow caught her under the chin like footlights and her skin began to burn. Instinct made Lucie quickly step back and finger her jaw line. She looked up, drawn to a dusky painting hanging on the stone wall: Saint Catherine, a fourth century martyr and haloed patroness of young maidens and virgins of Christ, hung there, frozen in time, just before she was to be torn to shreds by giant wheels studded with spikes. At her touch, according to legend, the instrument of torture was miraculously destroyed, and Emperor Maximianus, persecutor of fourth century Christians, had her beheaded. And now, in 1969, the Church historians had the gall to declare her nonexistent, erasing her name from the calendar of saints. Yet from this portrait positioned high above Lucie's reach, Catherine seemed to be looking down upon her with compassion—at this sister in agony who shared few of Catherine's qualities, namely fearlessness and virginity. The woman in this painting gazed down upon eyes giving up on life.

1954

A DECADE AFTER THE WAR, Lucie celebrated her thirtieth birthday with friends at *le Café des Ecoles* in the Latin Quarter. In the spirit of contradiction, they laughed and shouted and interrupted each other while discussing the rebuilding of Europe, General Charles de Gaulle, the possibilities of life under a Fifth Republic, the views of Jean-Paul Sartre and Simone de Beauvoir. After midnight, the group wandered off to *La Calavados*, an underground nightclub near the George V hotel. At *La Calavados*, ex-patriot Joe Turner, a black man more welcomed in France than in America, played stride piano until daybreak.

Lucie hadn't been with François since he left Paris nine years earlier. "I think about you often and miss you terribly," she wrote. "I miss your strong arms holding me. *Chéri*, I need your love now more than ever."

He had left shortly after Paul discovered him with Lucie one spring afternoon. Her brother arrived at the tiny apartment on *la rue Mouffetard*, eager to tell her of his new post with the St. Paul diocese in Minnesota. Finding the door unlocked, he tapped lightly, peered in, and saw the two, naked, in bed together. He slammed the door and rushed away.

"How could you?" Paul shouted at her the next day. "François! Our cousin, for God's sake! You disgust me."

"But we love each other," said Lucie, trying to keep her voice cool and even. "We want to get married."

"Impossible! You know very well the Church opposes such marriages. First cousins? How could you bring such shame to our family?"

A day later, Paul confronted François, who soon left Paris for Avignon.

"If I weren't a priest . . ." Paul's hands turned into clenched fists.

Lucie rushed over to embrace François.

"It's better that I go," he said, inching away from her. "Perhaps one day . . ." His voice broke. "I promise to write, *ma chérie.*"

And he did—every week during that first year. Less often after he married a woman named Catherine.

One September afternoon in 1956, a letter arrived that shocked and pleased Lucie:

Darling,

I think of you every day. Please forgive me for not writing more often. Our lives are not going well. I have a tremendous favor to ask of you. It is much to expect, I know. Catherine is very ill . . .

François had asked Lucie to come to Avignon. Catherine was dying and he needed help with their three children and the housekeeping. He didn't know where else to turn.

Lucie wrote back immediately. Of course, she would come.

It didn't take the children long to realize Lucie's primary role in their home. Robert, the youngest, liked her at first. Jeannine, who was ten, and Gabrielle, nine, did not. The two girls had discovered letters from Lucie to their father. When they showed them to their mother, Catherine remained calm and simply told the girls to return those envelopes to where they found them—inside their father's briefcase. With silence and burning looks upon Lucie's arrival, with a brisk turning away, the girls conveyed at home what Father Dubois would reaffirm inside the confessional at Saint Roch—that Lucie's deep love for François, her first cousin and not yet a widower, was a sin—twofold.

Reminders of her transgressions came daily to Lucie, through raging letters from her parents, admonitions from Paul, pointed sermons from the priest in Avignon, Bible passages that struck her like bullets. Even the brochures and posters on the church bulletin boards told her that she, descendent of Eve, was entirely to blame.

In spite of these constant reminders of her "sinful ways," she continued to love François, hoping for eventual acceptance by his children and her own family. She assumed that Catherine was too ill to notice, but one evening while Lucie was bathing the sick woman, Catherine pushed the warm cloth away.

"I've always known," she said. "François told me about you before he and I married."

"I am so sorry, Catherine. Please forgive me."

"There is nothing to forgive. It is life. He never stopped loving you."

Catherine was buried in the churchyard cemetery in Avignon.

Lucie stayed on, keeping house, knitting sweaters for the children, helping them with their schoolwork, and marking their birthdays with little parties and special cakes. Over time, Jeannine, as did Robert, grew to care somewhat for Lucie, sensing that this woman was treating them as her own, yet had no intention of replacing their mother. But Gabrielle would have nothing to do with her.

During Lucie's tenth winter with him, François became ill. Exhaustion and relentless coughing spells sent him to see his doctor who recommended a cardiologist in Paris.

With the children grown, François and Lucie closed the house in Avignon.

"At last," she said, "we will be alone together in Paris. And when the children come to visit, we'll show them our favorite places. We will be so much happier there. Besides, Father Dubois has been transferred to the parish of Saint-Roch. I need to find us an apartment nearby."

As the years passed, François' health worsened. The children and grandchildren seldom came to visit. Lucie grew thin and nervous as a sparrow. From a distance, she still looked chic in her wide-brimmed summer hat and breeze-rippled dress, but up close, her clothing was crushed, frayed, thread-bare, and gravy-stained.

Although Lucie's parents had been long dead, more than ever, she realized what a disappointment she had been to them. What a disappointment she was to the Church.

And then there was Paul, so far away in America. They had once been close, but now Lucie heard from him only on her birthday and at Christmas.

1974

"*Mais, que-est-ce que tu as, chérie?*" asked François, finding Lucie downcast, seated at the kitchen table with folded hands. "What is it, my dear? You are not well? One of us falling ill is quite enough."

"*Non, non, ce n'est rien.* It is nothing."

But gone was her little dance step, the humming of songs while she prepared their meals. Gone was the free-flowing patter of a happy woman.

On a lovely, warm Sunday in April, François clasped Lucie's hand as they left mass and lingered in the sunshine along the boulevard, admiring the yellow forsythia in full bloom. They stopped to pet and offer treats to a little terrier named Patoon who belonged to an elderly prostitute and was leashed for long periods, day or night, to a nearby lamp post, next to a crusty old dish filled with dusty water. Others looked after the small dog as well, including the neighborhood pharmacist who cleaned up after her on the sidewalk, and a police officer who kept Patoon company during his late-night shifts.

After caressing the little dog, Lucie stood up straight and glanced back at the church—her church—where she felt more connected than anywhere else on earth. *Saint-Roch* promised solace and protection with its tiers of wide steps and massive stone columns. The heavy cross at the peak watched over Lucie, beckoned to her. She reached into her pocket and dutifully fingered each bead of her rosary.

François, exhausted from the short walk between church and apartment, collapsed as they approached their building. Lucie called out to the neighbors, who helped carry him inside. She phoned *les pompiers*—the emergency number for resuscitating.

The next day, Lucie bought a bright red heart-shaped pillow that François could clutch to his chest whenever he felt a coughing spasm coming on.

Their last year together passed in a flurry of doctor appointments, house calls, and trial medicines. There were no more walks, no more gatherings with their few friends who called from time to time, asking if they could help.

"*Non, merci*," Lucie answered, "there is nothing anyone can do."

Apart from her time spent in church, she tended François until he died.

AFTER THE FUNERAL, Lucie never returned to Avignon. François was lost to her there in his grave next to Catherine. Yet she could not shut him out of her thoughts. "After the way you handled his final hours . . ." she said, shaking a finger at her own image in the mirror. "There he was, night and day, signaling to you, unable to talk. And what did you do?"

She couldn't bear to admit it.

A week later, Lucie began traipsing through the churches of Paris, talking to herself, searching for Father Dubois, who had been transferred yet again. That was all she knew, all she could find out. No one, it seemed, could tell her where he'd gone or why. She missed him terribly, especially his lovely, flawless, white hands—so young looking for such an elderly priest—exempt from physical labor.

Lucie sat for hours in front of crypts and vaults containing the long-dead remains of church hierarchy, dukes, and wealthy patrons. Loud, reverberating chords from pipe organs and the clear voices of chanting monks soothed her as she sat alone in the stone sanctuary, brittle as the floral arrangements whose dusty petals and faded ribbons crumbled a little more each day.

At times, Lucie forgot where she was and how to get back home. Once, when a priest asked her name, she wasn't able to answer and rushed from the church.

Wandering through cemeteries, Lucie spent hours near her favorite sculptures, tombs, and elaborate monuments. "They are like little houses," she said to no one in particular, "so easy to keep up. How I envy those inside."

Smoking settled her nerves. Alone in her apartment, she lit fresh cigarettes from the butts of others, tossing the empty blue Gauloise packages onto the floor. Ash trays overflowed. Burn spots appeared on the sofa and on Lucie's soiled blouses and torn camisoles. Unwashed dishes were stacked on every surface in the kitchen. Weeks went by. The telephone no longer rang. Through clouds of cigarette smoke, Lucie studied a snapshot taken at a picnic with friends beside the lake at *Bois de Boulogne*. François sat next to her on the grass, his arms around her waist, laughing. She was laughing, too. Laughing, but not smiling.

Lucie welcomed sleep above all else; for then she could lose the maddening thoughts that made her head ache. But with sleep came the repeat nightmare: François calling to her without a voice—just a mouth wide open and a desperate look in his eyes. In her dreams, Lucie was unable to reach him, for she was confined to a room with some man dressed in a black robe, a man who grew increasingly impatient as he directed her towards a giant flame, rushing her along as if he had more important things to do. "Please, please," she screamed at the man in black. "I will do penance! I will do anything!"

Upon awakening from these dreams, she lit more cigarettes, inhaled deeply, and pressed the glowing ends to the undersides of her forearms, next to healed scars.

LATELY, LUCY HAD GROWN confused by the compassion of Father André, a new young priest at *Saint-Roch*. He is so very different from Father Dubois, she thought. He knows *nothing* of the old ways. And why does everyone call him by his first name?

She didn't know what to make of his words: "With time, madame Moulin, your pain will lessen. Surely, you are left with loving memories of François. Now you must try to find happiness in your own life. Although I never knew him, I'm certain he would want that for you."

Lucie's voice traveled along the church's stone walls as she cried, "*Jamais*!

Never.

She repeated her confession every day for two weeks, until Father André became concerned and told her that perhaps once a week would be sufficient.

"Madame Moulin," he said, "I know of someone who can help you."

But Lucie was undeterred. She had to get through to this young priest. Make him understand. "I know that God took him from me because of my sins," she said.

"No, madame, your husband was not well. It was his time."

"Was he my husband?" she asked in a small voice.

The priest fell silent.

"You must listen to me, Father. I think about François constantly, day and night, and I cannot bear it. I also cannot bear it if I *don't* think about him. Because you see, if I don't think about him every moment, he will eventually be lost to me forever, in every way, and I cannot allow that to happen. Do you understand? This must *not* happen!"

"Madam Moulin, your pain is far too great. I will get you some help. No one should have to carry such a burden."

"But I must. I must force myself to remember the pain or all will be lost. Don't you see? I *must* continue to feel the pain, for I have sinned. You have to tell me that, Father. Tell me!"

"Please, madame. Stay here for a moment. I will be right back."

As soon as Father André left, Lucie rushed out of the church and into a late afternoon chill. A light rain began to fall. Down the street, she spotted the twisted dog leash still attached to its lamppost, and the water dish, crusty and dry. But there was no Patoon. Where could she be?

After wandering the streets, soaked to the skin, Lucie found herself in the middle of *la Place de la Concorde*, for the first time since the Liberation of Paris. She crossed the square, approached the cement wall that she had always avoided, and edged up against its cold, damp surface where sniper bullets had lodged thirty years earlier. She lit a cigarette, inhaled more deeply than ever, and reached up to feel the holes in the rough cement as she slowly exhaled.

Around the corner, she read the names of her dead friends on bronze plaques embedded in a low wall:

René Michaud ~ né le 7 septembre, 1922
             tué par les Nazis le 15 juin, 1945
Marie Lefèvre ~ née le 30 avril, 1923
             morte pour la Liberté le 15 juin, 1945

Lucie tried to remember their faces. And she found that their names seemed no different from all of the other names in the dozens of cemeteries around Paris: René, Marie, François, Lucie. Where is home? she wondered aloud, staring in all directions. Exhausted, she sat down on a park bench, imagining François at her side.

"Father Dubois, you know," she said, lying down on the bench, "brought me to *Saint-Roch*. Now I cannot find him. What shall I do without Father? Where is he? I have looked everywhere for him."

Sleep never came to Lucie that night, either on the park bench or at home, which took her hours to find. She had arisen from the bench and, with tiny steps, wandered among the trees, singing in a child-like voice, "*Sur le pont d'Avignon, l'on y danse, l'on y danse, sur le pont d'Avignon, l'on y danse tous en rond.*"

A circle of thoughts wouldn't let her be and she was finally able to admit her mistake. "If only I'd called the emergency number instead of the doctor," she cried. "François couldn't stop coughing, couldn't breathe, made a sign to me that he needed oxygen. And what did I do? I phoned the doctor instead of *les pompiers*. Why did I do that? Why?"

1930

LUCIE IS SIX, bouncing a ball forth and back with her playmates until it is time for them to sit quietly in rows on little wooden chairs like the big ones in church. They listen to Sister Magdala, who tells them stories from the Bible, while manipulating figures on a felt board. Afterwards, Sister passes out holy cards to the children.

Lucie's card has a picture of a saint with the same name as her own.

"How many of you little girls would like to become Sisters? Raise your hands high," sings *Soeur* Magdala.

Each child looks determinedly at the others in an effort to raise her hand the very highest of all.

"Jesus died for your sins. Did you know that, children?"

"*Oui, ma Soeur,*" they chant in unison.

"Repeat after me: I AM SIN."

"I AM SIN," cry the little girls, one louder than the rest.

"Very good, children." And Sister Magdala claps her hands three times.

1987

IN EARLY SPRING, two years before the bicentenniel, Paul flew to Paris to meet with Father André and several doctors. All of the men agreed that Lucie should be committed to *l'Hôpital-Asile Sainte Jeanne*. Upon completion of that task, Paul returned to Minnesota, to the archdiocese in St. Paul.

Several weeks later, Lucie escaped from the asylum in her robe and slippers and found her way back to *la Place de la Concorde*. She approached the wall and pressed her face to the cement. Raising her arms high, she dug her fingers into the bullet holes until the rough stone made her nails splinter and her fingers bleed. She turned, forced her back hard against the wall, and lifted her eyes toward the top floor windows of the building directly opposite the square.

"*Me voici! Me voici!*" she cried. "Here I am!"

She saw the glint of light off metal—a gun barrel.

Shadows flitted past curtained windows—snipers.

"*Me voici!*" she screamed over and over, stretching her arms straight out from her body, as if nailed to a cross. "*Me voici!*"

A police van arrived. Three gendarmes gently pried Lucie Moulin from the wall and coaxed her inside the van.

1989

THE FESTIVAL OF LIGHTS is over. Highlights replay on the television. Several patients doze in awkward positions in front of the screen. Others, with tired eyes, continue to watch a recap of the annual celebration venerating the revolutionary struggles of two centuries ago.

Lucie awakens in her bed and gropes under the pillow for her treasure—a wrinkled page that she has torn from a religious magazine. Clothed in a black cardigan and baggy pajamas, she snaps on the light and shuffles aimlessly about the room in slippers more suitable for an old man. All that remains of her hair are a few sparse patches of gray. She looks down, attracted by the glint of silver—a needle, barely visible—one that she had hidden in the crevice between the floor and the wall. Lucie bends over and picks it up. Pacing the length of her room, she holds the long, thin needle in one hand and the creased paper in the other. She stops to frown, remembering a conversation she'd overheard the day before in the lounge.

"Those attendants," she murmured, "they were talking about me. I know they were. '*Elle est belle,*' said one, '*mais elle a les yeux morts.*' She is beautiful, but her eyes are dead."

Lucie sits down on the edge of her bed, smoothes the shred of paper over rumpled sheets, and stares at the picture of a pious young woman whose head is draped in a black shroud—a saint who has pierced her own eyes in atonement and consummate devotion to God.

Clutching her worn rosary, she reclines against a pillow, serene, beatific, while her vitreous blends with blood and trickles in dark rivulets toward the upturned corners of her mouth.

Miserere Nobis.

14

Oh, That Charles Boyer!

How ya gonna keep 'em down on the farm
after they've seen Paree?
—lyricists Joe Young & Sam Lewis

CALLIE SHIVERED and gripped the steering wheel of her dad's car, recalling every detail of *Ego Te Absolvo*, grateful to have been raised in a slightly more liberal Lutheran tradition. As a young girl, one of the worst things she could remember was how, shortly after the controversial films came to Masterton, the pastor pounded the hell out of his pulpit, claiming that far too many Parisian women were of ill repute. Then he shamed his parishioners into tithing more for the church fund.

Now, the movie about Lucie Moulin was still showing in a few city theaters and when her friends commented at length about the screenplay and how much they liked it, Callie kept to herself the fact that she knew quite a few things that fed this story while growing up in Masterton, much as she had kept still about finding that trunk full of Uncle Amer's personal things inside the storeroom of her grandparents' cottage: old clothes and rare books, letters to the family, his prized violin, which now belonged to Callie, and a dark red album storage book with a dog embossed on the cover. In both instances, with regard to the intriguing life of Uncle Amer and that of Lucie Moulin, along with all of the other individuals whose lives she had considered during the trip back home, Cal needed time to process what she had discovered, witnessed, heard about, not only as a child, but especially now, as an adult. What was the meaning behind all of this powerful stuff and how might she learn from it?

Years later she heard that Father Paul Moulin had approached Selmer Johnson for a brief interview in front of the bank. Selmer, standing tall and rigid, patted that soft wallet tucked away in his back pocket, and said, "I'll cross the street before ever meeting up with the likes of you again."

Callie and her father continued north in the secure confines of their automobile, leaving Spring Green far behind, along with Readstown and Viroqua. They were not far from La Crosse and the Mississippi River Bridge that would take them into Winona, on the Minnesota side.

Splashes of crimson and pumpkin-colored leaves filled the river valley, intermingled with shades of lime and yellow. A flock of geese in V formation arrowed southward.

While driving along highway 14, Callie slowed down when she spotted a frame of activity in the middle of a long pasture between Coon Valley and La Crosse: a laughing woman in jeans, down on her haunches, welcomed a black lab that leapt towards her, followed by four chestnut horses running fast and wild, tails and manes flying in the wind, ears pinned back, eyes wide open. The woman jumped up with arms aloft and ran with the animals.

And then Cal drove past a dead skunk lying at the edge of the road; its strong odor filled the car. She held her breath, looked up at the rearview mirror, and saw the same woman, now a miniature image, still running with her dog and horses.

Callie continued to ponder the life and death of Lucie Moulin. In the film, there was very little mention of Selmer Johnson, who, according to folks in Masterton, had fallen in love with Lucie during the short time he was stationed in Paris.

So why was there no shame or guilt placed on Lucie's cousin? After all, François, played by Charles Boyer, had had an equal part in their love affair. Yet Lucie was forced to take the brunt of it.

"Dad, do you remember that old movie about Lucie Moulin, back in the late fifties? The one I wasn't allowed to see?"

"Who could forget it? Caused quite a stir among the locals, especially the Catholics. Your aunt Hazel refused to speak to Emily and me for a long time after we told her what a great show that was. Cecil was all right with it—greeted us whenever we saw him in town. And thank goodness, Marvin Slaybaugh didn't knuckle under, although he did receive threatening phone calls and nasty messages tacked to the door of his theatre."

"That's right. The Church tried to get it banned."

"Keep those reels in Hollywood, they said. Don't even think of shipping them to Masterton. The National Legion of Decency got involved too."

"More censors, huh?"

"Oh, yes. They graded movies as far back as the thirties. Gave a lot of them the big 'O' for being morally offensive. I believe they were in cahoots with the Vatican."

"Wouldn't you think the Vatican would have more important things on their plate than zeroing in a southern Minnesota small town movie theater? By the way, how did the League rate "*The Saga of Lucie Moulin*?"

"Restricted it to 'a limited adult audience.' At least that show made it to Masterton."

"So that's why I wasn't allowed to see it, even though we're not Catholic. What the hell!"

"You were only twelve or thirteen, Callie. Your mother and I thought it best for you to wait a few more years."

153

"Well, I sure got an eyeful with this new version that just came out."

"Oh? There's another one?"

"Hollywood reworked the story in time to celebrate the French Bicentennial. It's called *Ego Te Absolvo*. Hmm, let's see now. I'll have to rate that film with an 'O' because I've decided that it's a bit much for your sensibilities at this stage in your lives, Dad—yours and Mom's."

Callie laughed and patted Will on the shoulder.

"Oh, you do, do you? By the way, what does the title mean?"

"*Ego Te Absolve*? I believe that's what the priests say through the grates of confessionals when they absolve people of their sins."

"Sounds like Latin to me."

"You got it."

"I wonder," said Will, pausing to look out at the ever-widening river, "who absolves the priests of their sins?"

Imposing bluffs rose in the distance as Callie drove into La Crosse and found the Mississippi River Bridge. The land formation triggered her memory of that long ago afternoon with Jim, atop Queen's Bluff.

Autumn colors commanded the area on both sides, as though an artist had passed by with a giant palette, flinging gobs of her richest hues against the hillsides and over the trees standing guard along the river where boats of every size still dotted the water.

"That was some picture show, *The Story of Lucie Moulin*! But, you know Cal, I always felt a little sorry for Selmer Johnson. He was still going fairly strong when that movie came to town and we all thought it would feature his life as a soldier more than it did. He only got a brief mention. Must have been a disappointment for him. Your mother often wondered what would have happened if Lucie's cousin, François, had never shown up in Paris and Selmer hadn't suffered from shell shock."

"Oh, that Charles Boyer! I'll bet he made the ladies swoon."

"I should say so. I can't imagine linking up with a cousin, but I guess that sort of thing happens from time to time. If it weren't for that François guy, maybe Selmer and Lucie would have married and returned home to live on the Johnson farm."

"Question is, would she have been able to adjust? Masterton versus Paris—go figure."

"Good question, Cal. I'll never forget how old man Johnson worried so after his sons marched off to war. He was doubly concerned about losing them to the bright lights of Paris or New York City, 'jazzin' around and paintin' the town,' a carry-over from World War I. Which would mean no return and no one to take over the family farm."

"And who would have substituted for Selmer against that ledge in front of the Maywood County Bank, alongside Clarence and the others?"

"I know. They were quite the fixtures around town all those years after the war—one with a missing limb, the other shell-shocked."

"Sure as hell kept *them* home."

"But not of much use on the farm."

Callie imagined a different tombstone with Selmer's and Lucie's names etched on it. And perhaps, another for Clarence and a wife, planted next to their mother and father, the last of the hard-working Johnsons on an acreage that had been in the family for generations. And then she visualized the tombstones as they really were up there on cemetery hill outside of Masterton: one for Mr. and Mrs. Johnson and one for their two sons, Selmer and Clarence, highlighted by crinkly red paper poppies and miniature stars and stripes stapled to wooden sticks.

Other graves that Callie visited whenever she was in town included those of her high school friend, Laura Lambert, and Laura's father, Carl—gypsies who used to live in a boxcar north of Masterton. Although Mr. and Mrs. Lambert were extremely poor and endured a prejudice that would have destroyed weaker individuals, Mr. Lambert received a decent marker, dated 1955, thanks to the PCLC (Presbyterian Church Ladies Committee). In 1985, Laura's name and dates were chiseled onto a small piece of dark granite placed next to her parents' stone. She was 41 years old and Callie had been invited to speak at her funeral. As far as she knew, old Mrs. Lambert lived on, because there was, as yet, no death's date carved out for her.

The story of Laura and her parents, when Callie thought about it, seemed like a startling movie, worthy of a 360 degree panorama, for it was an unforgettable reminder of what unwarranted judgment and prejudice can do to a vulnerable family that had already suffered, among millions, across one of the widest screens in history: World War II.

15

The Boxcar

We had fresh air. And we seen the grass.
And when others had something to eat,
we went out to feel that grass.
—Marcelina Sobol

"LAURA WAS MY FRIEND," Callie began in a soft voice. She didn't need the microphone, because most of the dining hall seats were empty. Empty, except for the first row where their mothers sat. Laura's husband cast an apologetic look as he stood to greet latecomers—elderly relatives who bumped against their metal folding chairs in a rush to sit down. A cane tumbled to the floor. In quick succession, these noises sounded like a version of the old-fashioned theater signal: TAP-TAP-TAP! Let the play begin.

Afternoon sunshine poured through the tall church windows, warming Callie's back and flooding over the open coffin. Laura would have liked that. She loved summers, sunbathing on white sheets in Cal's backyard when they were teenagers, talking about boys, gently tugging up blades of grass to nibble their tender roots, listening to WDGY on the transistor radio: Buddy Holly and The Crickets, the Everly Brothers, the Big Bopper and his "Chantilly Lace." Feeling pretty, Callie and Laura would shout-sing, giggle, and swing their ponytails.

They named the shapes of clouds coasting along a powder blue sky and shivered in their hose-dampened swimsuits whenever a mound of cumulus blocked the sun. The second it drifted away, they stretched their limbs again, like a pair of lazy cats sprawling on the mid-summer-green grass.

Callie believed her friend would have liked the coffin her husband had chosen for her: creamy white and blue, like the interior of Our Lady of the Prairie Church. With pink flowers on the outside and pale pink satin on the inside, it seemed a casket for a young girl, really. But then, in many ways, Laura had always remained a girl, even in middle age.

Standing behind the podium, Callie thought back to a pajama party she'd organized in junior high. She was determined to talk of little before that, because prior to age twelve, her treatment of Laura Lambert had not been very kind.

"A bunch of us rode our bikes out to the lake," she said to the small gathering, eager to add special meaning to this day. "And we swam and roasted hotdogs and made S'mores and told ghost stories around the campfire, until we got so hyped up and scared that no one could sleep."

Recalling that adolescent scene, Callie glanced at Laura's husband who wore an expression of sad amusement. Elderly Mrs. Lambert sat tiny and bent with the look of old age resignation and the singularity of a mother who has outlived her only child. Callie's mother, Emily, smiled slightly and nodded in approval, doubtless recognizing that her long ago efforts to turn her daughter into a compassionate human being had finally paid off. Her sharp reminder of long ago echoed in Cal's mind: "Callie! You will be civil to that girl. She is in need of a friend."

As long as the anecdotes came to mind, she would fill the void and make things right with the Lamberts. But she had to be careful, because along with the good memories loomed the unpleasant ones—the mean ones. Which had no place in a eulogy. And so Callie stood at the podium, filtering out the shameful parts.

No one knew where Laura and her parents came from that summer of 1952. And were they really her parents? a bunch of school kids wondered. The Lamberts seemed too old and hard-worn to have given birth to her. So where did *she* come from? Gossip and rumors about the family, passed on by children and adults alike, flowed through the little town of Masterton like a spring-swollen river. Perhaps they'd stayed on when the County Fair ended, after the other Carnies had packed up and left. Or maybe they came from the Gypsy camp near Buffalo Ridge. Or the one between Currie and Lake Shetek. In any case, they'd moved into an old boxcar north of Masterton, next to the dump, where Mr. Lambert took a job as caretaker. He also stoked the furnace before dawn on Sunday mornings at the Baptist Church, an hour's walk as the crow flies, through cornfields and bean fields.

Mrs. Lambert oversaw the public toilet in the basement of doctor Bartel's dental office, a small dark brick building on Main Street. She scoured the floor on her hands and knees, scrubbed the stool, wiped down the sink, and handed out fresh terry towels, small and white. Callie went down those steps only when she had to—usually after a long siege by the dentist's jackhammer drill. Unlike the old woman who worked the public toilet before, Mrs. Lambert never said a cross word or gave Cal a nasty look when she failed to leave a coin in her dish. But neither did she speak.

On the first day of third grade, and every day for as long as he was able, Laura's father walked her to school. He looked as if he'd never had enough to eat, like those men in the concentration camps pictured in *Life Magazine*. Instead of a full head of thick shiny hair like Callie's father's, Mr. Lambert's scalp offered up only gray strands, just enough to cover his temples and the back of his head. A gray tinge lay beneath the surface of his dark skin. Every day, he wore the same clothes: gray pants, shiny and baggy in the seat and knees, a paper-thin gray shirt with frayed cuffs and brown patches stitched over the elbows, and scuffed brown shoes. Shuffling into town, he escorted his daughter bareheaded at a time when men never stepped from their homes without a fedora.

While the rest of the children ran around in sneakers and blue jeans and rode their bikes to school, Laura walked the distance from their boxcar, holding her father's hand, all decked out in white shoes, lace-trimmed anklets, and a flouncy white dress with a different colored sash each day. Her skin was the color of roasted almonds. Sometimes, she wore a small tiara or a ribbon in her dull brown hair. She looked like a fragile flower girl from another time, another place. Callie and her friends pointed and snickered, then pedaled on, wondering how this girl would ever manage to play tetherball or climb the monkey bars or swing from the giant strides dressed like that. And where did she get that white dress anyhow? And all those colored sashes?

After a time, Laura let go of her father's hand and scampered ahead or around him in circles, until he stopped, his arms hanging limp at his sides. He acted more like a grandfather, old and out of touch, uncertain how to handle this prancing girl who insisted on skipping over each crack in the sidewalk. "Step on a crack, break your mother's back," she'd chant.

Callie could see how awkward it was for Mr. Lambert to stand in the middle of the sidewalk, pleading with his daughter, trying to rein her in. She was like a puppy that had slipped her collar and refused to come back. It struck Cal that the girl wanted to join her and her friends, but didn't know how. Perhaps she was torn, sensing that her father might feel hurt if she abandoned him completely.

By fourth grade, Laura no longer walked alongside her father, even for a moment. Rarely smiling or speaking to anyone, Mr. Lambert, with his shoulders back and his head erect, followed his daughter several yards behind, making sure she got to school safely. He did this until his pace slowed and his shoulders stooped, sometime around the middle of fifth grade. Eventually, he became too ill to leave the boxcar. Or so everyone guessed. After that, Laura walked alone.

Once, when Callie passed Mr. Lambert while riding her bike, she slowed down, gave a little wave, and was surprised when he smiled at her and said with a curious accent, "Good morrr-ninngh, young lady."

All this time he must have been waiting for Callie to stop her snickering and recognize him in a civil way. After that, she always said, "Hi."

One afternoon, during recess on the school playground, Laura skipped over in her new sneakers and took the swing next to Callie. Breathless with excitement, she invited her to go along to the big amusement park near Spirit Lake, Iowa.

"Next Saturday!" she fairly shouted, a broad smile setting her thin, brown face all aglow. "Some people we know. They have a car. Papa said I could invite a friend."

"I dunno," Callie murmured, looking back at *her* friends who were motioning for her to join them on the Giant Strides.

"Papa said we could go on as many rides as we like. It'll be so much fun!"

Callie pumped higher on the swing, then flew out and away, landing with a thud feet first into the sandy hollow. "I'll have to ask," she called back over her shoulder.

Several days later, at the supper table, Emily told her daughter that she'd met Mr. Lambert at the grocery store.

"He wondered if you were going with them to Arnolds Park," she said. "He told me that Laura extended the invitation to you at school, but they hadn't heard back. Why didn't you tell us?"

"Because I don't wanna go."

"Why not?"

"I dunno. They're . . . so different. Besides, Dad and I are going fishing Saturday."

"No, Callie. Your father agrees with me. The Lamberts are decent, hard-working people. Their daughter chose you to spend the day with her. It would be a shame to refuse."

"She could ask someone else. Why does it have to be me?"

"Perhaps, because she sees something likeable in you. In any case, you *will* go. That's all there is to it."

Saturday was always Callie's favorite day of the week. But this particular Saturday morning arrived too soon. An ancient, rusty-brown

Chevrolet crept up alongside the curb and parked in front of the Lindstrom's house. Cal peeked out of the living room window and saw Mr. and Mrs. Lambert and Laura inside the beat-up car, along with another old couple. Strangers. Odd-looking. Spooky. Where would I even sit? she wondered, and balked again.

"What if we're in an accident, Mom? Or they steal me away? Gram always warned me about Gypsies. You might never see me again!"

Emily was having none of it.

"Some day, when you're older," she said, closing Callie's hand over a ten-dollar bill and prodding her out the door with fingertips against her back, "you'll realize how important this Saturday is for everyone involved, not least of all Mr. Lambert. You will go. You will have a good time. And you will be civil."

Callie stepped outside, hesitated for a second, then inched toward the curb, where Laura was motioning from the car's back seat. Cal got in and, with the door closed, looked longingly at her parents who waved from their front stoop. She missed them already, wishing they were the ones driving her to Arnold's Park.

Just as other people's houses smell foreign inside, so do cars. The old Chevy smelled musky with a trace of cigar smoke. The stocky, middle-aged driver, Mr. Biddle, and his heavyset wife, Flora, shared the front seat with Mr. Lambert. Mrs. Lambert, one of those women who seemed old no matter what her age, was seated in the back, on the other side of Laura. Wearing a long skirt and blouse with a scarf, she smiled and nodded at Callie.

"You girls going to have fun day," said Mr. Biddle, shifting to first gear. His manner of speaking was similar to that of Mr. Lambert who turned to say, "We happy to see you, Miss Callie. Laura wait long time for this day to come."

As they rolled away from the curb, Cal glanced over her shoulder and then looked back at Mr. Lambert. Seeing him up close for the first time, she was startled by how thin and worn out looking he was, with sparse hair and work-worn hands. Yet, he had the kindest eyes—eyes that seemed to have taken in more than most others in a lifetime. Although he looked different from the other men in Masterton, his welcoming smile and friendly words set Callie at ease.

During the hour and a half it took to get to Lake Okoboji, Mr. Biddle, whose first name was Stefan, sang peppy songs with strange words—words from another language—and Flora Biddle told stories: "One day," she said, "It was my turn to go fetch water from the well; I went off and played, instead—played for a long time before getting back to our wagons where everyone was waiting with mean looks or folded arms. So I lied and told them I'd seen two little fairies near the well. Everybody was talking about it, and next day one of the women went down to the well and when she came back she shouted, 'I seen the fairies too!'"

Callie and Laura laughed and poked at each other. Stefan Biddle started singing again. Flora and Mr. and Mrs. Lambert settled back in their seats to watch the changing countryside on their way to Iowa.

At Arnold's Park, Mr. Biddle found a parking place between the Roof Garden Ballroom and the Fun House. The girls hopped out just in time to see a large paddleboat, called the Boji Belle, leave the dock. To the left, across from the Nutty Bar stand, hung a large red sign advertising fireworks. And there, straight ahead, was a huge carrousel with galloping horses and a loud calliope playing "Over the Waves."

Lured by the music and hotdog/hamburger stands and riders screaming from atop the roller coaster, Callie and Laura peeled out toward the amusement park entrance with the grown-ups close behind.

Late that night, when Callie was delivered safely home, she wasn't about to tell her parents that she'd had a very good time and that Mr. Lambert insisted that the ten dollars remain in her pocket.

"It was all right," Callie muttered before trailing off to bed.

The next morning at breakfast, Cal admitted that she and Laura had had a lot of fun and that, although the Lamberts and the Biddles were generous and kind, they seemed odd. "They're so different from everybody else in town," she said, "the way they dress and talk."

"Good," said Emily. "Gives you a chance to learn something new about people."

During the spring of sixth grade, Mr. Lambert died.

How little anyone knew about this man and his family, understanding too late the simple things he'd wanted for his daughter: safety, acceptance, a sound education. Instead, the other kids obsessed about how peculiar they were, how strange and unsuited for 'our town.' Despite having taken that trip to Arnolds Park with the Lamberts, Callie said nothing to counter the impression when her friends jabbered on about the family. "They're so weird," they'd say. "Imagine, those Gypsies living in a boxcar out at the dump. Ugh!" And, "I don't think Laura is really their kid. I'll bet they stole her. Maybe even from another state. Or another country!"

Emily countered those ugly remarks with lessons in compassion, showing her daughter by example how to treat people she referred to as "underdogs." Callie bumped along this course by fits and starts, reluctantly accompanying her mother to the boxcar the day before Mr. Lambert's funeral.

"We're going to pay our respects," said Emily.

When Callie got home from school that afternoon, she found her mother wrapping a new turquoise casserole in flour sack dishtowels and placing the bundle in a large wicker basket. She'd baked a favorite hotdish of noodles, chunks of chicken, diced celery and onions, chicken broth and white sauce, with crunched-up potato chips sprinkled over the top.

She handed Callie the basket, picked up the envelope with the sympathy card inside, and ushered Cal out of the door, down the block toward Main Street, and north to the outskirts of town. As the two walked along the highway, Callie shifted the heavy basket from one hand to the other all the while chatting about school and how, although Laura had finally exchanged her frilly dresses and shoes for blue jeans and sneakers, she still didn't have any friends.

"Well, how about you?"

"What about me?"

"You could be her friend. After all, you went to the amusement park together and had a good time. Didn't you?"

Callie shrugged. At the turnoff to the town dump, she covered her mouth and nose against the stench of rotting garbage and smoldering ash heaps.

Emily briskly led the way, skirting mounds of trash: tin cans, piles of damp newspaper, moldy paper bags oozing everything imaginable, including stinky potato peelings and fish guts. The twisted metal of a rusty stove rose above one heap. An old wringer washing machine lay on its side, pocked with bullet holes.

"The boys come out here to shoot rats with their twenty-twos."

"I know that, Callie. Now watch what you say when we get to their home."

The wooden boxcar, gray and dilapidated, appeared out of place sitting flat on the ground, far from any railroad tracks. How did it even get there? Its weathered timbers looked thirsty. The large sliding door, normally on one side of a train car, had been removed, and the gaping hole boarded up to create a wall. There wasn't a single window along the front side. Just as well, thought Callie, since there weren't any trees or flowers to look at. And no grass. Only hard-packed dirt and stones with an outhouse nearby and the dump just yards away. Callie and her mother had to look twice to find the entry at one end of the boxcar.

Emily knocked at the flimsy wooden door. After a moment, Laura opened it a crack and peeked through. She was out of breath, as if she had twice run the length of the boxcar. Surprised to see Callie and her mother, she turned bashful and quickly backed away. Emily and her daughter stepped inside a cramped, partitioned space that was the kitchen. There were no appliances—no regular stove or refrigerator— only a couple of pans and a few dishes stacked next to a camping stove on a slab of wood nailed onto four stilts.

"Hello, dear," said Emily, reaching out to Laura and giving her a hug. "Is your mother at home?"

Laura nodded, then turned and hollered, "Mama!" in a voice at odds with her timid manner.

While standing there, Callie avoided looking at her classmate, focusing instead on the worn floor planks and the small rickety table surrounded by three mismatched chairs with broken backs. Everything looked like salvage from the dump. Cal glanced through the doorway into a larger room. The few inside wallboards not covered with faded yellow insulation were as gray as the outside wood. Stacks of boxes lined one side of the narrow aisle that ran back to another partition. Nearly everything the family owned must have been inside those pasteboard boxes.

Mrs. Lambert finally emerged from the rear, her head slightly bowed. Callie had only seen her up close a few times—downstairs at the public toilet and during the trip to Arnolds Park. She'd said very little in the car or when they sat down to eat in a restaurant. And here she was wearing those same clothes: scuffed Oxfords, turned down at the outside edges, and a green fringed shawl over an ankle-length brown dress that hung more loosely than ever on her tiny frame. Her long, ash-colored hair was uncombed and brittle looking—thirsty, like the boards on the boxcar. The skin on her face and hands was dark and withered.

"I am so sorry, Mrs. Lambert," said Emily, stepping forward and taking the woman's hands in her own. "My daughter and I have brought you something for your supper."

Callie held out the basket.

Mrs. Lambert glanced at the casserole, and then looked up at Emily for a brief moment. Her dark eyes shimmered with tears. "Thank you," she whispered, accepting the offering and holding it close for a long while before setting it on the makeshift counter next to the sympathy card. "We are most grateful."

"You have a very nice girl, Mrs. Lambert. A fine playmate for my Callie."

Laura's mother took her daughter's hand and smiled at Cal—a sad, tired smile.

And that was it. Emily gave each of them another hug, then handed the empty basket and wadded up dishtowels to Callie before saying their goodbyes.

"Why did you say that?" Callie hissed as they retraced their steps past the dump.

"What?"

"'A fine playmate for my Callie.'"

"Because I meant it. You're going to be kind to that girl. It will do them more good than you can ever imagine."

Out of the corner of her eye, Callie spotted a huge rat scurrying for cover under a rusted out stove. Emily must have seen it too, because she suddenly grabbed her daughter's hand and picked up their pace.

As soon as they reached the main road back to town, Cal tried to keep up with her mother's steady gait. Their shoes made loud crunching sounds along the gravel shoulder. On either side of the highway ran ditches filled with tall grass, and beyond those, long fields rich with black soil and the green shoots of sprouting corn. A hawk soared away from a cluster of oak trees, chased off by a smaller bird.

Callie looked closely at her mother. How pretty she was in her red print housedress that fell just below the knees. Her dark brown hair was fashioned in the latest style—medium length with smooth finger waves. The set of her face was kind, yet determined.

"No electricity or plumbing," she murmured, shaking her head as they marched along at a fast clip. "They are truly in need. Have been all along."

Callie broke stride in order to kick a stone into the ditch. "How do they cook?"

"A kerosene stove. And oil lamps for light, like when I was a girl. But this is 1955. People shouldn't have to live like that any more."

"What did Mr. Lambert die from?"

"I don't know, Callie. He wasn't a well man. He must have suffered a great deal during the war."

"Against the Germans?"

"Yes. The Nazis. I have a hunch this family has been through more than any of us ever realized."

"Where did they come from?"

"Poland. Warsaw, I believe."

"Some of the kids tell Polish jokes at school, but I don't remember any of them."

"That's good."

"What? That they tell Polish jokes?"

"No. That you don't remember them.

"Now Callie, I'm going to tell you a story, one that I remember from when I was about your age."

"Oh goody! Tell me a story, tell me a story . . ."

"This is no bedtime story, sweetheart. It's harsh and one you must think about and remember in years to come:

"After the war, a Jewish family settled in our little town, east of Masterton. They opened up a grocery and dry goods store, and lived in the space up above. Mr. and Mrs. Kaplan were refugees, and although they were the kindest people, friendly, and very giving, a few folks were bent on running them out—some because they were Jewish, others because they were German, even though they had fled that country.

"Mom and Pop lost their farm after the crash of 1929, and like most Americans, we were trying to survive the Great Depression that followed. Whenever we went inside Mr. Kaplan's store to buy groceries, he always tucked a bag of peppermint candy into Mom's sack, for my sisters and me.

"One night, less than a year later, members of the KKK broke in, ransacked, and set fire to the store. The Kaplans had to flee for a second time—where they went and what became of them, we never learned."

"What's the KKK?"

"Ku Klux Klan—groups of men who wear white sheets and pointy masks and hate people who aren't like them."

In silence, Callie and her mother walked the rest of the way home, turning onto Norwood Avenue and the wide sidewalk to their house.

Cal looked afresh at their white rambler with the green and white awnings and green trim around the windows and doors. From inside came the aroma of a second chicken casserole baking in the oven.

Before Callie fell asleep that night, she pictured clusters of vertical white sheets gathered on the streets at night. And she thought of the Kaplans trying to make a go of it in that little farmtown, what they might have looked like, and the impression they had made on her mother when she was but a little girl.

And then Callie thought hard about her mom's kind gesture toward the Lamberts, and how awkward she, herself, had felt, seeing Laura on her own turf, inside that boxcar.

The next day, Cal and her girlfriends attended Mr. Lambert's funeral, mainly for the wrong reason—they went because it got them out of school.

Sometime later, Emily delivered a package of clothing to Laura's mother, explaining that since the dresses and coat no longer fit her, perhaps Mrs. Lambert could use them.

During Callie's eulogy, she left out the fact that it was her mother who insisted on including Laura at a pajama party the summer before seventh grade. And how could Callie admit remaining silent after one of the girls told Laura, who was uncapping a bottle of Grape Nehi, that if she was going to eat the food and drink the pop, she should have brought something to contribute.

Laura's dark complexion paled. Her soft brown eyes widened and darted around like those of a cornered animal. An uncomfortable silence gripped the room. What was she going to do? Set the bottle down and leave? Bike the seven miles back to Masterton all alone? There was no telephone in the lake cabin. In case of emergency, Callie was to run down the line to the Johnsons' cottage for help. Like the summer she gashed the base of her thumb while cutting a willow stick and Mrs. Johnson poured sulfa powder in the wound and bound it up with wads of gauze and tape.

But Laura did not set the bottle down. Nor did she get up from the sofa. Instead, she raised the soda pop to her lips, took one tentative sip, and then another. Callie thought it was brave of her to drink it down and stay where she was, tucked into that snug corner, like a shy kitten.

Eventually, someone started up a conversation about boys, which got everyone talking. Laura unfolded her slender arms and legs, stuck her feet out and started giggling along with the rest of the girls. She had the prettiest smile and the most sparkling eyes of anyone at the party. Eventually, Callie was glad to have invited her. She didn't recall if her soon-to-be new friend ate any potato chips or peanut butter cookies or hotdogs and S'mores, because she couldn't bear to remember that the girl didn't. But Laura could tell the spookiest stories to everyone gathered around the bonfire on shore: "Thump, squish, I'm on the first step," she half-whispered in the fire's glow. "Thump, squish, I'm on the second step . . . on the landing . . . *at your door . . .*"

High-pitched screams carried across the bay.

After everyone grew quiet and there were no more sounds, except for the glou-glou of lake ripples and the snap of burning logs, and no light but from the flames and a zillion stars overhead, Laura said that she knew secrets the others could never guess in a million years—secrets her mother had revealed to her.

"But I can't tell you," she said, making the whole thing sound like a scary show. "All I will say is that they're about people getting killed."

Callie and her friends looked at each other, frowning in disbelief.

"Are you telling the truth?" asked Janet.

"Yes. Cross my heart and hope to die."

"You can tell us," said Karen. "We won't tell anyone else."

Judy leaned forward, close to the fire, her narrowed eyes alight through her glasses. "What secrets?"

"It was horrible," said Laura, shuffling her feet in the sand. "The way they did it."

"What are you talking about?" asked Callie, poking a stick into the center of the fire, stirring up red-hot coals. "Another Thump Squish story?"

She thought Laura was going to tell them more about the murder-ous man whose legs had been cut off at the knees and who hobbled up flights of steps on his stumps, bound to take revenge on the one who maimed and tried to kill him.

"You're just making stuff up," said Nancy, "to scare us."

"No, I'm not. They killed my whole family."

"Who did? Callie asked. "Who's . . . ?"

"Wait a minute," interrupted Judy. "What about your mom and dad?"

Laura picked up a small twig and tossed it into the flames. "Papa got us out."

"Where did you come from?" asked Karen in a gentle voice. "Before you moved to Masterton?"

"New York City."

"Wow," said Judy, leaning back against a log. "I've always wanted to go there. See the Statue of Liberty."

"And before that?" asked Callie, hoping to hear something about Poland.

"I don't want to talk about this any more."

"C'mon," said Janet. "Why did you even bring it up if you don't want to talk about it?"

Laura shrugged and examined the ground for more twigs.

Callie started to ask what it was like in Warsaw, but when Laura's eyes grew wide again, with that familiar frightened look, she said, "Aw, leave her alone. C'mon, let's roast some more marshmallows."

Several weeks after the lakeside pajama party, Laura invited Callie to her house. Cal didn't feel like going, but once she'd propped her bicy-cle against the gray timbered siding and knocked at the rickety door, it wasn't so bad. Probably because she'd already been inside once, with her mother—the day before Mr. Lambert's funeral.

This time, the girls went to the rear of the boxcar where Laura had a room of her own; it was the size of a large closet with space for a cot, a small chest of drawers, and a vanity, which her father had built out of wood scraps. On either side of a tarnished mirror, he had nailed pieces of old plywood to the wall. These Laura had covered with pictures clipped from movie magazines: Elizabeth Taylor, Audrey Hepburn, and Debbie Reynolds on one side; Rock Hudson, Sal Mineo, and James Dean on the other. A tiny window looked out on the ravine where a trickling creek bent its way to a larger body of water. Laura said she'd like to find some pretty pink cloth to pull across the window, especially at night when boys from town came out to the dump with flashlights and their twenty-twos.

Because it was raining on the day of her visit, Callie had brought along a large package of modeling clay from Buckles' Five and Dime: blue, red, yellow, white, and green slabs. They sat at the little table, fashioning silly faces, animals, and anything else they fancied. Laura preferred cats. Callie's specialty was palm trees in sway. Neither girl talked much and when they'd used up all of the clay, Callie left—without seeing Mrs. Lambert and without hearing any more from Laura about her family getting killed during the war. It hadn't seemed right for Cal to question her friend that day.

The following week, the girls played outdoors, opposite the boxcar and away from the dump. They trotted down to the narrow ravine and into the tiny stream, where they built a dam of stones, reinforced with dirt, clay, twigs, and leaves. Then they sat back in their muddy shorts and tee shirts to see if their dam would hold. Laura smiled at the rising pool of water.

"You should invite your friend to our house next time," said Emily as soon as Callie returned home. "It would be nice to reciprocate."

Cal shrugged, catching a whiff of the warm loaves of bread cooling on the kitchen counter.

"She's smart, loves to read, and cares for animals—same as you, Cal."

"Yeah. Maybe."

At the beginning of seventh grade, Laura and Callie did become fast friends. Not because Emily insisted on it, but because of what happened one afternoon.

A block from school, the girls came upon two fifth-grade boys about to hang Mrs. Holt's cat from the clothesline pole. They'd tied a noose around its neck with a long thin rope and were stringing it up. Its hind legs nearly off the ground and eyes bulging, the cat yowled, choked, showed fangs, and clawed at the air.

Laura snatched up a long stick. "You take Richard!" she shouted, sprinting toward the boys. "I'll get Jimmy!"

The girls tackled the culprits, Laura whipping the one with her stick and Callie pounding the other with her fists. The boys dropped the rope and held their hands in front of their faces while the girls screamed and beat them some more. Mrs. Holt exploded out of her back door with a broom, swatting up dust as the boys ran away, their voices trailing off in fractured falsetto.

Laura rushed over to the cat and loosened the rope, which had caught on one end of the pole. She slipped off the noose and dropped to the ground clutching the frantic animal, despite its claws scratching at her bare arms.

Mrs. Holt knelt down next to them. "This is the second time those boys have tried to hang her. Pretty soon she's going to run out of lives." She stood and took a long, thoughtful look at Callie's friend. "You like that cat?"

"Oh, yes, Mrs. Holt, I sure do." Laura stroked its fur, now only slightly raised at the shoulders.

"Well, my dear, since you saved her, she's yours."

Laura looked up at the elderly woman, grinning so broadly that Callie could see most of her teeth, which were very white and naturally straight, unlike Cal's, which required braces.

"I must tend to supper now, girls. Off you go, before I change my mind."

"I've always wanted a cat," said Laura, cuddling the orange tabby as the girls walked down the street shoulder-to-shoulder. "I just hope Mama doesn't kill it."

Callie stopped in her tracks, horrified. "What! Why would she do that?"

"For food."

"Food! You mean she eats cats?"

"In Warsaw, when we . . . oh, never mind."

"No, tell me."

"I was only three, but I remember what she did—how she skinned a little cat and roasted it in the alley, over a fire in a garbage can."

"Why?" gasped Callie. "How could anyone do such a thing?"

"There was nothing to eat, except for a stray cat or dog. And rats. That's what my mother told me. Sometimes, she found a potato or a piece of bread. But not very often."

As they headed north, Laura hugged her new pet, which by now had calmed down and was nuzzling her neck.

Callie wondered if Mrs. Lambert still roasted rats—from the town dump.

"Poland? Is that where you came from? Before New York?"

Laura nodded, but said nothing more. She just held the cat tightly against her chest as they neared the boxcar. Although Callie felt sick to her stomach, she went along home with Laura. Any girl who could tackle a mean boy and save an animal was her friend.

"What are you going to name her?" she asked, reaching over to pet the cat.

"I don't know yet. I'll have to think about it." Then with a dreamy look, Laura said, "It'll have to be special. Not just any old name."

The next day, Laura told Callie that her mother had let her keep the cat. And she had decided on a name.

"Tola," she said. "I'm going to call her Tola."

"What kind of a name is that? I mean, I like it and all, but it's sure different from any I've ever heard of."

"It means 'priceless' in Polish."

"Hah! So you *are* from Poland."

"What of it?"

"Laura doesn't sound Polish. Is that your real name?"

"Can you keep a secret?"

"Of course."

"I am Basia," she whispered. "That's what my mother told me. Basia Sobol. We changed our names when we came to America. Promise not to tell anyone."

"Cross my heart and hope to die," said Callie, drawing an imaginary X across her chest. "Basia Sobol—that's a pretty name." Then she began to giggle. "Sounds like 'Baa-baa, black sheep, have you any wool?'"

Callie's friend smiled. That afternoon, they played with Tola next to the ravine, not far from Mrs. Lambert's small garden and potato patch.

Sometimes, Laura (Callie wanted to call her Basia, but didn't because of her promise not to tell another living soul) and Cal rode bicycles into the countryside. Waiting for trains, they shinnied up trestles where the smell of gummy creosote filled their nostrils, especially strong on a hot summer's day. They entwined themselves around dark timbers beneath the tracks, ready to clap hands over their ears, shriek, and brush away sparks, as soon as the shaking metal thunder of an engine and boxcars rumbled overhead.

They sifted through dried up creek beds for tiny snail shells and waded in those same creeks after heavy rains filled them up again. Carefully tugging a wide blade of grass from the ground, Callie stretched it between her thumbs and blew on it. Laura clamped her hands over her ears against a sound the opposite of music—a harsh, screechy squawk, like that of a great blue heron chased from the end of a dock.

Sitting cross-leggèd in a grassy ditch, the girls picnicked on Hershey bars, crackers, and tuna fish, prying open the tins with their Girl Scout knives. They coaxed pastured cattle to the fence lines with saltines and fancy words. Cows, they learned, were the best audiences—attentive, silent, non-judgmental—and so they practiced their school speeches in front of those uplifted brown or black-and-white faces with the wide, unblinking eyes.

Every Saturday, Cal and Laura checked out books from the local Carnegie library: *Treasure Island, The Old Man and the Sea, Giant, The Yearling, A Woman Called Fancy, Peyton Place*, which they hauled up high into the willow tree in Callie's back yard. For hours at a time, those books, with the most wonderfully smelling pages and magical words, transported the girls far away from Masterton.

During Christmas vacation, Callie, Laura, Janet, Karen, and Judy popped corn and pulled taffy. After slathering their hands with butter to keep the molten candy from sticking and burning their fingers, they draped and folded the hardening strands and chewed the warm, sweet globs, until someone lost a silver filling or a section of Callie's braces came loose. After gorging on popcorn and candy, they pounded out *Chopsticks* and *Heart and Soul* on the piano, tittering, whooping, and nudging one another off the bench. Then they gathered in Cal's bedroom, closed the door, played with Tequila and Sam Cat, and talked about boys.

Callie and Laura went to the movies whenever Cal's father, Will, gave them each a dime—nine cents for the show, a penny for the gumball-trinket machine at the Milk Bar. As soon as the lights dimmed inside the theater, they slipped into seats saved for them by their boyfriends of the moment. Afterward, the four gathered on the playground behind the Catholic Church to act out whichever show they'd seen that afternoon—*Rebel Without a Cause, Rear Window, A Summer Place, Unchained Melody*—humming the theme music and arguing over who would play the leads.

The next time Laura invited Callie to her house, she asked, "Bring your paints along, will you?" in order to continue decorating her room at the rear of the boxcar. (The girls had already tacked up a small curtain scissored from several yards of pink Dotted Swiss fabric that Emily had given them. The remainder Laura used as a spread for her cot).

Callie had recently taken up oil painting, beginning with paint-by-numbers and moving on to her own designs. Because she was especially taken with pictures of Tahiti, everything she created had a palm tree in it: the shores of Lake Sarah with palm trees; cornfields with palm trees next to a farmhouse; canoes on a northern lake with palm trees in the distance. Soon, Emily asked her daughter to create small murals on the French door panels inside their house. Her mother's trust gave Callie confidence. And so, she was eager to make a painting for her friend.

Inside the boxcar bedroom, Laura had already removed her collection of movie star pictures from the plywood panels, and tacked them onto a different wall in order to clear the way for Cal's art.

While a curious Tola deftly wound around the brushes and tubes of paint, Callie worked all afternoon on the wooden panels with the ardor of a modern day Van Gogh, laying on thick greens and yellows and blues to create a brilliant sky and the largest palm trees and the widest seascapes she'd ever painted. Laura and her mother gazed in admiration at the bright colors.

Afterward, the three sat down for glasses of cherry Kool-aid. Mrs. Lambert was the most talkative Callie had ever heard her, adding to what had already been revealed the night of the girls' pajama party and the little bit Laura had mentioned about their past. While caressing Tola, Laura shot Callie a look that said, "See? I told you so."

"I make sure my daughter know what happened to our family," said Mrs. Lambert. "My mother and father, sister, brothers. All shot."

Laura stopped petting Tola. Her told-you-so look turned to one of nervous concern as she scraped her feet back and forth along the floor beneath her chair.

Although Mrs. Lambert frightened Callie with her direct talk and Gypsy ways, Cal was curious to hear more. Like the night she'd sneaked into the movie theater to watch *The House of Wax*, a horror show Emily hadn't wanted her to see. She went anyway, and experienced nightmares for a week. As Mrs. Lambert described what life was like in the Warsaw Ghetto—cold, hopeless, nothing to eat but field rutabaga and small animals, jackbooted Germans tromping through the streets in the light of day or the dark of night, Gestapo shootings of men and women, babies and young children—Laura began to cry.

"Stop, Mama," she begged, her wide eyes darting around the room as if she herself were a little animal searching for a place to hide. Tola jumped from her lap, landed with a thud on the wooden floor, and ran to the other end of the boxcar.

"Is true. If it not for your papa to get necessary papers, we would be dead too."

Laura clapped her hands against her ears. "I don't want to hear this again! Again and again!"

"You no forget how lucky we are to live in America," shouted Mrs. Lambert, shaking a finger under her daughter's nose.

"How could I? That's all you ever talk about!"

Laura jumped up and ran to her room, while Mrs. Lambert continued her tirade. Finally, in an angry voice, the woman began speaking a language that Callie couldn't understand.

Feeling sick in the stomach, her heart thumping against her chest, Cal set her unfinished glass of Kool-aid on the table, said good-bye to Mrs. Lambert in a voice that was barely audible, and left.

The smell and taste of that watered-down cherry flavor lingered with her as she tripped across the stones and dirt next to the boxcar, charged past the town dump, and practically flew the rest of the way home.

What especially stayed with Callie was Mrs. Lambert's description of how the family struggled to survive in the Warsaw Ghetto—containment surrounded by brick walls and barbed wire, the stench of feces and dead bodies lying in the streets for days, lice crawling over everything and everyone, Gestapo men beating women and children with truncheons studded with razor blades and hobnails, Jackboots killing Jews and Gypsies out of boredom.

Mrs. Lambert had spoken of how those who were left of her family escaped and found space in one of many boxcars that made up a long train to Eastern Poland.

"Eight or ten families hide in each one," she'd said. "We claim our own little spots on floor, where we sleep, sometimes eight people in family. Because we are only three, we take up much smaller space inside boxcar."

Mrs. Lambert described the awful smells when people couldn't hold their bowels or find water for bathing and drinking, and how babies cried nonstop from the stress of hunger and thirst. They cried and screamed until they became too exhausted even to whimper. Then they died without a sound.

"There was a time when all we had to eat was a pound of butter. We couldn't help but to shit for days and days after that."

For weeks, the train inched from town to town, stopping for an hour or two at each one, where families could spread out to beg for food or take whatever they could find: scraps meant for pigs, chicken feed, sometimes a live chicken, field rutabaga, old bread, which they soaked in water and spread with a little mustard offered up by one of the boxcar women.

"One time," said Mrs. Lambert, "we come to a town full of rubble. No people. Only broken bricks and stones and dirt everywhere. Empty town without any color. My little Basia, she find patch of grass near railroad tracks. I watch her run to that green grass and fall on her knees, her tiny hands in those bright green blades. Scouring, scouring, 'round and 'round. Laugh like a bell, so happy. She roll in them and tug a handful to nibble on. When others had something to eat and we didn't, I tell her, 'Little girl, go out and feel the grass.'

"We are lucky," said Mrs. Lambert, twisting hanks of her long, brittle hair around a finger. "My people—Romani—more than 500,000 murdered by Nazis. Out of one million. But we are lucky ones, what is left of family. We have something to eat now and fresh air to breathe when we stick nose out of boxcar.

"And we seen the green grass."

Several weeks would pass before Callie returned to the Lambert's home north of Masterton. Laura came often to the Lindstrom's to play with Cal's little dog, Tequila, and Sam Cat, and to listen to WDGY on the transistor radio while sunbathing in the back yard. Although they didn't speak of Mrs. Lambert's revelation, Callie would never forget.

The summer after eighth grade, Tola disappeared. The girls searched everywhere for her: the ravine, the dump, nearby fields. They set out a dish of milk and a can of tuna, then waited for the little cat to come home. She never did. Laura and Callie cried as hard as they would have for any friend or family member when they found Tola a week later at the far edge of the dump, shot. They wrapped her in a towel and buried her in the soft ground next to the ravine, where she used to play with the girls.

"It is only cat," said Mrs. Lambert in a harsh voice. "You girls stop crying. Be glad they not shoot people. Like my papa when he go for water."

Callie stopped crying out of shock and confusion. No one in Masterton had ever spoken to her like that. She had learned in school that people were killed under the Nazi occupation, but it was only a paragraph, a page, a chapter in their history books. It was never personal or described in such detail. Recalling what Mrs. Lambert had told her some months ago, and now learning about her friend's grandfather murdered on his way to find water, changed everything for Callie.

"That is right," continued Mrs. Lambert, pinning the girl with narrowed eyes. "Here in America, you don't know what life is like in Poland. Every day, since she's little girl, I tell my daughter many stories so she never forget how her people die in Ghetto. Papa and Mama shot like dogs in street. My sister, Marina, raped and killed, because she refuse to go with soldiers who drag her away. My brothers when they fight back, try to save Marina. All shot for trying to live. We come for new life here in America, so Laura can go to school. Her papa make sure she go to school and learn. I not let her forget."

Laura's eyes were as wide and full of terror as when she and Callie came upon those two boys about to hang Tola. "Mama," she sobbed. "Don't!"

The talking stopped. This time, Callie did not leave the boxcar. But because she didn't know what else to say, she asked, "What is *your* name, Mrs. Lambert?"

"Emma. Here, my name is Emma."

"And in Poland?"

"In Poland," she said, throwing her shoulders back, "I am Marcelina."

TIME PASSED, bringing an end to the girls' remaining years in school, highlighted by a class trip to the capitol in Saint Paul, their Junior-Senior Prom with a Tahitian theme (programs with palm trees designed by Callie), and the staging of Thornton Wilder's *Our Town*. Laura was chosen to play Emily Webb. Cal was cast as Rebecca Gibbs.

After high school graduation, Callie went away to college. Laura got a job as teller at the Prairie River Bank in Masterton.

Emily Lindstrom kept her daughter informed about the goings-on in town, especially the latest about all her friends.

"Laura has been dating a boy from Dundee," she said, "and asked us if the young man could pick her up at our house each time they go out together. She always arrives here an hour early, so we can have a nice visit beforehand. But you know, Callie, she always seems a little forlorn."

The following year, Laura and her mother moved out of the boxcar. In exchange for room and board, Mrs. Lambert worked as a companion and caregiver for the ailing wife of a prominent attorney in town. By the time the woman died and Mrs. Lambert's services were no longer needed, Laura had saved enough money to move away from Masterton.

After that, Emily and Will lost touch with them.

Callie wondered if the old boxcar was still standing.

"It is," wrote her mother, "but it's been vandalized. The last time your dad drove out to the dump, he made it a point to check on it. The door had been torn off its hinges and the insides were all broken up and strewn with beer and whiskey bottles. The boys had apparently been using the outside for target practice."

Callie imagined those parched gray timbers pocked with rifle shot. And the inside a torn up mess: the makeshift counter Mr. Lambert had hammered together for a kitchen; the vanity in Laura's bedroom; her small cot with the pink cover; the pink curtain at the window; the sections of plywood on either side of that tarnished mirror. Had all those thick colors from Callie's palette—depicting a wide ocean, soaring birds, and lush palm trees—survived?

Shortly before Cal's parents sold their home in order to move west of Minneapolis, they got a surprise visit.

"Laura is so fragile," Emily said over the phone. "Thin and very nervous. She married well—a history professor at the University. No family, but lots of cats. She takes in dozens of rescues and cares for them, I think, as if they were her children."

Callie flashed back to her friend cuddling a frantic Tola on the ground next to Mrs. Holt's clothesline pole.

"Where do they live?" she asked.

"Saint Paul. Her mother isn't well. Laura would like to get together with us. I gave her your phone number."

A month later, the three met for lunch at a café near the river between Saint Paul and Minneapolis. Callie was astonished at how thin Laura was. Her smile and laughter seemed forced and she continuously fingered the top button on her blouse. Her eyes darted about restlessly, recalling the frightened girl she used to be when the family first settled in Masterton.

When asked about her mother, she spoke instead of her many cats, barely holding back the tears. Several of them were ill and required special diets and more attention than she could sometimes muster.

"In fact, I can't stay long," she said, leaving her salad half eaten. "They need me. I have to get back to them."

The last time Callie and her mother saw Laura before she died was at her house in Saint Paul. Exhausted, she had recently placed her own mother in assisted living. The sick cats she'd been so worried about had been replaced with several more. She fretted over them as surely as one would worry about her babies. There were eleven special needs felines.

The house was clean and orderly and well equipped for her growing brood. Everything was made of wood—glowing maple floors, honey-colored walls and ceilings, pine tables and chairs with soft straw pads. Wooden gates blocked the stairwells. There were no carpets or upholstered furniture, just maple, pine, and oak, including the light fixtures, which were polished to a shine. Sitting on the kitchen counter were two framed photographs: one of Laura and Callie as young girls, taken in front of the Tilt-a-Whirl at Arnolds Park, Iowa. The other was a black and white picture of Laura when she was a child, standing next to her father and mother. It had been taken shortly after they'd arrived in New York City.

"What was your dad's name?" asked Callie. "I never knew."

"Alfons," she said. "His real name was Alfons."

Several weeks after Emily and her daughter visited Laura at her home, her husband called, late in the night.

"I didn't know she was that ill," Callie gasped, sitting bolt upright in bed and switching on the light. "What happened?"

"Cancer," he said, struggling to keep his voice even. "Esophageal. She'd suffered from acid reflux for years. I think you know she was in therapy. She had a nervous condition, could never find her equilibrium."

"I sensed that from the beginning," said Callie. "When we were young girls."

"Being around her mother didn't help," he continued. "Emma never let up with that constant diet of stories from their past. I encouraged her to get out of the house each day, be around other people, but she worried so about her cats. Didn't want to leave them. I took her to the hospital two days ago. It was a bad attack—she couldn't stand it any longer. We thought she'd make it. Just last night she was laughing with the nurses, telling them all about you and your mother and how much you both meant to her. Besides my family and her doctors, and Feline Rescue, your names are the only ones in her address book. She really loved your mother."

Callie's throat clenched and a knot gripped her stomach.

"Basia," she whispered.

"What's that?"

"I am so sorry," she murmured through her tears. "What can I do to help?"

"The funeral will be next Saturday. I hope you can come, maybe say a few words."

"We'll be there. What about Mrs. Lambert? How is she doing?"

"She hasn't been with it for quite a while. But she seemed to understand when I told her what had happened. No emotion, though."

Because it was very late, Callie waited until morning to call her mother.

"Oh, that poor girl," said Emily, her voice breaking. "That poor, poor girl."

AS CALLIE ENDED her eulogy, the sun's angle shifted away from her back and away from the coffin.

"She was my friend," Cal repeated in a strong voice, while glancing at her mother. "Basia was our dear friend."

At that, Emma Lambert quickly lifted her head with a momentary look of alarm. Then, in recognition, she gave Callie a little smile before her face clouded over again.

The funeral director approached Mrs. Lambert who stood up slowly and shuffled forward. She had hardly changed in looks since living in Masterton. Now here she was, the last survivor of her family, a woman who had made it clear to Callie what life had been like inside the Ghetto, and then inside those boxcars hooked to an engine that inched along through Eastern Poland.

How ironic that Laura had finished growing up in a second boxcar— the one north of Masterton—constantly reminded of the beatings and starvation, the shootings and the gas chambers. How fortunate they were, her mother kept reminding Laura, to live in a free country, where there were endless expanses of grass. Oceans of green grass, where they could get down on their hands and knees and run their fingers through the lush green grass, and "where you girls can spread out a blanket to play with your dolls and take a sunbath."

Mrs. Lambert stooped over the casket and tenderly kissed her daughter's face—a kiss on each cheek and one on the forehead. Then she stepped back and watched the funeral director close the lid. Laura's husband held onto the old woman's arm to steady her as they followed the coffin out of the church.

"She carried a heavy burden, that girl," said Emily, placing her arm around Callie's shoulders as they approached their car in the parking lot. "I'm so glad she had a good friend in you, Cal."

"And you, Mom. If it hadn't been for you and Dad . . ."

"Some of the people back home were terribly hard on that family. We all could have done better by them."

As they lined up behind the hearse, Callie recalled the big black vehicle that occasionally ghosted through Masterton. She and Laura were children back then, laughing and swinging high in the sky from the playground behind the Catholic church.

"I'm glad you mentioned her real name, Cal."

"Basia."

On their way to the cemetery, the two women spoke once again about the fate of Masterton's Polish Romano family.

"I wonder how many in our town knew the truth about them," said Emily. "Alfons, Marcelina, and Basia Sobol."

Several weeks after the funeral, Callie and her mother traveled to Masterton to visit their old neighborhood: the house on Norwood Avenue, where Cal had grown up and played with her friends and with her little dog, Tequila, and Sammy Cat; the streets where she'd roller-skated with Danny, and taken long walks with her father; the giant willow tree in the back yard where Cal and Laura used to perch on high with their bags of library books.

Finally, they visited the boxcar where Laura and her parents had lived all those years ago. Heading north, Callie and her mother turned off the highway onto the same dirt road they'd walked together several decades earlier.

The old dumpsite had been cleared and covered with earth and large patches of green grass. Parched weeds clustered around the collapsed boxcar, by now a tottery, worn out structure that looked like some strange animal fallen to its knees. And yet, there remained an element of stubborn strength among those gray boards that hadn't completely collapsed or been shot through with bullets and pocked by twenty-twos.

The two women circled the building and peeked through wide cracks in the timbers. There, at the rear, was Laura's old bedroom. The chest of drawers and cot were gone. Shards of mirror lay on the floor and on top of the vanity that her father had built long ago. A shred of pink curtain, faded to nearly white and snagged on the jagged edges of a broken windowpane, fluttered in the soft breeze.

"Mom, look!" Callie cried out.

They stood with their faces close together, eyes fixed on what was left of Callie's painting. Most of the colors had been scraped away, but you could still see the outlines of palm trees and a little of the green-blue sea.

16

Eavesdropper

We owe those who pass, not grief, but gratitude.
—*Thornton Wilder*

SPLASHES OF COLOR are rare in the dead of winter, especially within a snow-filled cemetery. But once a year, some mystery person waded through deep drifts at Hilltop in order to place a red rose on Helga Hoffman's grave.

Who could have been trekking through the snow each winter to insert the long stem of a bright red rose next to Helga's marker? She had no children or living relatives, and her husband had died years earlier.

Speculation about this sort of *homage*, unlike the stories about the Lambert family, and Lucie Moulin and Selmer Johnson, provided small town residents with little more than brief conversations.

Surprisingly, some of the goings-on around Masterton and neighboring communities had little gas to go on, such as Helga's annual red rose. For whatever reason, folks held to a *laissez-faire* approach for several incidents that might otherwise have exploded in other towns—the popular high school Latin teacher from Chandler, for instance, who married a former student, turned alcoholic, and drove his young wife nuts. Or she drove him crazy. In any case, stories like that remained mostly off limits, relegated to a nod of the head or discussions reserved for private coteries and confidants with little more to learn other than how the insidious effects of alcoholism spread outward in concentric circles, dizzying everyone in their ranges.

Callie could attest to that. Just drop a pebble (or in some cases, a boulder from the stratosphere) into a lake and watch those turbulent rings take off nonstop, until they reach a shoreline, leaving human debris bouncing around in their wakes. The lucky ones wash up on shore hefting tattered life jackets.

Other episodes around town did blow wide open, spouting details like a volcano spewing ash, as with Carl and Ruby Ryan, and Everett and Thelma Christensen. Because Carl went public, in part due to the self-confidence he'd gained, thanks to the weekly Dale Carnegie courses, nearly every detail sallied forth for all to know, surmise, and raise their eyebrows at. Over the years a lot of people around town acquired tell-tale furrows in their foreheads, including the Latin teacher's wife who wasted no time jumping into other people's swamps—likely, in part, to deflect attention from her own pit of potential quicksand. Eventually, she was able to leap in and help others after her own experiences had become concentric enough to create a survivor.

The best stories that blossomed, flourished, and gained momentum in Masterton were far-reaching in an exotically instructive way, like the one about Lucie, Selmer Johnson's Parisian lady. Despite the gossip, there was much to learn from this story. Callie supposed the idea of hooking far-flung topics, as from another country, assured safe distance—those human subjects at the center of matters that piqued creative curiosity couldn't easily show up in order to protest and set their records straight. Either they lived too far away from Masterton or they were dead.

If anyone knew the truth about Helga Hoffman, they were keeping it to themselves. Not that it mattered, in Callie's estimation. Hooray for Helga if she had an admirer. But unlike the intrigue about Lucie Moulin, Mrs. Hoffman's ended after a total of two or three sentences and a shrug of the shoulders. Whoever had planted a rose on Helga's grave each winter must have finally succumbed to his (or her) own long sleep. Callie wondered if anyone in town had paired a local death with the first January when the burst of red failed to appear atop that mound of snow at Hilltop Cemetery.

WILL LINDSTROM stretched and yawned. "I must have dozed off. That warm sun sure felt good. Knocked me right out."

Callie glanced through the side window toward the west. "Won't be long now, 'til sunset. "

"And the full moon," said Will. "I'm eager to get back to Emily. Don't like being away from my better half for too long."

"I'm excited to see Piper, too. He's such a great little dog. Great company." Callie switched on the radio and found a jazz station. "Whew! This is a long drive."

"You doing all right, Cal? After all, you're the one behind the wheel."

"I'm fine. Heaven knows I'm not at a loss for things to think about. I *would* like to stop for a bite to eat, though. How about you? Are you hungry?"

"Yes, I could go for a hamburger—and a basket of French fries. Oh, and a chocolate malt would sure taste good. Let's see if we can spot a joint along the way. And Callie, whenever you get tired of driving, just pull over and I can take a turn."

"You didn't renew your driver's license, though. Remember?"

"The hell with that. I can spell you for a bit. There's not much traffic."

"I don't think so, Pops.

"Well, at least we can stretch our legs, look around for a while. I'd like to take in that full moon tonight, the minute she inches up over the horizon, and starts to show her face. No more cemeteries, though. I've had my fill of 'em, at least for the time being."

The gravelly voice of Louis Armstrong came on the car radio. He played his trumpet and sang "We Have All The Time In The World."

PEOPLE TAKE FOR GRANTED that the dead get gravestones. Even the huddle of babies, who lived no more than a day, a week, a month, or a year, got markers. Most were without names, but at least they got a stone. Never a soul in Masterton, as far as Callie knew, was denied a tombstone for any reason, except, perhaps in the case of a drowning. Even then someone might twine a wooden cross together and plant it on a shore. And if marines and soldiers were lost at sea or on a foreign battlefield, white marble crosses sprang up like cornstalks, in perfect rows, right down to the diagonal.

If need be, church members took up a collection, as for Mr. Lambert, Laura's father. But that was unusual, because most families were too proud to accept aid, and would go without in order to set the stage for that final curtain drop: the installation of a tombstone. In Mrs. Lambert's case, however, it made perfect sense, for she had already gone without for most of her life.

Everyone Cal knew of had a marker, except Uncle Amer, back in Rockford. And that she hoped would change. After all the years of growing up, hearing Amer's story, reading his letters, knowing how hard he had worked to make a life for himself in Eastern Montana, Callie clung to the idea that her dad would rethink their visit to the Swedish Cemetery and suggest ordering a stone, which, in itself would be monumental, given that he'd have to come to terms with the fact that Uncle Amer was gay. Although his reaction was far less caustic than that of his cousins, Callie could sense that it was an idea with which her father struggled.

Moreover, he had visibly become tired of undertaking many of life's simpler and more pleasant tasks like rearranging his tackle box, lining up bait, and organizing the Crestliner for an early morning outing on Cook's Bay. Their talks and silent understandings were no longer as profuse as in old times. With Will in his eighties and battling melanoma, they had come to a place where long stretches of silence became interspersed with fond and sometimes not so fond reminiscences—such as long-ago Sundays on their farm near Hadley.

"Folks came calling unannounced in those days," said Will. "From the living room window, Dad would shout out to Mother, 'Better kill another chicken, Julia. Here come the Brewsters!'"

Mr. and Mrs. Brewster, along with their four children, occasionally drove up the lane after church, just in time for noon dinner.

"If it was too late to dress out another chicken, Mother would tell Ray and me to take a wing from the platter. She and my dad would split the neck and share the back."

"Who ate the breast meat?"

"The Brewsters. Legs and thighs went to their children—the oldest snatched up the wishbone from his mother's plate."

Callie recalled how her own mother had taught her to link a pinky on one side of a slender wishbone while Emily curled her little finger round the other. Sometimes, Cal was too eager to make a wish and her mom would say, "Not yet. We have to let the bone dry first. Otherwise, it won't snap. Patience, dear girl, patience."

"Didn't the Brewsters ever bring a dish to pass? Or phone ahead that they were coming?" Callie asked her father now.

"Nope. Not everyone had a telephone in those days. But that kind of thing happened all the time back then. Not so much now. She always helped with the dishes, though, Mrs. Brewster did."

With the door closed on that story, Will let loose with a few unrelated comments (mini-lectures, in Cal's estimation), left over from the 1940s and into the 50s, such as how speed wears down the tires and wastes gasoline.

"Our entire country had to ration during the war. Not only gas, but tires. That's why the national speed limit was set at 35 miles per hour. Folks should still be able to take a lesson from that period. Slow down!"

"I remember the sign you posted in our garage back in Masterton: "Is this Trip Necessary?"

"And there was another one attached to gas pumps: "When you ride ALONE you ride with Hitler! Join a Car-Sharing Club TODAY!"

"Whoa! That's a tough one."

"You see, the Japanese took over rubber plantations in the East Indies, so our government warned us that if our tires wore out and couldn't be replaced, the war effort would come to a halt, ending in a win for Hitler."

"I do understand where you're coming from, Dad, but we're living in the 80s now, and a lot has changed—synthetic rubber tires, for instance."

"I don't care. All that was ingrained in my generation. So let me remind you, Cal, always check the oil and tire pressure before driving off. And be sure to leave your car in the garage if your errands are within walking distance."

"And what would that limit be?"

"A couple three miles." Will leaned over from the passenger seat for a peek at the speedometer. "Better slack up, Cal. Haste makes waste."

Although she was tempted to floor the foot feed, Callie complied by lowering her speed from sixty to fifty-five.

"How fast could your old Pontiac go, Dad? Any faster than this slow tub?"

"A fine car, that one. Lots of chrome and white-wall tires. I think she could go pretty fast—up to a hundred on the speedometer, but I generally kept her under fifty-five. Traded the Nash for it, you know, the one that dropped its gas tank.

Callie remembered the outside visor on their black 1950 Silver Streak 8; it ran across the entire windshield with a spotlight at the side. And then there was that Chief Pontiac hood ornament centered above headlights that meant business. The grill reminded Cal of the braces on the teeth of a boy in her junior high class. Whenever he chomped into a California burger, shreds of lettuce stuck in the metal. With a broad grin, he'd exhibit his own silver grill with hanging greens. Then he'd dance the Twist, waggling his meaty behind for all to see.

The car's rear end looked strange too, like something moseying down the street with an extra set of hips slapped onto the sides. It was a four-door sedan with bench seats and small triangular windows next to the main roll-downs. In the back seat, on the left side, Will had pasted a sticker from their family trip to Manitoba on the triangular glass—a picture of a grazing buffalo that Callie studied on their way home from Canada, and then to and from Lake Shetek, and then late at night before falling asleep, stretched out on that long seat, on their way home from Aunt Hazel and Uncle Cecil's farm near Lake Wilson. She loved that buffalo.

Cal's favorite memory about the Pontiac was driving it down a country road at age six. Will had hoisted her onto his lap, ran the foot feed, and let Callie steer.

Now, on their way home from the Swedish Cemetery, he alternately kept one eye on the Cadillac's speedometer, dozed off, glanced absentmindedly at the scenery, and continued talking about old times— times when he was still firmly entrenched in the big picture. Times when he even participated in a few raucous stories, one of which, long ago, Callie wasn't supposed to hear, even though, as a little girl, she was usually invited to join Will and his friends down the basement of their home in Masterton, while they plucked and singed game birds or cleaned fish, while listening to a baseball game or big band music on the radio. When they were finished, the men filled their pipes or lit up cigarettes. Sometimes, they smoked fresh cigars, presenting Callie with the paper rings, which she wore on her fingers. When the rings tore, she taped the ends together so she could continue wearing them. Eventually, due to age and sweat and washing her hands, they fell apart, reminding Cal of the sopping wet chewed ends of Mr. Claussen's cigars.

One evening, when Callie was ten, she eavesdropped from around the corner in the basement. The radio had been turned down low, the ducks were gutted and singed, and the conversation among the three men took such a turn that Will sent Callie off to bed early.

Instead, suspecting a tale reserved for adults, she tiptoed back down the basement stairway, planted herself on the second step from the bottom, circled the gift of a paper ring around her index finger, and pricked up her ears to a most shocking story as told by their neighbor,

Mr. Claussen: it was about Bud Gleason, originally from Masterton, and a friend of his, named Louie March. After high school, Bud ran off to the Twin Cities and turned wild.

His kid brother, Curtis, was just the opposite—studious, political, lawyer-like. By the time Curt Gleason, two years older than Callie, entered high school, he was elected president of the student council, which consisted of all boys. In private, several of the girls, including Cal, said that he acted like a mean judge. Or a Nazi.

Curtis Gleason urged the council members to vote for a dress code ruling he'd composed, which applied to girls only. He then convinced the administration to back it up with punishment. The code stated that all girls must wear skirts or dresses to school and on school property, except during physical education classes, at which time they were allowed to wear shorts in the gymnasium.

Slacks and jeans were not allowed, even in the depth of winter.

The town girls, walking to school barelegged in sub-zero temperatures, eventually contracted chill blains and frozen patches that mapped their skin. Until Doc Dohms and her parents got involved, Callie had been sent home several times during January and February, ordered by the principal to change into a dress, then forced to stay after school for having worn jeans those mornings.

Doc Dohms finally met with the school board to inform them that he had been treating too many girls at the clinic, whose legs were frostbitten, some seriously. After that it was decided that they could wear slacks beneath their dresses, but would have to remove them as soon as they entered the school building and arrived at their lockers. When Callie, afraid of being tardy one morning, rushed into class without having removed her jeans, she was compelled to stay after school, not only for that, but for sassing the teacher and the principal, because she still felt bitterly cold.

The girls of that era had been forced to establish what would become popular many years later: "the layered look"—headscarf, jacket, sweater, skirt, pants, leggings, kickerinos.

One day, Callie had to stay after school for an hour, because she'd been caught swiveling her hips in the hallway while removing her jacket and slacks, laughing and prancing around like Mamie Van Doren.

But back to Curt's brother Bud: because Mr. Claussen was certain his audience consisted only of Will and another neighbor, Mr. Ryan, the language that went into its telling left Callie agog, shocked by the shift in Mr. Claussen's word choices, and, at the same time, somewhat inspired. A decade later, she would make up her own version, using many of those vulgar phrases that had spilled from the teller's mouth. She filled in a few gaps, modernized the details—especially the boat and motor central to the story—and added a tackle box full of embellishments. She even made up a title for this new yarn: "A Lunker for Louie."

While Will dozed, Callie continued driving northward, from La Crosse toward Red Wing, recalling the tale she'd inflated all those years ago, on the back of Mr. Claussen's account. Because the language ended up being cruder than her parents would have tolerated, she'd kept this version to herself. However, one day, she gave it to her sister to read, in part because Liz knew Bud, who had graduated a year ahead of her.

"Hey, Cal, I like this story a lot," said Liz. "I have to say, though, it is a bit vulgar. But now that I think about it, that's how Bud was, even back in high school. Didn't he have a brother?"

"Yeah, Curtis, a defense lawyer in Minneapolis. Quite successful, from what I understand, specializing in murder trials."

"Well, the only time I ever hung out with Bud," said Liz, "was the night he drove a bunch of us out to the middle of Lake Shetek for a spin on the ice. He had one of those beautiful two-toned Chevys, turquoise and cream, and when he got too close to The Narrows, the front end started to go down. He grabbed his six-packs and we all jumped out just in time and raced to shore. Bud was so mad when he lost that car! All he could do was cry and get drunk. The six of us stood watching it sink, imagining what it might have been like to be trapped inside."

"How come you never said anything about that?" asked Cal. "You never told me. Did you tell Mom and Dad?"

"Nope. But they certainly would have known if I'd told you."

If that was the kind of thing Bud did, thought Callie, taking a chance with his precious car loaded with teenagers skimming along on thin ice, spinning round and round in circles, then that next yarn, regarding his boat, might be true as well.

As for the ending—who knows?

17

A Lunker for Louie

By
Callandra Mae Lindstrom

"FOR CHRIS'SAKE, STOP PISSIN' in the wind," shouted Bud. "I ain't got no towel back here."

"Sorry!" Louie March zipped his fly just as the boat sliced through a large wave that forced him to sit down. Huddled in his parka, he squinted at Bud through an early November dusk. "Hey, toss me another brewski, will ya?"

Bud Gleason, steering his boat through a heavy chop, reached into the cooler, threw a can to Louie, snapped open the beer he held gripped between his knees, and grinned, pleased with himself. He cast an eye on the darkening lake, proud that even when a little drunk he could sense approaching waves and cut through them before they broadsided his trusty fishing rig.

"Check your line, guy, I think ya got somethin'," he called out between gulps of Schlitz, his favorite beer.

Bud slowed the engine and looked closely at the yellow fluorescent line angling into deep water, bending the upper half of Louie's rod.

"Easy, now. Don't horse him in."

"Yeah, no problem. I got him." Tension rose in Louie's voice as his heart beat faster. He had fished only a few times prior to going out in Bud's boat, always without luck. "I'll land this sucker if it's the last thing I do."

Bud, hoping to see his buddy catch a big one, reached for the landing net. "Easy does it, pal. Play him out now."

Too soon, Louie jerked his rod straight up. The line went limp. He couldn't see the look of disappointment on Bud's face.

"Hell, you're too damned impatient, Louie. How many times do I have to tell ya. They bite soft at first."

"Yeah, shit. I just got excited."

"You gotta let him run with it."

"Wish I coulda seen what it was."

"Well, next time let him travel awhile before you reel up the slack and set the hook." Bud guzzled the rest of his beer and smacked his lips. "You'll get the hang of it."

NOVEMBER NIGHTS come down early and cold over Minnesota's lakes. Fresh water fish—walleyed and northern pike—become siren songs, especially on Mille Lacs, a magical lake that summons fishermen with the promise of big ones. Lots of them.

Clouds scudded across the sky to disappear in the drop-down dark. Bud flipped on the boat's stern light and focused on a cluster of distant beacons along the southwestern shore. Every time he motored out, Bud remembered what old Jake Cooper, owner of the Ruddy Duck Saloon on the western shore of Mille Lacs, had told him the first time he'd fished this lake:

"At night fall," he'd said, "you don't want to get caught without a light from shore to help you navigate. Make sure you've got flares and a reliable anchor. When the wind blows on Mille Lacs, it whips up the ghosts . . . you don't want to end up bein' one of 'em."

That was the time when, out back of the Ruddy Duck, Jake had put on a fish fry for everyone in the bar. All of the regulars had had a hand in it, pooling their catch, which Bud helped clean. Jake dredged the filets in a mixture of corn meal, flour, and a dash of salt, then deep-fat-fried them over an open fire. Those golden brown filets were the best pike Bud had ever eaten. And he'd eaten a lot of fish in his thirty years of life.

"We don't give a damn where the hot grease spits!" Jake had announced, waving his spatula around like a cowboy twirling a lariat. "Fish! That's what we're here for, ain't that right, guys?"

"Huzza! Yippee!! Fuckin' right! Hey, hey! Hear, hear! You called it, Jake, old buddy!!"

Mostly men, plus a few women, raised their tall, dripping bottles and cans of beer, shoulder-butted whoever stood next to them, and cheered. Anyone would have thought they were watching a Vikings game.

STEAM ROSE in the cold night air as Bud peed into an empty beer can at the stern of his boat and poured the contents overboard.

"Gotta get serious here," he said, wiping his hands on the oily rag kept under the seat.

"Yeah, we can't go back skunked," chimed Louie. "Hell, we'll stay out all night if we have to."

Bud gulped a fresh beer, tossed both cans into a cooler of mostly empties, and zipped up his jacket. Running his fingers over the puffy thermal fabric decorated with a dozen fishing contest patches, he felt warm and happy, remembering all of the trips he'd made in this brown jacket, and the prized fish he'd caught from his rig. No one could separate Bud from his lucky fishing jacket—or from his boat and motor.

The motor was almost too powerful for his rig, but that's the way Bud liked it. The engine, a Max Mercury 125, hung like a black monolith strapped to the narrow transom of his eighteen-footer. Bud had fiddled with the tilt and figured out just how far he could up the throttle before the boat dug in and threatened to take on water over the freeboard.

A long time ago, his dad had shown him how to allow for weight and speed and the roll of back wash against the fortified stern. Bud had swamped his boat one summer afternoon before he came to terms with the mighty engine and the fact that it required a gradual slow-down instead of a sudden halt. Yes, he had definitely made the transition from teen-ager to adult.

Bud had finally figured out the sweet spot—like the perfect balance on a surfboard; it depended on the correct positioning of everyone and their gear in order to keep the wake at bay. It was tricky sometimes, especially with a big guy like Louie.

BUD AND LOUIE had met at McGinty's Pub in St. Paul. They and their wives were among the regulars who hung out on Friday and Saturday nights, as well as Sunday afternoons and Monday nights during football season. A large-screen television blared from one end of a long bar ringed milky from drinks and scarred black by forgotten cigarettes. A newcomer at McGinty's would most certainly smell stale beer and urine as soon as he pushed open the door.

The place was home-sweet-home to the regulars.

Between games, they talked mostly fishing: crank baits, graphite rods, spin reels, powerful motors, sexy boats, sexy babes, and the best lakes for bass or walleyes.

Bored, the wives eventually stopped going to McGinty's, which was okay with Louie, especially since a couple of cute twenty-somethings had started showing up at the bar. He liked to stare at their bulging halter-tops and low-rider jeans. It excited him the way they flipped their silky blond hair, then screamed and grabbed at the nearest guy whenever the Vikings scored.

"Hell, dude," Louie said through a mouth full of greasy onion rings, "we might be headin' for our fourth down but we ain't outa bounds yet." He looked down at his fly. "Ol' Junior here's still got a good passin' arm."

Bud slapped Louie on the back. Beer splashed onto the bar as the men guffawed themselves off their stools.

"WE AIN'T HAVIN' much luck trolling," said Bud, reeling in his line. "Too damned windy. I'm gonna shut 'er down and drift 'til we get to a spot I know of."

"All right by me." Louie belched, sounding like a peal of distant thunder.

"Get ready to dump anchor."

Louie quickly drained his beer, tossed the can overboard, and began working the anchor release until yards of rope slipped through his stiff fingers.

"All set!" he shouted. "Toss me another brew."

"Why don't you drink from your own damn cooler?"

"Hell, I polished those off an hour ago. C'mon, Bud, you've got another six-pack back there. Maybe we ought to break open the schnapps. It's gettin' to be kinda cold out here in the dark."

"Here ya go—a double-fisted catch." Two cans landed with a clunk in front of Louie. "That oughta hold ya."

"Shouldn't shake up a good beer like that." Louie stashed one can in his jacket pocket and snapped open the other. He sucked up the foam, took a long swallow, and squinted into the black night. "Jeez, I can't see a fuckin' thing out there."

"The stern light's on," said Bud. "Work off the rear. How about if I go with crank bait and you try a leech and bobber?"

"Okay by me."

"Got any bobbers in your tackle box?"

"Yeah, I got a good bobber right here." Louie tried to sound like Jack Nicholson. "If ya know what I mean."

Bud laughed. "Christ, talk about a one-track mind."

"Well, hey, that was one hot mama back there at the Ruddy Duck... maybe we oughta go back pretty soon."

Bud got Louie started with a leech and fluorescent bobber, then cast his own line, neatly placing his jig far from the boat; he let it lay there for a few seconds before reeling it in with quick, jerky turns.

After a quarter of an hour and no luck, Bud said, "That's enough of this bullshit. Let's pull anchor. Head on in."

Louie reeled up his line. "Lost my leech, anyway," he said, making an effort to stand up. He fumbled with his zipper, then stood precariously near the gunwale, raising the lake level by another pint.

Bud leaned over to clamp the lid down on his tackle box and stow loose gear for the beat back to shore.

"Is it up?" he asked, ready to start the engine.

"Sure as hell will be. And damn soon."

Bud couldn't see the go-get-'em grin pasted on Louie's face as he zipped his fly and turned to reach for the anchor line. After hauling in only a few feet of rope, an idea came to Louie: he let go of the long line, paid it back out, and reset the guard. He'd always wondered what would happen under such conditions.

"All set? You ready?" asked Bud, starting the engine.

"Sure thing!" Louie grabbed hold of the V gunwales and smirked into the dark like a brat up to no good.

"Okay! Here we go!" Bud opened throttle and charged full speed ahead. The boat plowed forward for a few seconds, then lurched to a violent halt, twisting around like the prey in a wild dog's jaws. Louie hung on, but the unexpected jolt threw Bud overboard.

With the anchor as fulcrum, the boat roared around in circles. Each time she found the spot where Bud tried to stay afloat there came a loud thud and clunking noise.

"Oh Jesus, Bud! Oh Christ! Oh my God!" wailed Louie, frozen to his forward seat.

The anchor had hooked itself to the bottom of the lake, lodged among hefty boulders. Around and around went Louie, screaming into the wind, sickened by the intermittent chopping sounds of the propeller, shredding Bud to pieces.

Overcoming his shock, Louie lurched toward the stern, sprawling along the bottom of the boat, feet tangled in the landing net and bouncing tackle boxes. He clutched at the rear seat where Bud had sat just moments before, reached up, and turned the key.

The circling stopped. It was suddenly quiet—quiet but for the slapping of waves against the drunken boat.

For a moment, Louie sat with his face in his hands. "Oh, my God, what have I done?" Then he grabbed the starboard gunwale, got onto his knees, and screamed over the water, "Buuud! Buuuuud!"

The wind howled back at him.

Then from the dark, he heard a voice: "Help me into the God-damned boat, you *fucking* asshole!"

Freaking out, Louie fell forward against the gunwale. He rubbed his eyes and spotted Bud thrashing and kicking towards the boat.

"Oh, Jesus, Bud, you're alive!" Louie began laughing hysterically, in wheezing spasms. "Thank God, you're alive!"

He grabbed an oar and stretched it out as far as he could. Bud clutched at the blade and held on while Louie drew him in. The boat pitched and threatened to capsize as Louie tugged at his friend. In the struggle, Bud's jacket slipped off and floated away.

"Oh, man, your good-luck jacket."

"Never mind. Just get me the fuck into the friggin' boat. I'm dying out here."

It took long minutes to haul Bud in. He wasn't so tall or heavy, but when he kicked his legs and leaned on the gunwale, Louie had to shift to portside and still hang on to Bud's wrists in order to keep him from slipping back into the lake.

Finally, he landed him, and the two men lay on the bottom of the boat, moaning and gasping like muskellunges. When they were able to sit, Louie helped Bud out of his wet clothes, and offered him his own parka. He uncapped the bottle of schnapps, held it to Bud's lips. Then he took a long pull for himself.

"Jeez, I thought you were a gonner, ol' buddy," said Louie, shivering and wiping his mouth on the sleeve of his flannel shirt. "What was that clunking sound? Every time we circled around . . ."

"Me, asshole! Kickin' the God-damned boat! Why didn't you pull up the fucking anchor when I told you to?"

"I'm sorry. I was just foolin' around, playin' a little joke on you."

"You son of a bitch!" Bud's teeth were chattering so hard he could barely talk. "I'm gonna beat the crap outa you as soon as we get back to shore." He tried to stand. "Here's a taste of what you're gonna get, you God-damned fucker!"

The boat rocked unsteadily as Bud threw a weak punch, missed, and sat back with a lurch. Louie crept forward and struggled with the anchor rope; the entire line had threaded out and the anchor was stuck.

"I can't get it up, Bud! It must be wedged between some rocks!"

"Cut the damned thing."

Louie pulled a pocketknife from his jeans, open it, and severed the anchor line.

"Nothin' left but this little prick of a rope," he said, holding up the remains. "Christ, what will they say at the Ruddy Duck? And, at McGinty's when we get home?"

"Not a God-damned word . . . that's what, 'cause you're gonna keep your fucking mouth shut, you idiot!"

The engine was idling, ready to take off. In spite of his anger, Bud remembered to zero in on the familiar lights flickering along the distant shore. And because he was angry and had lost his jacket and anchor and new rope, he gave it the gun. Spray flew in all directions as the boat pounded through wave after cresting wave.

Louie hung on, teeth chattering, his pale fingers curled around the gunwales. Above the roar of the engine, he could hear Bud swearing at him, his voice pitched in a fierce staccato that carried across the lake, screaming until he choked and gagged and couldn't utter another sound.

Louie figured the shouting would help keep Bud warm, so he sat and silently took his due, his face and knuckles the color of whitecaps. He would wait until they reached the dock to apologize, then he'd buy him a couple of drinks at the Ruddy Duck. Maybe that girl would be there.

As Bud held a steady speed, he replayed the disaster in his mind. It had seemed like hours, but only a few minutes had passed while he kicked at the boat each time it circled toward him like a phantom out of the dark. He'd had to listen for the approaching motor and time his lunges, launching himself off the stern and away from the propeller. But the waves kept pushing him back. If it hadn't been for his jacket bulging with trapped air, he'd have gone down. Even so, he had felt himself growing numb from the cold water, nearly ready to give in to hypothermia after the third pass. That's when Louie finally got the bright idea to turn off the engine.

Bud, now gunning the boat fast and hard, settled into a groove and watched the cluster of welcoming lights get closer and closer. He couldn't wait to get into warm, dry clothes and throw back a couple of hot buttered rums.

As for Louie? Bud would soak him good. And if Louie were ever to catch a lunker, it would have to be from someone else's boat.

Just then, two monstrous rogue waves angled in, one after the other, and broadsided the boat. If Bud had seen them coming, he might have had time to turn the bow into those mountains of ice-cold steely black and white liquid. But angry as he was, soaked and freezing, his teeth chattering like a steady drum roll, and wanting to be rid of that joker perched in the bow, he'd kept his eyes on the shore instead—on those warm, welcoming neon lights that would fade come morning.

18

Frozen on the Hoof

There are as many pillows of illusion as flakes in a snow-storm.
We wake from one dream into another dream.
—Ralph Waldo Emerson

EN ROUTE HOME, Callie gave her father a shortened version (minus the indelicate language) of that tale she called "A Lunker for Louie." He said he remembered something like it years ago, when his friend, Mr. Claussen, told about a couple of young guys, one from Masterton, who had drowned in Lake Mille Lacs back in the mid-1950s.

"As I recall, Claussen's account was a little too spicy for your ears, Cal. You were just a kid back then."

"Did they ever find them? Bud and Louie?"

"I don't know. That lake isn't very deep, so it would stand to reason they'd eventually rise to the surface. Lakes like that one usually give up their dead, especially in summer."

"I wonder where they're buried."

"On second thought, it could have been a watery grave for that pair, considering they went down in November. All those long winter months with ice cover, on into April. Who knows what they found come summer? If anything."

Callie gripped the steering wheel and stared at the long road ahead. She remembered what that man from out West had told them one night while they were sitting around a campfire near Leech Lake on a chilly summer's evening, just outside of Federal Dam. Callie was poking at the hot coals, watching the sparks fly. Her parents had become agitated when John Delmore started talking about his job diving for submerged boats and motors—and bodies: ". . . like any lake, you don't fool with Tahoe . . . Leech is shallow . . . dangerous in a high wind. Tahoe runs deep and doesn't like to give up its dead. When the bodies do surface, *if* they surface, they're unrecognizable. All of the soft tissue is gone. Oh, the fish and turtles do have a feast."

Shivering at those comments and at the memory of her mother abruptly leaving the bonfire and rushing back into their camper, Callie inadvertently pressed down on the foot feed.

Will leaned over to eyeball the speedometer, then settled back against his seat. "How're we doing for gas?"

"Still half a tank. I think we can make it home on that. But we'll see."

"Sure is pretty around here."

In the late afternoon sunlight, a small pond north of Red Wing shimmered like the translucent green of a fresh dragonfly wing. Surrounding the pond, dry, colorless stalks left over from recently harvested cornfields bent as if bowing to one another.

"We should be out there hunting pheasants, Cal. With all that water and loose corn on the ground, heck, we'd fill out in no time. Lucky for my brother and me that our dad decided to leave Illinois and come up here to lake country—for the hunting and fishing, along with the farming. Yes indeed, I've been a fortunate man to live my whole life here in God's Country.

"Except for the winters."

"Well, yes. But on either side of those, I'd say . . ."

"Remember the blizzards? How you had to shovel the car out so we could make it back home from Aunt Hazel and Uncle Cecil's farm?"

"Those were quite the times, weren't they? You were just a kid."

"And nothing could make you leave your seat at that Pinochle table next to the woodstove. Not even a storm."

"I had my eye on the weather. You may not have noticed, but your mother and I . . ."

"Oh, c'mon, Dad. Don't you remember? Once we got started through those drifts, Mom was so upset, she belched all the way back to Masterton."

"Quite the times. I told her, 'Emily, have a little faith in me. We'll make it through. You know we always do.' Course, I was pretty confident back then. And a bit more agile."

Callie pointed from left to right across the windshield, as if she were tracing a big screen. "I can still picture you out there in the middle of a blizzard, shoveling like crazy to get the car unstuck, your storm coat whipping in the wind. Seems like we always stayed too long at the farm, 'cause some nights it took us nearly two hours to drive the ten miles home. I thought we were all going to die out there, along with the cattle."

"No, no, I'd never let that happen, Cal."

HEAVY SNOW AND A WHISTLING WIND circled the old farmhouse as night came down. Icy air seeped through its seams. The four adults inside failed to take notice.

The women (Callie's mother and aunt) had paired up against the men (her dad and uncle) for marathon hands of pinochle at a card table next to the piping hot Acme Queen wood stove, the only source of heat throughout the two-story pine board house.

Every other Sunday, Will drove his black 1950 Pontiac to Aunt Hazel and Uncle Cecil's farm north of Lake Wilson. Aunt Hazel was a relative who'd converted to Catholicism in order to marry Cecil who loved dogs and was kind to the family. Hazel, however, seemed allergic to animals and still treated Callie as if she were totally responsible for Emily's difficulties giving birth eight years earlier.

In retrospect, before the age of detailed forecasts and country snowplows, the ten-mile drive from Masterton was a risky venture in southwestern Minnesota, renowned for its pocket of heavy weather sock-ins.

Cal's sister, Liz, a junior in high school, was given the option of staying home. Callie wanted to stay back too, but Liz convinced their mother that she wouldn't be able to look after "the little brat" what with all she needed to do—mainly "studying" with friends.

This particular Sunday started out in typical fashion—a sunny afternoon drive to the farm under mackerel skies and mares' tails, a roast chicken supper, and the usual pinochle games that began after the dishes were done. The card playing lasted long after a test pattern would have come on the screen of a television set, if there'd been one inside the old farmhouse.

With nothing to do and no one to play with, Callie plopped down in the sitting room and bounced for a while on the easy chair with coiled springs, her legs not quite reaching the floor.

The glow of lamplight shown on the onyx black panther that paced stealthily along the small buffet. On the wall above, hung a picture of an Indian warrior astride a horse that stood with all four feet tight together. In the falling night and isolated on a hilltop, surrounded by the bitter cold, they seemed to be caving in on themselves. To Callie, they looked like a fragile triangle—the dying Indian and his horse.

Cal shivered and pulled a green and gold knitted afghan from the back of the couch, wrapped it around her shoulders, and began fiddling with the record player set up next to her chair.

She found two black vinyls that Uncle Cecil had placed next to the vintage turntable—first, some man named Tex Williams with a cowboy voice, singing "Smoke! Smoke! Smoke! (That Cigarette . . .)" Then she played the second record: "Serenade of the Bells," sung in the pretty voice of Jo Stafford, about how a gay *señor* and a gay *señorita* in the sleepy town of San Juanita would be allowed to marry only if the broken mission bells began to ring. Callie played both songs over and over, until she'd memorized the lyrics.

While singing "Smoke! Smoke! Smoke! (That Cigarette)," alternating with "Serenade of the Bells," Callie left the sitting room to wander through the wind- and snow-battered frame house, inhaling the lingering smells of supper, and taking notice of country habits as compared to town life: flowery wallpaper pasted to the dining room walls with a flour/water mixture; baited mousetraps in the kitchen corners; teaspoons standing upright in a jelly jar; a pipe-curled ringlet of sticky flypaper still hanging above the kitchen table, even though fly season was long gone. The mousetraps made sense, especially at the first signs of winter, but the flypaper? Midwestern winters shut down most insect and some animal life, either killing them off or forcing them into hibernation. Callie counted six dead flies still attached to the amber-colored glue—the same number as during her last visit several weeks ago.

Will had told her about when he was a boy and had a threshing crew out on their farm. His mother and several other women had been cooking for a week in order to feed the men. "The flies were so thick that day," he said, "there was no meringue left on the lemon pies."

Suddenly, over the sounds of the storm, Cal heard a scratching noise at the door and a desperate whining. It was Sport, Uncle Cecil's Border Collie. Just as she opened the door and called out to him, Aunt Hazel rushed into the kitchen looking and sounding the only way she ever appeared to Callie—like a churlish old spinster.

"Leave him be!" she shouted. "He ain't no indoor dog!"

While Hazel rummaged for leftovers, Callie stared through the glass at Sport's soft brown eyes, which seemed to say, "Please let me in."

He sank into the snow to chew at the pads of his feet while Aunt Hazel took up a grimy, greenish brown crockery bowl from the sink, and filled it with chicken skin and bones, leftover mashed potatoes, a glob of cold gravy, cooked carrots, green beans, and chunks of biscuit. She opened the door just enough to shove the bowl out onto the snow-glutted step, straightened herself, pushed aside a hank of coarse brownish-gray hair from her forehead with the back of her hand, glowered at Callie, and high-tailed it back to the card table where the halted game resumed.

While Callie watched Sport gulp down the soft food and crunch the bones, she gave but a moment's thought to her aunt's attitude towards her. Ever since she was a tiny girl, she had felt the woman's hostility, which, as it turned out, stemmed from the fact that Cal, an unplanned member of the family, was the cause of Emily's difficult pregnancy and near death.

Over time, with her mother's love and reassurance, Callie had learned not to take Aunt Hazel's demeanor to heart—except last summer, when the woman had been instrumental in getting rid of Uncle Cecil's favorite dog, simply because he had found his way, once too often, into the henhouse. Callie hated the woman for what she did.

As Hazel put it, "I won't put up with a farm dog that sucks eggs for a living."

After licking at the snow for moisture, Sport looked up at Cal once more. He seemed to smile before turning and slowly making his way through the spindrifts back to the barn.

She could tell that Sport had wanted to come in and play with her, knew that look from her own little dog, Tequila, who was waiting back home in Masterton, cozy and warm inside a house with central heating.

Callie closed the main door and walked over to one end of the countertop, where she pinched off a hunk of the rhubarb cake her mother had brought, stuffed it into her mouth, and grabbed a second chunk before heading upstairs to the cold, spartan second story of the farmhouse.

Because the door to the staircase always remained closed, a big chill awaited Callie at the top of those hard, narrow, steep risers, which she no longer had to crawl up in order to reach the slanted hallway covered in dark green linoleum, scuffed and torn in spots.

Of the two closed doors upstairs, one led to a large storage room filled to the ceiling with boxes and old furniture (some of which reminded Cal of the things inside the store room of her grandparents' cottage at Tepeeotah), and the other to a small bedroom, once belonging to

Aunt Hazel's daughter, Lena, who had died several years earlier, at age twenty-five, from what Uncle Cecil called "a defective heart." In private, Callie's mother said she thought her death was more likely due to a "broken heart" after Lena's fiancé severed their engagement in order to marry an eighteen-year-old from Pipestone.

Callie stood for a moment to gaze about the tiny room papered in large floral designs of pink, yellow, and green. Aunt Hazel's feather stitched piece-quilt covered a lumpy mattress on the iron frame bed. The single narrow window that never knew a curtain was caked with frost on the inside. Blown by the wind, fine snow sifted through cracks and into the corners, creating triangular piles that looked like little mounds of chalk dust.

Callie's fingernails clawed down each windowpane, sending near colorless curls to the scuffed wooden floor. She liked the feel of thick frost beneath her nails and on her fingertips. While scratching her name into the top piece of glass, she looked out through a break in the storm, and saw the whirring windmill churn like the side paddle on a speeding riverboat. Although she couldn't hear them, she watched clusters of naked trees at the edge of a massive grove clack against each other. The dark red barn loomed large. Cal wondered if Sport and the cats and livestock—pigs and cattle—were going to be all right throughout the night. Or would some of them freeze on the hoof like those cattle her mother and dad had seen years ago, the morning after a harrowing blizzard?

She sat down on the bed, remembering how Lena had played "Patty Cake" with her when Callie was two or three years old. Pretending that her cousin was facing her once again, Cal clapped her hands together and then outward to slap at where Lena's hands would have been. Her breath streamed into the cold air while she chanted the words Lena would have spoken: "Pattycake, pattycake, baker's man, bake a cake as fast as you can. Roll it and roll it and mark it with a 'C,' and throw it in the oven for Callie and me."

Enveloped by cold drafts, Cal began to shiver uncontrollably. Her chattering teeth sounded like a tiny motor. She jumped up and rushed down the steps, through the kitchen, and into the only room thoroughly warmed by the stove. The four adults, their eyes intense with concentrating on fans of face cards, glanced for a second at Callie.

"What've you been up to, Skeeziks?" asked her dad, shifting a few of his cards around to create a different order.

"Mmm, a little of this and a little of that," she answered, still shivering a bit. "Did you know it's snowing out? And the wind is blowing awful hard."

"Oh?" they all said, except her mother, who stood for a moment to peer out of the window.

"Maybe we'd better start for home, Will."

"A couple more hands," he said, "then we'll get a-going."

With a look of concern, Emily sat back down while Cal cozied up to the woodstove and held her hands over the hot metal.

Because blizzards erupt and sweep over the prairielands as commonly as gales beat across the Great Lakes, no one else seated at the card table bothered to glance outside until much later, when they had finished several more rounds of pinochle.

After counting the numbers of jacks, queens, and kings in each player's hand, Callie left to curl up in the bedroom just off the kitchen. She burrowed under her mother's black borgana coat, rolled her dad's wool storm coat into a pillow, and fell asleep to the steady drone of voices coming from the distant parlor. Well after midnight, she awoke to a shift in sounds and movements that indicated it was time to go home.

The cards had fallen quiet, the conversation changed in words, tempo, and volume, and soon Will was gently tugging his coat out from beneath Callie's head.

"Gotta go warm up the car, Snookums," he said, tousling her hair.

Cal tumbled from the bed and quickly prepared for the ride back to town.

"I can still smell supper," said Will from the entry, brushing snow from his coat and hat. "It's blustery out there. A near white-out."

"No school tomorrow!" shouted Callie, eager to hear her prediction validated on WCCO radio come morning. Relayed from the Twin Cities, the list of school closings nearly always included Masterton, the Snow Belt's county seat.

By the time Will, Emily, and Callie huddled inside the Pontiac, it had stopped snowing. Drifts had piled high in unprotected spots all around the farmyard. The temperature dropped as the wind picked up, blowing the fresh snow in thick white rivers across glutted fields where honeysuckle and milkweed once stood tall.

The inside of the car felt toasty as they fish-tailed down the lane, avoiding the ditches, heading for home, with the white hills of Buffalo Ridge no longer visible in the distance. Through the rear window, Callie watched the farmyard's tall beacon of light fade and melt away, swallowed up in a final flurry of snow. At the last second, she saw Sport stick his head and shoulders out of the barn door. Although she figured that he wouldn't be able to see her, Callie waved big.

At the end of the lane, it was nearly impossible to see where the road's edge gave off and the ditch began. Will managed to turn right onto the snow-filled gravel road and pick up speed. That's when Emily began to belch.

Accustomed to hearing her mother respond that way to alarming situations, Callie placed her mother's cake pan on the floor and stretched out on the back seat, searching through a side window for the familiar rhythmic dip and rise of the high-line wires that jetéd all the way into town. But this night, she couldn't even see the telephone poles, much less the overhead wires. Instead, horizontal white streaks, like tracer bullets, raced sideways behind the Manitoba Buffalo sticker affixed to the little window glass. It had started to snow again. She sat up and, with her chin resting on the seatback, stared straight ahead through the windshield, a focal point for zillions of atom smashers. Will's left foot pressed the floorboard headlight button, demonstrating how impossible it was to see anything other than white tracers against a high beam. You couldn't tell where the edge of the road gave off and the ditch began. Within seconds, the car lost its momentum, swerved, slid sideways, and lurched to a stop.

"Well, I guess we're stuck again," said Will pulling the earflaps down from the inside band of his hat, as if what he was about to do simply existed as a carry-over from last winter—more shoveling, all in a night's work.

Emily handed him a woolen scarf to wrap around his neck and then began more audible belching—lightly, at first, then in long, drawn-out burps that sounded like those from the rude boys in Callie's third grade class.

Will struggled to push open the car door and plunged into the storm, leaving his wife and daughter inside. Callie climbed over the seat back and huddled next to her mother. They heard the trunk lid open. And they heard Will scoop mounds of snow away from the back tires and along the sides of the car. When it got quiet, they knew he was sprinkling sand from a bucket he kept in the trunk all year long. Leaning into the wind, Will's bent form appeared dim and disappeared, until he waded back into the glare of headlights like a phantom haunting a lonely road, his face turned sideways as if to avoid a blow from an unseen fist. They lost sight of him as he scooped long paths far ahead of the front tires. Just as Callie began to worry that she'd never see her father alive again, he reappeared like a different ghost out of the wild white frenzy before trailing off once more with his pail of sand.

"I'll never forget the blizzard of thirty-five," murmured Emily, between belches. "It snowed and snowed and it got so cold that the prairie was dotted with cattle that froze on the hoof. There they were, next morning, standing in those fields like statues or heavy cardboard cutouts, figures on a game board. Frozen to death. Oh, it was awful to see."

"Do you think they cried, Mom?"

"I don't know, dear," she answered, holding her daughter close. "It's not something I care to think about."

Whenever Cal asked her dad about those freezing cattle crying out there in the pastures, he answered in his usual way whenever a question took him off guard: "Could be, Callie girl, could be."

As she was visualizing this scene, fearing that a repeat of it was taking place that very minute in the pastures on the other side of the snow curtain and roadside fences, Will yanked open the door and zipped in behind the wheel, enshrouded in the cold and powerful smell of ozone.

"Brrr!" Snowflakes from his hat and coat whipped about the interior as he slammed the door and handed his fogged-up glasses to Emily. "Oh, to feel spring in the air again," he intoned. "Think apple blossom time, gals."

Callie climbed over to the back seat and sat with her chin resting close to her parents.

Will shifted into first gear, eased the clutch, and picked up speed while Callie called out, "Give 'er hell, Dad! Give 'er hell!"

And he did. And so did Emily, moving her upper body repeatedly forward as if to help keep the car inching ahead, until the next drift, which brought on another round of belching and more shoveling.

"Mom, are you going to be all right?"

"I'll be fine, dear. Just a little gas." She handed Will his cleared spectacles and reached over the seatback to shake a finger. "And by the way, Callie, you'd better watch your mouth."

All quiet during the last few miles, the three finally made it back to Masterton, to their house with a furnace, where Liz and Sam Cat and little Tequila awaited them.

19

The Prettiest Little River

Have you also learned that secret from the river;
that there is no such thing as time?
—*Hermann Hess,* Siddhartha

SEATED BEHIND THE WHEEL of her dad's Cadillac, Callie checked the rearview mirror and watched the plowed fields fade into the distance outside of Red Wing. A herd of Red Angus grazed in a grassy pasture with a freshly painted red barn beyond.

"Those are some healthy looking bovines," said Will, keeping them in view as long as he could.

"Remember when so many cattle perished, Dad, all those years ago? Frozen on the hoof?"

"That was an awful sight. Your mother and I could hardly bear to see it. Not much anyone could do to save them back then. The storm and bitter cold came on so fast it caught everyone off guard. And so little shelter available in those days."

Callie remembered asking Will on their way home from Aunt Hazel and Uncle Cecil's farm about those animals out there in the cold, snow-filled pastures. Now she asked once again.

"Did they . . . do you suppose they cried, Dad? I've read that they do," she said, recalling the line written by Edgar Lee Masters: "While he wept like a freezing steer."

"Could be, Cal, could be." He shook his head and made his usual chirping sound from the corner of his mouth. "Not something I like to think about."

"Me neither."

"Well, aside from the snow and cold, it's a hell of a nice country we live in, Cal-girl; a place where the living is easy."

"'Summertime,'" sang Callie, " 'and the livin' is sleasy. Fish are jumpin' and the' *co-orn* is high."

"That doesn't sound quite right."

"Ever see any cotton growing around here?"

"Can't say as I have. At least the fish are jumping."

"When the water's open."

"I thought you were tougher than that, Cal. Sounds like the winters are getting to you."

"Not really. Not yet, I hope, at this stage of my life. Just the extreme ones—winters *or* summers—and I dare say those affect most everybody."

"As do the tolerable ones. Remember those beautiful summers on Pine River?"

"All the great northerns we caught?"

"And frying them up over an open fire. Delicious."

"Oh, and all the wood you chopped. That was hard work."

"Enough to see you through, I hope."

During those cold, dark months of winter, as Emily called them, Callie and Liz, each in her own home, portioned out logs from the neatly stacked rows inside their woodsheds, counting on the fact that they'd last at least a couple more seasons.

"Wish I could still accommodate you girls, but there *will* come a time when you'll have to do for yourselves along those lines. After my supply is all used up."

NORTH OF LAKE MILLE LACS, where those two young men drowned, Will Lindstrom, at age eighty-five, had found a small campground next to Pine River, discovered while returning home from Federal Dam on Leech Lake. He and Emily had taken a detour, done a little exploring, and there it was—that beautiful river connecting lakes from north of Backus, gurgling through Ding Pot Swamp, hooking up with Norway Lake, becoming a long river again, rushing over the dam, traveling to the Whitefish chain, and purling on down to meet the Mississippi River.

The Lindstroms immediately set up their Hi-Lo camper and, as Will often said, "There we lived for several weeks, before the summer gave in and fall forced us to skedaddle back to our apartment."

Having left off wintering in California, Will and Emily had settled on a second-floor apartment in a small community west of Minneapolis—a confining space that Will skipped out of whenever possible.

"Even though the air got nippy and the leaves began to drop, it was hard to go back," he said, "when we had the biggest, most luxurious living room in the whole wide world. Step out of that little Hi-Lo and there it was! Groves of trees, pines, acres of fields, and dozens of lakes just around the bends of the prettiest little river shimmering in the sunlight."

At nightfall, after their fish fry, Will and Emily sat next to the campfire with all those stars overhead—like quiet company winking down at them. Once in a while, they'd hear the wailing yodel of a loon. And nearly every evening, a black lab from town trotted over to sit down next to them, happy to be petted, smiling, eyes closed, his damp snout reflecting the fire's glow.

"Now I ask you, Emily," Will said each time the flames died down or the sun rose to burn off an early morning haze, "what more could a fella want out of life?"

Each day of the week, while camping by the river, Will shoved out from shore in his Crestliner first thing in the morning and, during a full moon, the last thing in the evening. Which is what Will loved most during those final summers of his life.

Rowing and trolling along with the current, or against it, gave him the leisure to consider his lifetime of years. As with the water's flow around boulders and tree roots, thoughts and memories washed over him, circled about in his mind, and moved on. Just as a familiar cluster of pebbles under watery sunshine caught his eye each time he approached the giant willow tree before the next bend in the river, some thoughts stayed with him, while others left him guessing: Thoughts about his older brother, Ray, for instance. Would he ever see him again? And if they did get together, say one last time, would they get along?

There were times when Will's mind seemed blocked, like an ice-covered bay with all kinds of activity swirling beneath, waiting to surface. Those were the gray times when he felt little shocks in his brain like sudden cracks in the ice. They only lasted for a second or two, before his thoughts and memories came back to him, like free water surfacing through those fissures in a spring-thawed bay.

Being on a river, it was as though time didn't exist. Everything that mattered was there. Unchanging. At least during Will's time spent on it. The stream was complete from beginning to end, from its source to its flow into every other body of water, until finally it met up with the big one—*Old Man River*—which urged those brisk northern waters on down to the summery Gulf, as if moving along with the deep, warm notes of Paul Robeson's voice.

Alternating between a strenuous row and motoring, Will made daily runs up Pine River and across Norway Lake. Along the second stretch of the river, in the direction of Ding Pot Swamp, he found a secluded stand of timber, some of it chewed through and felled by beavers, which made his work easier.

"All I had to do," he said in a grateful voice, "was cut up the lengths of maple and oak and some pine (hard work but good exercise) with my bow saw, then split the bigger chunks with my iron wedges and a big axe."

Those iron tools he had inherited from his father, Vic.

Loading the wood into the Crestliner required strategic planning so as to keep her evenly afloat on his way back to camp, especially when the wind and waves decided to threaten the small boat.

Emily routinely packed a bag lunch for Will, consisting of a salami sandwich slathered with mayonnaise and mustard, a nice big Greening apple (similar to those they raised back home), and a thermos of strong coffee. None of that "drag-a-bean-through-the-water" stuff he used to grouse about when they lived in Masterton.

"It took a number of years after the Great Depression," he said, "before Emily felt flush enough to make a decent cup of coffee."

Then she'd remind Will of the "extraordinary care" he took of his vehicles—especially that 1950 black Pontiac Silver Streak—and how he overly conserved on gas and wear-and-tear of its tires, well beyond the recovery years, and how he . . .

"A gem of a car!" he'd shout, as if he were still posing between it and his 1943 war poster tacked to the garage wall, postulating, "Is This Trip Necessary?" Only now Will was more concerned about where his ill health was taking him.

Near Pine River, while Emily collected wildflowers, worked on her crocheting, coffee-klatched with the neighbor ladies, and worried about her husband out on the water, Will spent entire days in the woods next to the river.

"That was some wonderful spot," he said. "And quiet, except for saw teeth against timber—the kind of place where you don't need a watch. A fellow forgets about everything but the task at hand, and how beautiful and silent it is. Nothing else matters, at least for the time being. What more could you want? Being there, you have all the time in the world. That's what Uncle Amer used to say when we broke from hunting ducks around Moon Lake, a little way from our farm in Hadley, and Big Slough, south of Masterton."

Bits of sow thistle grabbed at the cuffs of their overalls as they stepped over fallen timber and through soft goldenrod at those places, and between the shoreline and woods of Bear Lake.

"'We've got all the time in the world, boys,'" Amer would say. I'd study him and my dad—two brothers sitting side by each on boulders or dry ground, beneath a butternut tree, eating lard sandwiches, sipping coffee from a Stanley thermos. And next to me sat my brother Ray."

On Pine River in summer, Will used to wave at Emily, who stood before their camper window, wearing her usual look of concern. Or she might walk to the little knoll at water's edge minutes before sunrise, twisting an end of her pink-and-white checkered apron while Will rowed or motored out to the middle of the river where the current ran smooth against his boat. He was often the only human out at that hour among the mallards and geese and red-winged blackbirds and a pair of swans called Bert and Hilda, named after an elderly couple—friends who lived in a trailer near the third bend in the river.

"After a while," he said, "I lost count of how many boatloads of firewood I brought back to the dock. Some afternoons, she rode pretty low in the water, barely an inch or two below the gunwales."

Sitting perfectly still, he held the Johnson at trolling speed and plied his way back across Norway Lake and through the turns of Pine River. Seldom one for sentimentality, he occasionally allowed himself to feel as though his father Vic and his uncle Amer were keeping an eye on him, making sure he'd learned his lessons well from their forays on the southwestern Minnesota lakes that figured into his early life—Great Oasis, Bear, Rush, and Crooked Lakes—home to tens of thousands of waterfowl whose numbers began to dwindle with the draining of those bodies of water.

And then there were the lakes that figured into his adult years—Sarah, Maria, Shetek—plus the sloughs in between, all flocked with waterfowl in season.

All those lessons held. Will pictured his father's silent nod of approval as he loaded his fishing boat with firewood and still managed to snag a good-sized northern pike on his way back to camp. Spotting Emily, he'd shout, "I caught our supper, Em! Heat up the lard!"

There she'd be waiting near the small dock, still wringing a corner of her apron, chastising Will for being gone so long, floating up to the gunwales, and wasn't he a lucky man that a fierce wind hadn't blown in to fill his boat with water and sink "the whole dang load" and him along with it. Each time, he'd issue a gentle reminder for her to calm down, followed by his standard retort: "My dear Emily, the fates and Pine River seem to be on my side yet another day."

One August morning, during his last summer on the river, Will piloted Callie up to the forest where he had spent many hours sawing thick limbs for firewood. As soon as she stepped from the dock into the boat and took her usual place in the bow, she seemed a girl again, as if she and her father were together once more on Lake Shetek. Except this was a river. And unless you have a reliable motor or arms strong at the oars, a river will take you where *it* wants to go.

River residents, Bert and Hilda, the ornery old swans Will had tried to befriend, surged mightily to attack their boat. The two birds thwacked the gunwales with powerful wings and hissed until you could see clearly into the sharp-tongued insides of their mouths—pink tongues splotched with black, as if from spilled ink. Black bumps swelled between their eyes where more black trim highlighted their orange beaks.

Will and Callie fended them off with oars extended. But the swans beat at the blades and stabbed at father and daughter, until Will upped the throttle and left the great white birds behind to shake their feathers, ruffle and refold their wings.

While Bert and Hilda bobbed up and down in the boat's wake, Callie hummed a few strains from Saint-Saens' "*La Cigne*," giving those exquisite birds the benefit of the doubt as they paddled on down Pine River with their wings half raised.

"Swans are unusual creatures," Will called forward to Cal whose own feathers had remained unruffled through such harsh treatment from such beautiful birds. That sort of thing no longer surprised her. People could be like that too, for whatever reason. How could she ever forget the performer who sang the loveliest lyrics at Orchestra Hall, in such a way that his entire being seemed linked to truth, beauty, and near-perfection? But after the performance, backstage in the green room, where Callie and her friends were allowed entry, he spewed venom at everyone around him, and made belittling, misogynistic remarks to the women in his entourage. After that, Callie realized that things and people are not always as they appear "on stage." A crooner doesn't necessarily live the lyrics he sings.

"All summer long, I've had quite the experiences with these swans," said Will. "They're elegant and graceful from a distance, but, by God, once you're up close, look out. They can be treacherous."

Recalling a poem she'd learned, Callie pointed at the sky and measured out,

> *"You've seen Balloons set—Haven't you?*
> *So stately they ascend—*
> *It is as Swans—discarded You,*
> *For Duties Diamond— . . ."*

"Unusual words, Cal. Is that a . . . ?"
"Wait, I'm not finished.

> *"Their Liquid Feet go softly out*
> *Upon a Sea of Blond—*
> *They spurn the Air as t'were too mean*
> *For Creatures so renowned—"*

"Emily Dickinson." Callie pointed back at the pair. "That's swans for you."
"Yup, Bert and Hilda own this river."

STARTING OUT FROM NEAR THE DAM on Pine, there are six turns in a river marked by snug cabins, tipsy wooden docks, a few rickety boat houses, and towering trees filled with red-winged blackbirds singing, *Thweee!* as Callie trills when imitating them. (She can also caw like a crow and howl like a wolf.)

Will always felt buoyed up when making a turn on a river or channel or from an inlet—final turns that deliver a fisherman (or any lover of the great outdoors) onto big waters. "Maybe that's what a good death is like," he once said—"taking that final turn onto the big waters."

In his younger years, he had boated thousands of times through the long inlet connecting the Des Moines River to Lake Shetek. He'd carved through the channel out of Federal Dam onto Leech Lake, and traced Pine River as it allowed him to enter Norway Lake and beyond. More than once, he traveled Pine, crossed Norway, continued along the next portion of Pine River, then meandered all the way up to Ding Pot, a trip that required two salami sandwiches and all the time in the world—or at least an extra-long day, shoving off from the dock well before first light.

"Uncle Amer would have liked these lakes and rivers," he told Cal. "Might even have found a place to be himself. A place to grow old."

"Wish I could have known him," said Callie, "besides what I learned from his letters and all that other stuff in the trunk."

Callie loved playing Uncle Amer's violin and his records, especially those slipped out of the Victor Record Album jackets inscribed with "His Master's Voice and the picture of a little fox terrier staring into the horn of an Edison-Bell. She had read that whenever someone played the early home-recorded cylinders with his dead master's voice on them, Nipper would race to the horn, cock his ear, and listen.

"There are some simple truths," wrote Joseph Duemer, "and the dogs know what they are."

On that day in August, it took Will half an hour to motor and row Callie to the spot where he'd spent summer afternoons cutting up those stacks of wood that he hauled back to the campground by boat, and then loaded into the trunk of his car for delivery to Cal and Liz. The fresh morning air breathed cool with the reminder that autumn would soon be dropping in. Beads of dew sparkled like rare gems on fading green leaves and blades of grass. The only telltale signs of Will having been there before were mounds of damp sawdust near the bases of tree trunks where beavers' teeth had already made their marks. Will pointed out the downed saplings he'd left in case those same beavers needed them for their dams, explaining that he didn't wish to impinge on *all* their hard work.

In the grass, next to one of the saplings, lay the fragile, cellophane-like skin of a garter snake.

Facing the river, Will and Callie sat down on tree stumps to take in the scenery beyond the slow-flowing current where boulders lined the opposite shore and tall grass bowed in one direction, as if it had been combed that way. A cluster of cottonwood trees kept company, surrounded by fields of corn, still somewhat green, but with a tinge of russet. Above the treetops hung a faded, partial moon, barely visible against the blue sky.

Will pointed it out and said, "You know, the moon has a life of twenty-eight days before it disappears and then comes around again. And each of those days represents that which is sacred to the Indians."

"Such as?"

"Father Sky, Mother Earth, the sun and the moon, the Morning Star. And then there was the honored buffalo with their twenty-eight ribs."

"I didn't know a buffalo had twenty-eight ribs. How did you come by that, Dad?"

"Remember when I was invited to smoke the peace pipe with some members of the Ojibwe tribe on Leech Lake? It was the time when your mother and I were camping just outside of Federal Dam. I struck up a conversation with those men and they asked me to join their circle."

"That's when Mom got so worried about you, the way you staggered back to the camper. She said you were really out of it for a while."

"Well, I didn't realize that I shouldn't have inhaled all that smoke when the pipe came my way. Kinnikinnick—that's what they called their tobacco. Anyhow, they talked about Black Elk, a Sioux medicine man, and how he divided those twenty-eight days, matching them up with what is sacred: the spotted Eagle; the four directions; earth, wind, and fire; the Great Spirit." Will shook his head. "That was quite an evening there by the lake shore. Unforgettable. They said that the one true thing Black Elk believed in was the pipe religion."

Looking out over the river, Will nodded, and then fell silent.

In the quiet, Callie recalled a dream she'd had shortly after her dad had been diagnosed with melanoma, several years earlier. The setting for that dream was along a very wide river, much wider than Pine. Wider, even, than the tea-colored Mississippi as it rolls south. Callie, her sister Liz, and their mother Emily stood on one side of the river while a huge gondola, decorated in red and gold, with a square room in the center, surrounded by golden curtains, floated slowly across the water. Although there was dance music, the only person on board was her father. The song was *O Mio Babbino Caro*, a tune her grandmother used to play on the upright piano, and Uncle Amer played on his violin. Callie tried to leap into the river and swim out to join Will before the boat could carry him to the other side, but Emily and Liz gently held her back. Her father, smiling all the while, stood tall before the golden curtains, like the proud captain of a ship, waving with his fingers, palm up, the way a grownup waves to a child.

Callie had awakened from her dream crying and reaching out toward the wall. It had taken her a long time to recover from that image, even though there was nothing but a sense of calm surrounding it—calm and acceptance by everyone but Cal.

Seated on the tree stump next to her dad, she glanced at the surgical scar on his face, leaned sideways and, for a moment, rested her head on his shoulder, remembering when she was a little kid, completely unaware of time. What did she care about time back then? She laughed and shouted and ran and played with her friends, assuming that everyone's time on earth would be forever. That is until she began to overhear people say that they were feeling "a little punk" or that they had "the heebie jeebies of the globber lobbers."

Looking down at the water's edge, Callie spotted a small arrowhead among the pebbles. She stood and walked over to retrieve it.

"Oh, that's a nice one," said Will. "A perfect souvenir of our day on the river."

"It is. I wonder whatever became of the Indian who created it."

"Say, how about if we toss out a line? I brought a few worms."

Callie placed the gray arrowhead in her jean's pocket and slapped her hands together. "Sure! It's been a while since I've threaded one on a hook."

She stepped into the boat and snatched up two cane poles and the red Folger's coffee can filled with moist black dirt.

"You can dump it all out on the ground, Cal. I don't think there are too many left."

Running her fingers through the damp clumps of soil and leaves and small twigs, Callie picked out a couple of earthworms, handed one to her dad, and began stringing the other onto the long-shank hook tied to the end of her line. As she was threading the worm, it broke in half and both parts suddenly curled in a violent struggle, especially the tail end.

"I hate when that happens," she said, continuing to guide the tense sections of worm up along the shank. "I know they have to die in the water, among the fish, but I hate to tear them apart like this."

"Did you know, Cal, that a worm has five hearts?"

"No, I've never heard of such a thing."

"I hadn't either, until recently. If segments break away, only the pieces that have no heart die off. The rest will live."

"You mean they can regenerate?

"Exactly."

Before leaving their side of the river, Will left the remaining worms on the ground, then gathered a few stray branches from his work area and made a pile next to the trunk of an intact white pine.

Cal found a small chunk of wood etched by beavers' teeth, which she would take home to place on her mantle—another souvenir from this singular afternoon.

And then there would be one more memory: on the opposite side of the river, a pair of sandpipers jitterbugged along the sand bar in search of sustenance.

"I can do that." Callie tossed her head back and skittered over to their rowboat.

Heading back to Emily, as Will liked to say, they let the boat drift while devouring their lunch: liverwurst-mayonnaise sandwiches stuffed with thick wads of lettuce, and black coffee still steaming from the thermos. In a cloth bag were two chilled cans of *7-Up* wrapped in tinfoil and newspaper, and quarter-pound *Baby Ruth* candy bars.

"Too bad Emily couldn't figure a way to pack a couple of ice cream cones," said Will, referring to the triple-scoops they used to buy for a dime on their way out to Lake Shetek from Masterton, a part of their routine when Callie was a girl. First they stopped at the Five-Mile Corner gas station for ten-cent quarter-pound *Baby Ruth*s, then at the Currie Corner for triple-scoop maple nut and butter brickle cones, then at Breezy Point for soda pop (*Coke* or *7-Up*). After that, they spent the rest of the day on the lake, their bait and lines sharing the water with Blue-Winged Teal, Coot, Mallards, and an occasional turtle.

Early evenings, they cleaned their catch, then sat on the dock to unravel a backlash from one of the reels. Callie always sat close to her father in order to watch how he untangled those black lines. She studied his eyes and mouth, wondering if he felt irritated about the mess she'd made while practice-casting, a jumble that resembled thin tangles of a thousand skinny worms. But she saw only patience written across his face, and occasional glances over the lake and at the sky as a great blue heron returned to her nearby nest just before the day gave over to night.

"No problem, Cal," he offered, noticing his young daughter's furrowed brows. "We'll work it out. We have all the time in the world."

And they did, for a long while, until Callie reached the point where a deep awareness began to set in: the realization that nothing or no one is forever—physically, that is. But there would always be the memories and lessons learned, along with the whisperings of oft-said phrases: "It's a good day for ducks. Hey, Snicklefritz, how's your gizzard? Are you up for all day? We've got fish to catch. And Cal, there's one right there with your name on it."

In Callie's estimation, her dad fished the way a great blue heron fished from a dock—quiet, patient, still. "No rush," he'd say. "All the time in the world."

Before locking up the cottage on Tepeeotah Hill, Callie often skipped around to the side where a little wooden box inscribed with the words "Leave a Message" hung on a nail. As far as Cal knew, she was the only one who ever opened the cobwebby door. Each week, before she and her dad drove back home to Masterton, she snatched up the nubby yellow pencil and wrote something on the white pad: "BOO!" or "Hi, we caught two northerns today!" or "I hate Bobby Keeler!" or "I don't want our cottage to be sold!"

The last time Callie opened the message box, a huge black spider, nearly half the size of the paper pad itself, spun around on its web to face her. Startled, Cal jumped back for a second, then eased forward and gently closed the door. The only thing that stood out on the page behind Mister Spider was the word "sold."

THE DAY CALLIE AND HER DAD DRIFTED together along Pine River was a warm and lazy one. After shoving off from the bank where Will sawed wood, Cal reached over the gunwale to let her hand wash through the cool water. Little bubbles formed in the shallows where small fish and turtles surfaced for insects. A soft breeze whisked through the cottonwood leaves. The air smelled of moss, soggy leaves, and river water. With varying pitches, red-winged blackbirds sang away the silence: *Thwee! Thweee!*

Will pointed out a portion of the river where the water was wide and deep, like a pool. "Let's anchor and see what's in there," he said.

Cal lowered the mud hook with ease. From her tackle box, she picked out the Lazy Ike—a favorite since she was a kid—and clipped the chunky red and white lure to the end of her line.

Will dropped a yellow-green Rapala overboard and worked it along-side the boat, through sunlit ripples. "Just look at that action," he said, admiring its simulated minnow maneuvers. "Now I ask you, what fish could turn his tail on that?"

Cal smiled and cast her line, watching it arc toward shore. Within seconds after *Lazy Ike* plopped into the water near a boulder, a long pike swirled, struck, and took off with the lure.

"Did you see that?" Cal stood up, excited, tightening her grip on the rod. "He's huge!"

Will stowed his own gear and reached for the landing net. "That was a hell of a strike. Hang in there now, Callie girl. Don't horse him along."

She laughed. "You always say that, Dad." Reeling in slowly and remembering what her father had taught her, she eased her thumb off the reel and let the fish run several times before bringing him in next to the boat. He zinged out once more, stripping the line, before the flag went out of him, and Will could scoop him up with the net. Finally, he held the heavy fish aloft and reached over to squeeze the back of Cal's neck. "We eat tonight, kiddo! Six pounds if he's an ounce."

The thrill of that catch left Callie's hands shaky and her heart beating fast. She sat down on her seat in the bow and stared at the fish bent into more than a half circle inside the net.

"Good work, Cal. I'd say that's the biggest northern you ever caught."

"Yes, I think so," she said, catching her breath.

"Enough for a feast."

"And then some—leftovers for breakfast."

"Yup, cold and dipped in mayo." Will ran a metal link from his stringer through the lips of the northern pike, clamped it shut, and lowered the fish into the river, next to the boat. "What say we pull anchor and work our way back to the lake?"

"I'd like to row for a while before you start the motor," said Callie, "stretch my arms a bit."

As the Crestliner moved quietly along Pine River toward Norway Lake, a large doe came out from the trees, froze in the clearing, and kept watch with round, liquid eyes.

"That's one beautiful sight," Cal whispered, letting the oars go still in the water. "Aren't we lucky?"

They floated past her on the current with only a faint tapping of loose oars against the boat's hull. The deer stepped to the river's edge, switched her white tail, then lowered her head and relaxed into a long drink, while Callie rowed slowly, far and away, the sun warm on her back.

For a time, the sole sounds on that river rose from the rhythm of the oars, forward and back, metal against old metal, pins on oarlocks. Cal swung the blades low over the water, the way she'd been taught. Dip, pull. Dip and pull.

BEHIND THE WHEEL of her dad's Cadillac, Callie talked about that day in August when she had caught the big fish, and quietly passed the white-tailed deer who didn't feel the need to run away. After she had rowed along that part of the river with a light breeze ruffling her hair, Will took over. With his left hand easy on the throttle, he motored across Norway Lake, back to the first stretch of Pine River, and the rest of the way home.

"Rowing back to Emily," said Will, glancing through his car window at the remains of harvested corn and bean fields. "I'm glad you got to see that wonderful place where I cut firewood. Wish I could get back up there and chop some more, enough to see you and Liz through a few more winters." He turned to rest his head against the seat back. "But my sawyer days might be over." Suddenly, he sat up straight and looked at his daughter. "I've had a good run, though, Cal. A real good run."

"After we get back home, Dad, say next week, let's launch the boat, if weather permits. Go for a spin before the bay freezes over."

"I don't think so, Cal. We put her away for the winter. No sense going through all that rigmarole for just one more day. Getting everything lined up, hitching the trailer. It'd all be a little much."

"I can do all that rigmarole, Dad. I know how."

"But there's the motor. That old Johnson has become more temperamental than ever."

"We'll leave it then. Just take the oars and life jackets. Keep it simple, do a little casting."

Will turned to look at Callie with that old familiar shake of the head and a chirp from the corner of his mouth. When his dimple deepened on the side of his face that wasn't paralyzed, she knew they'd soon be making a few more waves with the sixteen-foot *Crestliner*, perhaps for the last time.

It's hard for everyone to have to give up doing the things they love. It's an especially cruel time when a man can no longer drive the car he worked so hard to keep spotless and in perfect running condition, or launch his fishing boat with that former fluid ease, or repeatedly pull the cord on his Johnson 10-horse for as long as it takes to start the motor, in order to make his way through favorite channels out to those sparkling gray-green bays where he fished ever since he was a boy.

All of that, Callie and her family were already witnessing. What she was about to see, but could not or did not want to imagine, would happen incrementally over the next year.

There would come a day when Will could no longer step out onto the balcony, into the sunshine and fresh autumn air in order to look up at the sky where flocks of Canada geese practiced the neat formations that would arrow them south. He would stop eating, no longer wishing to sit up to the dining table with the rest of the family.

"Flying south?" he questioned. "I'd like to travel down to the Gulf coast, sit on the deck of a really good restaurant, and eat a big plateful of shrimp."

Emily reached over to touch his arm. "We can't drive that far, Will."

"I'll take a train."

"You know you're not up to that."

"I'll go with you, Dad," said Callie, feeling suddenly hopeful. "I'll take you there. When shall we . . . ?"

Moments later, she would ask Will if he'd like to go out and sit on the deck of his apartment. He would shake his head no.

And finally, he would give in to those vile tumors and take to his bed, until it was time to let go his oars, close his eyes, and let the river deliver him back to where he came from.

And what would Callie do? She would always remember how, early one morning, she took her own small boat out alone, intent on catching and frying up some panfish for Will. But nothing was biting that day, except for a huge bullhead with scars around his head and a rusty hook and leader hanging from his lip. She clipped the snell of the hook with her small pliers and removed the barb. Her hands pulsated with the fish's heavy underside and powerful quiver. He slipped from her grip and lay along the bottom of the boat. Cal scooped him up, leaned over the gunwale, and eased him back into the water, where he hung for a moment before swimming deep and away—back to where he came from.

20

Loneliness versus Solitude

She was stronger alone . . .
—*Jane Austen,* Sense and Sensibility

SHE TOOK LONG WALKS with Piper, watching him run and cut across last winter's frozen lake, herding make-believe sheep, plowing through a dozen crows fighting over panfish stilled beneath the surface. When he raced over to her, yip-yapping away, Callie called back to him, yet sometimes missed hearing a human voice in return—especially, words from a man. Not the blasting kind, but those spoken out of a warm and caring soul—like from her first love, a boy she'd dated in college; the young man who was later killed in Viet Nam.

Forever nineteen, the image of Chuck Edwards returned to Callie's mind as easily as if he had just stepped through the door of her old campus apartment. Dressed in black slacks and the black and white ski sweater she had given him for Christmas, he resembled a youthful Tyrone Power with a touch of Brandon deWilde. He laughed a lot, played guitar, and sang folksongs.

'You're a loser unless you end up with a man in your life' was the old college maxim, especially parceled out among sorority members.

After Chuck left for the army, Callie turned her back on those organizations that hung on such precepts. She studied hard and remained a GDI for as long as she could, until the pressure of that earlier dictum won over. Like her mother and sister, she would enter a union where she could be herself.

But Robert Burns got it right:

The best laid plans may end up thus: "Wee, sleekit, cow'rin, tim'rous beastie, O, what a panic's in thy breastie!"

And so it goes: "Thou saw the fields laid bare an' waste, An' weary winter comin fast, An' cozie here, beneath the blast, Thou thought to dwell—Till crash! The cruel coulter past Out thro' thy cell."

And so it went in translation: "But little Mouse, you are not alone, In proving foresight may be vain: The best-laid schemes of mice and men Go often askew, And leave us nothing but grief and pain, For promised joy!"

Now, with the end of her marriage to Jim, Callie needed to recover, learn how to move forward, count on herself, and build another nest. Efforts at figuring out the difference between loneliness and solitude, turning away from sorrow to make time for creativity, were slightly set off balance when a visiting family friend greeted Cal with a hug. It was when he gripped her shoulders, smiled tenderly, and reached out to touch her face that she fell back into a depth of longing. Not for him, not for her first love, and not for Jim—but for someone new.

Contrary to her ideals, Callie began browsing through the dating ads in the *City Pages*, responding to several who had written intelligent, thoughtful introductions, and managed to put a best foot forward by telephone.

Meeting each one for coffee or lunch, however, revealed the unforeseen: a nonstop talker who looked away at other women while speaking only of himself; a middle-aged businessman with a single saber tooth poking out from between his lips, making Cal wonder how the hell he could eat or drink, much less kiss someone; a guy who sat at the table, texting, calling, receiving calls from his fancy new cell phone; a short, stout man with a mild case of Down Syndrome: the kindest of all, for he had brought Callie a long-stemmed red rose.

And then, there was that final blind date, which turned out to be such a shocking experience, it hovered over Cal like an unforgettable *film noir*—bleak, ominous, Stygian.

And she was in it.

21

Gunny

Then a soldier, full of strange oaths . . . Jealous in honour,
sudden and quick in quarrel, Seeking the bubble reputation
Even in the cannon's mouth.
—As You Like It, *William Shakespeare*

"WHAT'LL IT BE COWBOY?"

Gunny swiveled on his stool to face off with the bartender. "Hey! I don't put up with no shit from nobody. Got that?"

"Yeah, sure." The bartender stepped back with his hands up. "No problem."

Callie felt the blood drain from her face and thought of bolting back to the warm safety of her car.

"Let's try this again," said the bartender in a calm, polite voice. "What's your pleasure?"

"A couple a drafts." Gunny pointed at a gold lever, then snapped his head around to case the room. He reminded Callie of a hawk.

I'll stay a few more minutes, she thought, plugging the silence with small talk that came out shaky to her own ears: "Quite a few boaters here tonight."

"Yeah, I noticed. Bunch a rich Republican Chris Crafters."

Earlier that evening, Callie had pulled into the parking lot next to Wayzata Bay. Christmas lights dotted the shoreline. Because there was no snow that clear and cold night, zillions of extra bright stars reflected off the wide expanse of black ice. Diners hustled toward the *Home Port* restaurant, their breath hanging like smoke signals in the air. Cal sat huddled inside her car with the heater blasting, fiddling with the radio, watching for her blind date.

At seven o'clock, a green Silverado turned in and parked at an angle, taking up two spaces. The door opened and out stretched a pair of tall, black cowboy boots with tucked-in jeans, followed by the rest of a short, wiry man who hopped off the running board, slammed the door, adjusted his cowboy hat, and headed for the restaurant, sauntering like John Wayne.

There aren't many cowboys in Minnesota, especially around the cities and suburban lakes. Something about this guy—he didn't seem like a real cowboy. He wore boots and jeans and an authentic hat, but then there was that military jacket.

Taking cover behind her steering wheel, Callie felt like a spy, watching this man pause to hitch up his dungarees before entering the restaurant. She considered stealing out of the parking lot with headlights off, and rushing back home. But then what? Watch an old episode of "Frasier?" Read a stack of her students' research papers on classical composers? She'd planned for this date, spent time getting ready. He'd sounded nice on the phone. Besides, she could hear her mother's admonition when Callie, a reluctant teenager, antagonized over an invitation to the Prom: "He may not be your type," said Emily, "but he has feelings, too."

Cal shut down the engine and left the refuge of her car, the last bit of interior warmth, to cross the frigid street. A bitter wind swept up from across the bay and beat the chained *Home Port* sign against its moorings. The icy gust caught in her throat and she quickly stepped into the cozy restaurant filled with the rich smells of pasta sauces and grilled steaks. Her date was waiting inside the entry, unsmiling, standing at attention.

He looked at Callie briefly from beneath the brim of his beige cow-boy hat, glanced around while shaking her hand, and nodded when she said, "It's nice to meet you."

After this brusque introduction, Gunny shouldered through the main part of the restaurant, cased the room, and headed for the bar, leaving Callie to trail behind.

I could still get out of this, she thought. *Just turn around and run back to the parking lot.*

Several diners looked up and smiled as she stood for a moment, try-ing to decide what to do.

Despite the apprehension, a smidgen of curiosity and her mother's words won over. She slowly made her way to the bar, where Gunny had chosen a pair of stools at the short end of the reverse L, away from the crowd, so he could sit with his back to the wall.

Plastic menus shaped like sailboats skimmed the shiny surface of the bar, advertising a dinner special in celebration of the Festival of the Lakes: Champagne, Shrimp Scampi, Barbecued Ribs, Cherries Jubilee.

Hundreds of playing cards plastered the ceiling above the bar. Like Fifty-Two Pickup upside down, the idea seemed chaotic and out of place, like something one would see in a sports bar.

The restaurant quickly filled up with weekend partiers: women dressed in pastel sweater sets, like Callie's; men in fleece vests. They were mostly handsome, wealthy yachtsmen with wives or girlfriends, discussing the stock market and vacations in Aruba.

What Gunny said for openers took Callie by surprise. She wasn't sure how to respond.

"Hell, I know I'm not good looking," he said, glancing around. "I got an ugly mug and tough skin from all the years I spent in the Marines. Been to all sorts of places, mostly outa doors. Got me a pit bull to train. Gotta give him wide berth, though, lemme tell ya."

Although he spoke without glancing her way, Callie stared at Gunny, noticing how he kept an eye on everyone but her. His skin was like tanned hide with deep lines carving parentheses around a down-turned mouth. But for his ears, the sweat-stained leather hat might have covered his entire head. He sat tall for a small man, but he didn't sit still.

Cal noticed how others around the bar and in parts of the dining room seemed to be sizing them up—longer than usual, especially after Gunny's outburst. And they watched and held off on their own conversations as the bartender returned with their beers. Glad for the crowd, Cal smiled at them as if to convey that she'd probably be all right in the company of this man, but that she appreciated their awareness all the same. Toying with her napkin, she turned her attention back to Gunny.

"Like I told you on the phone," he said, "I just got me a new bass boat. You like to fish, right?"

"Yes, but I haven't been out in quite a while. One of the last fish I caught was a big old lunker with . . ."

But Gunny wasn't listening and so Callie never finished what she'd started to tell him—that the bullhead, giving off the powerful stench of a warm, algae-covered lake in August, did not belong on her table, and so she let it go.

Gunny was describing his new boat when he noticed Callie focusing on the insignia stitched to his jacket.

"Vietnam Special Forces," he explained. "I was tail gunner in 'Nam. That's how I got my name."

"You shot from the rear of an aircraft?"

"Nah," he growled, emptying his glass and signaling for another beer. "A tail gunner's the last man on foot patrol. You got your point man, then slack; he's backup for the point man. Followin' him are four other guys. Then comes the drag man—that's me."

"I had a boyfriend who died in Vietnam. His name was . . ."

"Yeah, well, I lost a lot of buddies over there."

"His name was Chuck Edwards. He was only twenty-four. Ever hear of him?

"Nope."

Callie looked down at her right wrist. Although it had been years since Chuck was killed, she'd never removed his gift of the ruby red artillery charm from her bracelet. It was in the shape of a tiny shield with the design of a canon. Which, unless one looked closely, resembled a heavy cross.

The bartender, still with a wary eye, set down a fresh beer and turned away.

"I got a temper if you haven't figured that out by now," said Gunny. "I can get pretty mean if I'm provoked. I know that much about myself. But mainly, I'm your regular guy who ain't gonna take no shit, 'cause I seen stuff in 'Nam that makes every other game nothin' by comparison."

In spite of the tough talk, Callie no longer thought about leaving. She sensed that Gunny had checked his trigger temper by talking about it. Unless someone inside the restaurant did or said something provocative, it would stay checked. Besides, she wanted to hear about what had happened to him in Vietnam. Most of the vets she'd met over the years couldn't or wouldn't talk about their experiences. She'd always ask if they'd known Chuck. They hadn't. But then, it was a big, lonely war.

"Like I said," Gunny repeated, looking at Callie openly for the first time, "I seen stuff in 'Nam you wouldn't believe."

She knew then that he was inviting her to hear what he had to say. Cal would also learn that she wasn't to participate in any conversation with this man.

"What stuff?" she asked quietly.

Gunny cased the room once more and took a long swallow of beer. With nicked fingers, he reached out to wipe away a ring of moisture from the bar. Thick veins and sinewy tendons patterned the backs of his hands like old trail maps. The cuffs of his faded olive-drab jacket were frayed. He turned towards Cal. "You sure you wanna hear this?"

She thought about Chuck, handsome in his neat, crisp uniform, laughing dark brown eyes taking her in, a boyish grin on his smooth, unlined face. Boarding the train at the Great Northern Depot in Minneapolis, he turned to wave at his mother and dad, and at Callie. He blew kiss after kiss out of the window as the train pulled away from the station. How storybook, where the three left standing on the platform could not have guessed that within months, Chuck would die while piloting an assault helicopter. His Cobra was shot down during a night-time gun run.

What? That was so unlike the boy Callie knew. He would never assault anyone. He read poetry, played his guitar, and sang pretty songs. He loved people and nature. Shortly after Cal had met him, Chuck shared a quote he had received from one of his professors at college, words spoken by the Lakota: "When a man moves away from nature his heart becomes hard." Legends tell us, said Chuck, that hummingbirds float free of time. Their delicate grace reminds us that life is rich. Beauty is everywhere. Well, almost everywhere. And every personal connection has a special meaning. Laughter is life's most pleasurable creation.

Who would Chuck be had he lived—that sweet, laughing boy? What might he have become had he been able to return home again—vertical?

Wars: started by politicians and old men, fought by brainwashed boys. Where is the redemption?

"I said," repeated Gunny, "are you sure you want to hear this?"

Callie looked him in the eyes and then focused on his Special Forces insignia. "Yes, I want to hear your story."

"WE WERE JUST KIDS. Hell, we didn't know it then, but a bunch of us were goin' straight from Howdy Doody to body bags. I was seventeen when I learned to play the game, went in with a lot of other guys who didn't go to college. No future. Nothin' to lose."

Callie thought of her university friends who had avoided going to war through education deferments—all except Chuck. He was on grade point average probation that semester and failed an Econ class. It was painful to imagine. . . . No, it was heartbreaking to know for a fact that the passing or failing of a single college course in Economics meant the difference between his living and dying.

"We went to play the game," said Gunny. "You know, like Russian roulette. We didn't go in for all that honor and glory shit. But, by God, we had to protect America from Communism."

Gunny sneered with his last comment and shot Callie a quick look to make sure she was getting it.

"That's what they wanted us to believe," she said, primed to discuss some of the political and corporate implications of Vietnam—the economic ramifications.

"Boeing damn near went under before the war," said Gunny. "Did you know that? Shit, they got tons of contracts; all pumped up just like the other big corporations. Made their millions on 'Nam."

Callie nodded, ready to tell him how she'd rallied with other college students, chanting, "Hey, hey, L.B.J., how many kids did you kill today?" But he shook his head; as if he didn't want to hear anything she had to say.

"Hell, I'd go back in a minute, though, to protect America from Communism."

"Wait a second," said Callie. "I thought . . ."

Gunny drew himself up straight and gave her a severe look, a warning. That's when she realized once and for all there'd be no discussion, that she would hear conflicting thoughts from this man. Once she supported a comment, he would pull a bait-and-switch. She sipped her beer, wadded another white paper napkin into a damp little ball, and sat still, determined to hear him out.

"Then Kennedy gets shot," said Gunny with a downward grin. "And Johnson's sworn in. Pissed me off when I heard the son-of-a-bitch got his mitts on 35% stock in Colt firearms—listed under his wife's name. Talk about your sure-fire investments, except the damn things didn't fire half the time.

"Anyhow, I'm a long way from playing war with my buddies back home; we grew up like a lot of other kids, a bunch of big shot punks with our dime store cap guns and toy rifles. Shit, they wouldn't know I was the same guy if they coulda seen me in 'Nam."

Gunny fell silent for a moment. Overriding that quiet came a jumble of cheery voices from the dining room, silverware clattering against plates, steaks sizzling in the kitchen.

He wiped his mouth with the back of his hand. "If only they coulda seen me. I'm goin' for the big show now. This here is the fuckin' big test:

"We were like a branch swaying in the breeze, seven marines bending our way through the Central Highlands near Dak To. Tight? *We were tight.* Hell, we'd trained together for eight months.

"It was a sterile mission, searching for Viet Cong along the Ho Chi Minh Trail. When you're on that kind of patrol, you leave all identification at base camp in case you don't make it out. All we had was a map, compass, and survival gear.

"Everything was so quiet it spooked you—like you were part of the forest and something could take you out any second. If you could of seen us weaving back and forth, hour after hour, without a sound, you'd of thought we looked like a dance line. But, hell, we were jungle animals. I don't care what anybody says. Tuck—he's one of the vets I drink coffee with on Saturdays—he says, 'You guys were wusses, nothin' but a bunch of animals trained in a fuckin' zoo back home.' Tuck's off his fuckin' rocker! He don't know shit! I was there and we was jungle animals!

"My buddy, Frisbie, he was point man. The one thing he hated to leave behind was his dog. That's all he cared about. The only thing left alive in some burned out village we came across. Everybody outside their huts had been shot, except for that puppy. There he sat in a little clearing, just staring at us. Frisbie scooped him up and took him back to camp— saved from a stew pot. Named him Dingo.

"Bryan came next—the music man. After Bryan was Stan and Billy. Then Dave and Crow—that guy could caw like a goddamned crow, no foolin'.

"I brought up the rear—I was tail gunner.

"We were workin' the thickest woods you ever saw, wet and green with layers of trees that rose up so high you couldn't even spot a patch of sky. Strange, but just before we took the hit, the last thing I remember was a leaf brushin' my shoulder; I saw every green and yellow vein in that leaf, and I remember how quiet it was, like everything was holdin' still, holdin' its breath. Even the birds shut up. Come to think of it, I don't remember the last time I heard a bird sing other than Crow cawing his goddamned head off down at base camp.

"Those sons-a-bitches jumped out from nowhere. Nowhere, man. Like Ninjas hacking at us. They fuckin' slashed my men to pieces. We tried to scatter. Where the hell they came from I'll never know. Their camouflage must of worked right in with the brush 'cause they were on us before we knew it. I couldn't even fire off a round. All I could do was make a run for it. And I ran like hell.

"You want to know what a hunted animal feels like? You run and you don't look back. You run 'til your mouth goes dry and the wind catches in your throat and you gag and when you can't run no more you hit the ground, lay dog, until you're part of the fuckin' ground. You suck in air without making a sound. You cock your ears and your M16 when you think it won't give you away.

"I was small and fast—got me deep into the jungle. I could hear them gooks chopping at the underbrush—missed me by a few yards. I listened hard until their slashing and high-pitched yammer faded and I couldn't hear 'em no more.

"I made it without a scratch—a goddamned miracle. But you know what bothers me to this day? We had no warning to shit and git. Not a sound. No guns, nothing. It was some crazy new way to attack, slicing men to pieces instead of shooting them.

"I laid on the ground for a long time, just squeezing dirt between my fingers. Nothin' else to do. I'll never forget how soft it was—that dirt—soft and sweet smelling—like when you make a garden, you know? Not like at the lower elevations where you take cover behind sandbags. Six-inch centipedes live in those bags and they crawl out and bite you like snakes. One bit me, that son-of-a-bitch! I tried to kill him, tried to grind him into the ground, but he wouldn't go in. You couldn't kill 'em—too goddamned many. You just couldn't kill 'em all!"

Gunny's scarred fingers dug into the bar's surface as he stiffened and twisted his lips in disgust.

"Anyhow, it got dark and started to rain. I laid there all afternoon and into the night. Sure coulda used a smoke. I sucked on leaves instead, and pissed my pants. The rain and piss made mud underneath me. Then I drifted in and out of sleep, thinking about my buddies, wondering if any of 'em got away besides me. I dreamed about them, a weird dream, never forget it long as I live: we was kids, hiding out, watching for enemies from a platform we nailed high up in the giant maple tree at the end of our road. Bryan was shouting, 'Pow, pow, you're dead!' The other guys screamed and laughed. 'No fair!' Frisbie hollered. 'Didn't see me! Ain't fair if you don't see me.' Then I shouted, 'Gotta go!' cause I heard Mom callin' and I smelled supper on the air.

"I snapped awake and jerked my head around, thought I heard somethin'. But it was just my brain playin' tricks on me. For a minute, I thought I was back in Wisconsin and I could hear my buddies. Except nobody was laughing anymore.

"It wasn't supposed to turn out this way, you know? This wasn't how we practiced it.

"The next morning, when I woke up, one side of my face was full of mud. And mosquitoes were dive-bombing the shit out of the other side. Fuckin' leeches were stuck to the back of my neck. Had a hell of a time pulling those suckers off. I vomited, man—nothin' left in me, but I heaved all the same. Then I rolled onto my back, sweaty and soaked from the rain and piss, and stared up through the trees. I remember how beautiful it was under them trees, all shades of green. Must of been old trees, 'cause they rose up real high and kinda nestled into each other.

"By morning of the second day, I turned my radio on, signaled for help. Then I couldn't move. It was like I couldn't leave my goddamned nest. I knew what the Viet Cong did to guys they captured—how they gutted and burned 'em alive and left 'em in clearings, half-dead decoys, so the rescue helicopters would fly in and get blasted to hell. I sure as fuck didn't need a ride in no Johnny Jump Up—get riddled with bullets on my way up into a chopper.

"I finally made it onto my hands and knees, then crawled a little ways and stopped and listened. When I didn't hear nothin' I hunkered low and ran toward the spot where we was ambushed.

"That place was somethin' I never want to see again. Like you could never imagine. My buddies—what was left of 'em—were scattered in pieces. I recognized Brian's right hand, the only one with long nails, for playing guitar. I used to tease him about them nails. Otherwise, I couldn't tell one from the other 'cause their heads were gone. I ain't even gonna tell you what the Viet Cong did with them.

"I reported my position, then hauled my guys to the clearing. When I heard the chopper blades in the distance, I wondered if we'd even get outa there.

"Finally, I waved my orange flag and gave the call sign and password: 'Casper Ghost and out.'

"The Huey moved in for a touch down—too big a load for the McGuire rig. The crew stowed me and my buddies, blades worked up to speed, and we dusted off—fuckin' outa there, man. Fuckin' outa there!"

GUNNY LEANED BACK on his bar stool and rubbed his hands hard across his face. "As if that wasn't enough, we had to go through all that shit when we got back to the States. Jesus Christ, we got guys barely made it out of 'Nam getting spit on and pelted with garbage. Right here at home! What a loada shit!

"I made training sergeant after that—a damned good one too, except the military didn't see it that way, didn't appreciate what I done. Hell, I knew what those rookies needed to survive, but the fuckin' brass eliminated me, said I was killing my men. I wouldn't do that. I was just toughening those guys up. If that one soldier would of stopped crying long enough to listen, he'd of learned how to survive. Your buddies depend on you, for Chris' sake. All you got is each other.

"I didn't mean to choke him, but the fuckin' baby just wouldn't shut up.

"So, they said they didn't need my kind anymore. 'You are relieved of further duties and service;' What the hell does that mean? 'My kind?'

"You know what the tour sergeants told our folks when we went in for basic training? You know, the stuff to get us ready for war?

" 'We take your boys and we wipe out everything you ever taught 'em. Then we build 'em back up, build 'em up the way we want 'em—as MEN! So they can survive! So you can be proud of 'em! So they can go out there and kill!'

"And that's what I did. That's exactly what I did."

Gunny's rigid jaw worked the veins in his neck like guitar strings ready to snap with one more turn of the peg. His eyes blinked away a last flicker of anger, then shaded over with fatigue.

Callie felt sick inside. Questions like, 'Will you be all right?' or 'Where will you go from here?' seemed empty. Any gesture or word, condescending. Her mind raced to understand what she'd just heard: a story that had gone from boy to man to warrior to soldier to murderer.

"You know," he said in a tired voice, "when I got home, to my folks' place, the Goddamned ketchup bottle was still in the same fuckin' place in the refrigerator."

Callie shook her head and held his gaze.

"I thought I'd be all right 'til my old man told me how in the middle of the night I was all the time crawling around and running and hiding in the lilac bushes in our back yard. I didn't know I was doing that. And I don't know when I stopped doing it. Must have thought I was a kid again, playing war with my buddies, taking aim with my dime store cap gun."

Speechless, Callie fixed her eyes on Gunny's, as if that alone might help keep him on this side of it all.

"It's okay," said Gunny, tossing back his last warm drops of beer. "I'm too much for a lot of ladies."

The two might have talked of other things before leaving, but Callie couldn't remember what. She did know that they sat quiet for a long time while dishes and silverware clattered around them.

22

Minions of the Moon

. . . a sweet natural eye to the new hip moon.
— Allen Ginsberg

CALLIE'S KNUCKLES TURNED A SHINY WHITE as she gripped the steering wheel. Will, alert in the passenger seat, kept to himself, as if sensing some needed quiet time.

Cal remembered leaving that restaurant with Gunny walking ahead of her. It was frigid outside and the streets ran empty. Christmas lights along the far shore had gone out. Clouds covered the stars. For several minutes, Gunny stared those thousand yards across the ice-blocked bay, and then he turned to look at Callie. She thanked him and they shook hands. But when Cal leaned forward to give him a hug, he didn't bend.

She stood on the sidewalk and watched him march to his truck and climb inside. She watched as he eased out of the parking lot and drove slowly down the cold, hollow street, his cowboy hat framed by the truck's rear window.

This was a man who had suffered trauma in all three worlds: the human, the warrior, and his own world. What was keeping him going? Would he ever find himself again, like when he was a young boy who left off playing army with his friends as soon as he heard his mother calling him home for supper?

Callie took a deep breath and exhaled. "I'm so glad you never had to fight in a war, Dad."

"I know. It was a fluke that I missed out. Too young for World War I, too old for the Second. And every war after that."

"You were lucky to be born when you were. Fortunate for Mom and Liz and me."

"To think I might have never known you gals."

"And our perfect ways."

"Oh, I wouldn't go so far as to say that."

"Even after all these years, I still think about Chuck and how the military changed him, turned him into a killer. No way could I have been the wife of a soldier, expected to follow the rules of warfare. Can you imagine me living on a military base?"

"Not your cup of tea, Cal. As things turned out you would have ended up a young widow."

Callie thought about how Chuck and thousands like him never had the chance to draw a breath and remain standing beyond the 1970s, for all of the birthdays and holidays and the just plain living. For Cal, he would always sport a fresh face, his foot beating time with the songs from his guitar.

"I sure miss the boy that he once was," she said, "a real sweetheart."

"You'll meet some new gentlemen, now that you're on your own."

"Gentlemen callers," she laughed and thought about the man who was having trouble with his boat motor and happened to drift over to tie up at her dock last summer. She'd gone down the steps to see what was going on and found that he had a motor similar to her father's. It was all about the lean-rich adjustment to get it running again.

And then there was Bobby Keeler who, as a young boy, had accidently crashed his bicycle into the rear end of a neighbor's Buick. Swinging in the park, Cal and a friend had shrieked with laughter as Bobby gathered himself and his bike up to trudge home in silence. The next day, as he passed Callie's desk at school, he swiped her pencil onto the floor, stuck out his tongue, and shot her a cross-eyed glare.

But all that had happened several decades ago, and during their recent class reunion in Masterton, they had hugged each other and laughed about what it was like to be a bratty kid.

"Well now, Callie girl," said her dad, "I've been giving some thought as to what we should do about a stone for Amer."

"Oh, yeah?"

"I've come to the conclusion that we ought to order one up as soon as possible. We'll look into it when we get home."

"Really! What changed your mind?"

"I've had plenty of time to ponder what happened back there in Rockford. And, of course, growing up on the farm with Uncle Amer— why, he was like another dad to my brother and me. When we received that telegram from the sheriff of Garfield County all those years ago, I knew that we could never leave the burial up to strangers, unattended by our family."

"Without a marker, Dad, he might just as well have stayed right there in Montana. In fact, those officials might have done better by him than Hannah and Nellie's folks. That is, unless the Church got involved. Then he would likely have been placed in a potter's field, away from the orthodox cemeteries, because of who he was."

"Could be. Although, the McKammans were his good friends. I'm sure they would have seen to some kind of a headboard wherever he was buried.

"You know, Cal, all our talk about people's lives being like in the movies reminded me of a show I saw on television a while ago. It was called 'A Death in the Family,' starring E. G. Marshall—a hell of a fine actor. Anyhow, that little speech he gave has come to occupy my memory and won't let go. You know how some things stay with a fella and never fade—pictures, words, deeds. In this case, it was words."

"How did they go?"

"'When a man dies,' he said, 'it ought to be everyone's business. You can't bury a man in an unmarked grave.'"

"Or a woman."

"Somehow, I knew you'd say that, Cal. Of course, that's a given. Still, I'll never quite understand."

"Understand what?"

"About Uncle Amer. Why would anyone want to make such a choice in life?"

"You mean homesteading in Montana or being gay?"

"The gay part."

"It's not a choice, Dad. People are born that way. It's genetic."

"Oh?"

"That's what makes it such a tragedy. It's hard enough when society rejects them, but when families turn against their own, when parents disown their children, as if they were to blame for what nature turned out, that's the killer. One of the teachers I work with volunteered for several summers at a hospice in Oregon during the AIDS epidemic. Those young men who were dying, he said, all they wanted was to see their families. They desperately needed to be with their moms and dads one last time. Resolve issues. Receive their blessings. Feel a little love. They simply longed for some comfort on their way out. Now how hard is that?"

"And did they go? Their folks?"

"A few. But many of them didn't. They rejected their sons right up to the end."

Will shook his head. "I can't imagine any parent doing that to his children, for any reason."

"Exactly." Callie took a deep breath. "It's settled then? About Uncle Amer?"

"Yes, Cal, it is. We'll take care of him. His memory, at least."

"And how will it read? His tombstone."

Will raised his right hand and traced above the dashboard with his thumb and forefinger:

AMER LINDSTROM
1880 – 1919
DEVOTED UNCLE OF WILLIAM AND RAY

"I like that, Dad. And while we're at it, we should get decent markers for your grandma Ernestine and Auntie Edna—something other than those sketchy little bronze squares tucked under the grass."

"Yes, we'll take care of them, too. Take care of what Nellie and Hannah's folks were supposed to do and never bothered. Talk about tight, those uncles. Damn close to the vest! As if we hadn't done enough, my dad and I, traveling to Montana to retrieve the body. Guess I'll just have to see this through to the end, the way we did with Amer's dog—that good old boy."

"How long did Radge live after you brought him back to Hadley?"

"He was my buddy for a lot of years, made it to around fifteen—a fine herder, as devoted to us as he was to my uncle. He never left Amer's side when he passed away. We made damn sure to give him a good home after all he went through out there in Montana—getting kicked around, watching his master die. Dad and I were surprised the Carmichaels didn't shoot him when he tried to defend my uncle during that first attack. Even stayed by the pine box at the railroad stations every chance he could during those three days it took us to bring Amer back to Rockford for burial."

"Did you take Radge out to the cemetery when they lowered the casket?"

"No. I think that would have been too hard on him. He might have wanted to stay there from then on. I've heard of dogs doing that, you know, spending the rest of their days lying next to their masters' graves."

Callie glanced over at her father as he suddenly leaned toward the steering wheel. He was checking the speedometer again.

"Keep 'er under sixty, Cal. We're in no rush."

"Woof, woof."

"Now see here, young lady!"

"Just kidding, Pops."

"Highly unlikely. As I was saying, under sixty, you hear?"

"I'll think about it."

With a brisk toss of the hand, Will shook his head and grinned, reminding her of the young father he once was and how he almost always condoned her adolescent attitudes.

Keep it up, Cal, she told her middle-aged self. If you stay young and sassy, maybe he won't grow any older than he already is—at least, for a while. With silver hair and worn out wingtips, let's hope he'll still be dancing. Dancing the old soft shoe.

She thought about a fascinating dream that had repeated itself during the past months, where she walked along, able to dance, step, bounce straight up, and linger at her leisure thirty feet above everything and everybody. She could descend slowly and re-ascend whenever she wished, in order to jump hurdles in her path or to amuse herself. Not yet into flight or somersaults, she preferred always to remain vertical with her feet pointed downward for landing. Some said she should sign on with a corporate tennis shoe label and become rich through advertising.

"Well now, isn't that the American way?" she'd mutter with a laugh, after sleeping like an old dog, legs twitching, eyelids fluttering. "I guess there's no such thing as a real utopia. After all, nowhere is perfect, but the trail seems a heck of a lot smoother.

She flipped on the car radio. Tony Bennett was singing "Fly Me to the Moon."

"How much farther do we have to go, Callie girl?"

"About ten miles to Long Lake."

"O. K., let's make a detour north for a couple of miles, to some wide open space. Since there'll be that full moon tonight, I'd like to have a clear view of it rising. After that, I'll drive the rest of the way home."

Callie looked at her dad with arched brows. "Are you sure? Your driver's license has expired."

"Yes, I'm sure and I don't care. It's nowhere near dusk. I can see just fine."

"Okay, but be sure to keep 'er under a hundred."

"Well, I guess that's what the fates have in store for me."

Before trading places, Callie and her dad stood for a time at the edge of the road, next to a long stretch of harvested fields. Breathing in the cool fall air, they watched the brilliant top of the moon rising while a pair of black and white dogs chased it across the soybean field as if to hop on for a ride.

"No need to reach for the moon any longer," said Will. "There she is. Reminds me of the evenings I took Radge out to run the fields under a saucer like that. We never did do any night hunting, though. Just loped along in the moonlight."

While the scarlet sun got ready to set in the west, a hunter's moon, deep gold and streaked with crimson and orange, rose out of the east. The enormous disc seemed so close, Callie imagined running wild with those herders—moon-doggies—jumping on top of the rim and riding it all the way up into the sky.

She would always remember that certain dog who came to lie down next to her in the country cemetery of an autumn afternoon and stayed by Callie's side for a long time, until she was able to rise again.

Slightly off-key while humming their favorite tune, Will held out his arms and invited his daughter to dance, just as he had when Cal was a little girl. Shuffling in ¾ time over gravel and weeds, they sang and three-stepped next to the ploughed field where those two dogs cavorted before the moon.

Calm and commanding, the gigantic ball hovered for a moment along the horizon. For a while, the sun and the moon faced off across the prairie—two ancient, fiery globes acknowledging one another as they'd done every autumn for eons. As soon as the sun gave over, the lady in the moon, profiled on the butter-yellow disc, smudged in red, seemed to smile down at Cal and her father as she traveled higher and higher into the night sky.

"Looks like your face up there, Cal, ridin' high."

Despite stiff knees from the long trip home, Callie took off running. With arms aloft, she danced in circles along the edge of that expansive field, a huge stage stretched out between the sun and the moon. Until these floodlights click off for good, she thought, we can only guess how our lives are going to play out.

Slowly returning to the car by walking backwards, Callie gave a final nod to all those whose destinies she had considered during the drive back home: Chuck, her first love; Gunny, likely primed for another Viet Nam; Bud Gleason, thrown from his beloved boat; Laura Lambert, growing up in a boxcar; Lucy Moulin, torn between love and religion; war-maimed Selmer and Clarence Johnson, whiling away the rest of their days in front of the bank on Masterton's Main Street; Auntie Sarah, saved by her music; Jean Moulin, vertical to the end; and all those dogs who made a difference, especially that farm dog she would refer to as Bobby, who remained by her side in the cemetery when she thought she was going to die.

And there was her mother, Emily. Callie remembered a line from the poet Edgar Stafford: "I have woven a parachute out of everything broken." Those words described how Emily lived her life and interacted with others. Adversity never won a match with her. Disappointments got swept aside. Not only was she the rock around which water flowed, she was also the water, which, when coming up against the rock, swirled on by.

"There's nothing softer than water," she'd say, "yet it can wear away the hardest things," followed by, "I should worry and lose my shape."

And then there was her sister, Liz, who was always there to help, especially when Cal's marriage began falling apart, as if it were a gigantic slab of ice beating against the closed grates of a dam, without so much as a trickle of hope.

And finally there was Callie's dad, Will Lindstrom who stood in the moonlight, leaning against his Cadillac, arms crossed. All the time in the world had started to run out for him, but he would leave his daughter with an unparalleled legacy: keep on rowing.

As long as the sun and the moon hang around and the rivers keep flowing to the sea, there'll be all the time in the world.

And what about her own self, having approached the half way mark in life—what would the fates have in store for Cal? As a child, witnessing human frailties and tragedies, she wondered how one person could come out of a terrible circumstance relatively unscathed, while another just went to pieces. Her mother, a gifted seamstress, called those instances "the nubby weave of life." When told that others had it far worse than someone else, Callie wanted to know which living thing on earth had it the worst of all. Who merited the single darkest prize atop that needle-tipped pinnacle?

She took another look at the sky and imagined herself sailing around that hunter's moon, free at last. The dark side of the disc no longer existed for Callie, even in her thoughts and dissolving memories.

"Time to go, Cal." Will entered his car and buckled up. "It's been ages since I was in the driver's seat. For once, I want to step out from behind this wheel and wave at Emily. She'll likely rush out onto our deck, you know, as soon as she sees us."

"Have at it, Pops. I'll be the doggie in the passenger side now." She laughed a happy laugh. "Just call me Miquette."

"Well, we're almost home now," said Will, replacing his hands at ten and two on the steering wheel.

Callie lowered her window, inhaled a gust of cool country air, and waved big at the hunter's moon. When she turned back to look at her father, she saw how almost vertically he sat, with his head held high, eyes focused straight ahead on the last stretch of road. Soon he would pull up next to the curb in front of his apartment, shut down the engine, forget to unbuckle his seatbelt for a second, step hesitantly onto the street, work the kinks out of his knees, hitch up his suit trousers, wave and call out, 'Halloo, Emily, we're home!'

IT WAS EARLY MORNING, Callie's favorite time of day, when energy levels were high, choices plentiful, and yellow chrysanthemums upstaged everything else in the fall garden.

And though it was autumn, a time when bay buoys cluster together like worn out gossips soon to wear wigs of snow, clucking and wagging in November's wind, the blue hours of winter waited impatiently in the wings, sending out sharp-eyed emissaries over black water and tinkling shards; Bald Eagles, poised like cold water sailors in high water pants, hopped clumsily along the edge of an ice shelf in search of prey, and then unfurled their wings to catch pockets of air, and sail away like old sea captains.

In the depths of winter, while low-slung beams of sunshine crept along the horizon, Callie and Piper would race across the ice-glutted bay, confident that they wouldn't fall through. That is, until several months later, when warning sounds erupted and the crisp clean air gave way to earth smells. Like a giant's grumbling stomach, the eerie groaning of bay ice in late March meant, "Off with you!"

And then would come the warmth of spring, with the last of the tinkling shards, that long-awaited time when the rising sun casts a long, flaming candle across open water before commanding center sky—all light and diamond glitter.

Cal hummed the beginning notes of "*Chanson de Matin*" and thought that Elgar might have composed his "Morning Song" with a place like hers in mind. Those lyrical phrases and trills were the painted prelude, followed by fluttering rays peeking over the treetops. Determined final chords announced a full sunrise.

And she thought of her father, borne out of a lifetime in the natural world, and all he had taught her while living on the prairie under changeable skies, along lakes and rivers, taking only what he needed to exist. No matter where she found herself in the world, Cal would keep on rowing.

"At midnight," offers a Chinese proverb, "noon is born."

And there it will be—a brand new morning with the slow, rhythmic sounds of lake water lapping against the shore, a breeze stirring up a zillion maple leaves, and finally, the call to show by leaping fish, sassy gulls, and a dancing Piper at Callie's side.

About the Author

Connie Claire (Peterson) Szarke, award-winning author, came of age in Southwestern Minnesota, influenced by life on the prairie, among farms, small towns, woods, and lakes. As a former high school French teacher and lifelong pianist, Szarke's links with European culture, history, and the arts provide her with additional material for her novels and short stories. She currently lives on a lake west of the Twin Cities, where she sings Mancini's "Two for the Road" while kayaking with Kipp.